# EARLY AMERICAN
# STENCILS

## ON WALLS AND FURNITURE

BY
JANET WARING

DOVER PUBLICATIONS, INC · NEW YORK

Published in Canada by General Publishing Com-
pany, Ltd., 30 Lesmill Road, Don Mills, Toronto,
Ontario.
Published in the United Kingdom by Constable
and Company, Ltd., 10 Orange Street, London
WC 2.

This Dover edition, first published in 1968, is an
unabridged republication of the work originally
published by William R. Scott in 1937.

*International Standard Book Number: 0-486-21906-2*
*Library of Congress Catalog Card Number: 68-19166*

**Manufactured in the United States of America
Dover Publications, Inc.
180 Varick Street
New York, N. Y. 10014**

# LIST OF ILLUSTRATIONS

*\* Houses are identified by the names of their builders or original owners as far as possible.*

vi

*The first color illustration, following page 80, was reproduced on the cover of the*
*original edition of this work. It gives a detail of the parlor overmantel,*
*Josiah Sage house, South Sandisfield, Mass. The decorations*
*in this book were reproduced from original stencils*
*in the author's collection.*

# THE AUTHOR'S PREFACE

Most prefaces come as the final word to a book, and these pages are not an exception. I should like them, however, to express something of the pleasure and adventure which the gathering of the material has brought to me. Begun as a casual interest many years ago, it has been continued when leisure and opportunity permitted and has widened through the help of others. The mere word of a recently uncovered wall, an unknown set of stencils, or a well-preserved chair has led me on, and has also drawn into the work—or play rather, for much of it has seemed that—many strangers who have become friends. It has taken me into quiet villages of New England, into shops of old artisans whose training reached back to the crafts of the past, and into houses which still retained the memories, traditions, and belongings of their first builders and owners, and in so doing it has made me realize anew the charm and dignity and practicality of the manner of life in early America.

It is impossible to acknowledge my debt to those who have opened their doors to me and given largely of their time, their quiet hospitality, and welcome. No inconvenience has been too great, no interruption too long. Furniture has been brought down from attics, paper stripped from walls or plaster chipped away, the keys found for locked and unused houses; family papers have been consulted for a needed fact, older people questioned for an almost forgotten memory, letters generously answered, and many acts of gracious cooperation, without which it would be impossible to collect facts about any subject that touches so intimately the homes or possessions of others. How large their contribution has been is evidenced throughout this volume. I am especially indebted to Mr. and Mrs. Alfred A. Carter, owners of the Sage house in South Sandisfield, which was my first introduction to a stencilled wall. The many hours spent in these rooms enabled me to study the method of the unknown artisan who has left numerous traces of his handiwork in this region. Such kindness at the beginning of a search fortifies one's spirit for succeeding efforts.

Perhaps a word of explanation should be given as to the arrangement and plan of the book, for each part is a separate unit. Although the introductory material on the stencil came last in my experience as the result of a very natural desire to know what the stencil as a tool had accomplished for the decorative crafts, I have placed it first because it not only shows some of the possibilities of this method of producing ornament, but also gives perspective and a sense of continuity. It does not, however, furnish antecedents of a direct kind, for there is every indication that America developed the craft in her own way to meet the special needs emerging out of the conditions inherent in a new land.

The introductory pages on the use of the stencil in foreign lands are little more than suggestions; those on the stencilled wall in America have another purpose, and one perhaps not without a hint of the didactic, for these walls have aroused less general interest than has been accorded to some of the more trivial possessions of our forefathers. Yet the very fact that stencilled walls were so much a part of the everyday life of their period may in itself account for the ignorance of our own generation in regard to them. Many of the patterns have been covered with paper again and again, obliterated with coats of whitewash or thin plaster, or left to fall into ruin, until they have seemed mere remnants, worthy only of the neglect they have received. But if one has had the good fortune to find a well-preserved stencilled wall as the setting for its contemporary furniture, the experience has brought into the present, as nothing else can, a simple and dignified way of life, which makes significant every fragment of other walls that retains an old pattern. If the descriptions of the walls seem detailed, it is because I wanted them to serve as a basis of comparison with other walls which might emerge from under paper or paint, as well as a guide for those who wish to reproduce these rooms in houses of the period. Colors, paints, original stencils, whatever has been salvaged of the old technique have also been included for the same reason. The battered kits, the worn brushes, any facts about their first users add to our knowledge and appreciation of this craft, just as the histories which surround the individual houses give personality to the walls themselves.

While my account of stencilled walls has been as complete as I could make it in the localities I explored, that of furniture has been selective rather than inclusive, and generally chronological. Something of the background, the rise into popularity, the spread, and the decline of the fashion has been illustrated by examples chosen to suggest the variety and range of ornament and the types of furniture on which it was placed. Those who would like to follow the craft will find that all the phases of technique practiced by the old artisans have been included, not in a separate section, but where they could be shown best either through illustrations of furniture decoration or of the cutouts which produced it, or by the precepts of some worker who has handed down his own experience. In this way, together with biographies of the artisans and the many stencil patterns whch placed the design, they are a part of the development of the craft. We need all these things to understand this furniture and its place in both the industrial and domestic life of the last century. Although we may not wish to duplicate it, we may be able to put its methods or its designs to new uses, for, at its best, this gold stencilling has a quality and beauty that should not be lost.

These records of walls and of furniture could only come to life through the excellent photography which has been done by William F. Winter, William Manahan, Burton E. Moore, and Arthur C. Haskell. They have given far more than their technical skill through their interest, their thought, and their patience. The difficulty of securing a needed fact or picture in some distant place has enlisted the kindness of many. Professor

E. W. Tristram has given his opinion in regard to certain English stencilled work; Dr. Joan Evans with Mrs. Hamlin Hunt made a special journey to take photographs of motifs on rood screens in East Anglia; Mr. George Dickinson, over cups of tea, has discussed many early aspects of the craft of japanning and called my attention to some stencilled papier-mâché trays, Mr. Arthur M. Hind before the publication of his book, *An Introduction to a History of Woodcut*, directed me to additional early prints colored by stencils; while the personal inquiries of M. René Saulnier brought information about the methods of stencilling used in the Imagerie Pellerin at Epinal, France.

The staffs of the various libraries and museums to which I have had occasion to turn have shown that readiness to cooperate which makes their contribution so real to the work of all who come to them. The Bibliothèque de l'Union Centrale des Arts Décoratifs, the Staats Museum, Berlin, the Victoria and Albert and the British museums, the Metropolitan Museum of Art, and the Museum of the City of New York, the Boston headquarters of the Society for the Preservation of New England Antiquities and the Essex Institute are among those which have been most helpful. To Miss Laura Bragg, Director of the Berkshire Museum, Pittsfield, Massachusetts, I owe a special word of thanks for her interest in the material and encouragement to make it available in published form, and to Miss Eva Judd O'Meara of the Yale University Music Library for her stimulating research on stencilled choir books. The experience of Miss Alice S. Erskine in the use and the value of stencils as wall decorations has served me in various ways. Sincere thanks are due to Miss Anne E. Lincoln for her constructive criticism, her many helpful suggestions, and for her valuable assistance in the presentation of the material and preparation of the manuscript.

Finally I owe a debt of gratitude to those who with enthusiasm have accompanied the making of this book from its beginning. For them it has meant hours of waiting through the heat or cold of the day, sitting by the roadside or in stony pastures while I traced patterns, matched colors, or pried off hard layers of whitewash. Without the encouragement of these special few, the material might not have been collected.

# THE STENCIL: AN INTRODUCTION

THE word stencil is surrounded by prejudice. To many in America it means something commercial—a stamp for marking packing boxes, or a painter's catalogue with figures of pond lilies and sturdy Dutch boys in wooden sabots. To those of longer memory it recalls the high walls and ceilings of the Eastlake period when elaborate stencilled designs in pale color or blatant borders in reds and browns, often Egyptian in inspiration, became the setting for curtains banded with heavy plush and for ornate furniture of black walnut. To others more familiar with recent trends in our decorative arts, the term may have a pleasanter connotation. It may suggest a landscape or interior by Emil Ganso or Conrad Cramer, or the many stencil plates with which T. M. Cleland has composed his well-known prints, for, perhaps under the inspiration of their French predecessors and contemporaries—Picasso, Jean Saudé, Guy Arnoux, E. A. Séguy, to name only a very few—these American artists have found in the stencil a means of achieving pattern and color for pictures, reproductions, or book illustrations that is gained by no other method.

To a few the word brings back some almost forgotten wall of old New England, still vivid with the bright tones and strong patterns stencilled over a century ago, or perhaps a chair or other piece of furniture of the same period, with overflowing bowls of fruit or clusters of flowers done with metallic powders in shades of bronze and gold, lustrous even today. It is these two chapters of its history which for me have given the stencil so much of its fascination as a tool, leading me to look into the past for records of its other contributions to the decorative crafts which will help us better to appreciate its accomplishments and possibilities.

It is as impossible to gather these records with completeness as it is to reconstruct perfectly the patchwork of any phase of man's cultural heritage. We find a fragment here, another there, and from them we sense something of the finished design. This difficulty, great in any art, is even greater when a craft does not exist in its own right, but is thought of merely as a method; for stencilling, like engraving, has been adopted by various arts as an element of their technique, and so its contributions must be sought in many fields. Walls, textiles, books, games, furniture, a hundred and one objects and surfaces, have at one time or another known the stencil, traceable today by the distinctive quality of its decoration. When and where some artisan first began to repeat with exactness by means of a cut-out pattern the motifs of a design, or the symbols of his language or of his ideas, we can only guess. All we know is that the stencil is an extremely old tool, which by its very nature may have had many separate origins. The simple process of applying form to a surface through openings made in a superimposed material can easily have been the discovery of different peoples at different times.

Fancy may lead us to a cave of prehistoric man or to the steppes of Central Asia where civilization was cradled, but if we cannot point to some illustration of stencilling in the caverns or among the remains of our Cro-Magnon ancestors, we do have one which comes from a culture scarcely less primitive in its state of progress than that of the Stone Age. Almost the first historical accounts of the Fiji Islands tell us that the women, unlike any of their neighboring inhabitants of the South Pacific, decorated their bark cloth with wide geometric borders stencilled through openings cut in dried banana leaves with dyes of "vegetable charcoal and water or red earth liquefied with the sap of the candle-nut tree."[1] Mr. Henry Balfour, in considering possible origins of this method of decoration on these islands, has offered a theory as plausible as it is unusual for an indigenous development. He suggests that the natives adopted stencils ready-made by nature, for the larvae of certain tropical insects bore through a tightly rolled young leaf, which, when unfolded, results in a duplicated, perforated pattern very like that obtained by the child who snips through a paper folded lengthwise many times. Innumerable decades and even centuries may have elapsed between the first "stencilled pattern," perhaps accidentally made by some woman idly rubbing red earth over one of these pierced leaves, and the later complicated borders upon which an early missionary reports his observations:

> The operator works on a plain board; the red dye gives place to a jet black; her pattern is now formed by a strip of banana leaf placed on the upper surface of the cloth. Out of the leaf is cut the pattern—not more than an inch long—which she wishes to print upon the border, and [which she] holds by her first and middle finger pressing it down with the thumb. Then, taking a soft pad of cloth steeped in the dye in her right hand, she rubs it firmly over the stencil, and a fair, sharp figure is made.[2]

And so we first see the stencil—a cut-out pattern through which design is applied to a surface in contrasting color—in these small islands of the Pacific, used how long we can only surmise. The probabilities are that the stencil was not brought to the islands by these primitive people at the time of the "great migrations"; and indeed it is very difficult to isolate the tool in any ancient civilization where various other arts reached a high perfection. Paul Lacroix cites[3] somewhat vague authority for the belief that stencils were employed by the Egyptians in the decoration of their mummy cases, although the evidence is not as yet conclusive.

When our thoughts go back to ancient cultures they naturally turn to the Orient and to China guarded by its great wall. According to a Chinese legend it was Shem, the oldest son of Noah, who was the first instructor in the arts of painting and sculpture and

---

1. Quoted in "The Origin of Stencilling in the Fiji Islands," by Henry Balfour, reprinted from the *Journal* of the Royal Anthropological Institute of Great Britain and Ireland, 1924, p. 347.

2. Williams, Thomas: *Fiji and the Fijians*, 1860, vol. I, p. 63.

3. *Histoire de l'imprimerie*, "Le livre d'or des métiers," p. 56.

in the preparation of silk for many uses. We are not asked to believe that the stencil was in his paint box, but it did have a place in the kit of later artisans, who used it in Buddhist monasteries as a means of reproducing sacred texts and of placing pattern on the walls of temples. Buddhism began its conquest of China a century before the Christian era, but invasions and anarchy brought the "dark ages" which hindered its progress and flowering for seven hundred years. Under the T'ang Dynasty, which began in 618, the former glories of the Empire were restored, and, in a period of religious toleration, Buddhism, competing with Confucianism, Taoism, and Christianity, became the dominant faith and influence—a conquest perhaps largely due to the stress on exact reproduction of religious images and texts. In this duplication, which was one step in the development of block printing in the East, the stencil played a real if humble part. If it had not been for the dry air of the Chinese Turkestan desert on the western rim of the great Empire and the patient exploration of archeologists, we might have known nothing of the stencil's contributions to the spread of this great religion, for the destruction of the monasteries after 845 and the damp climate of China wrought havoc with manuscripts and other records. From the litter piled knee-deep in ruined monasteries in the Turfan Oasis the Prussian Expedition, which finished its work in 1907, gathered many woodcuts, sheets of hand-colored stamped Buddhas, and "bits of silk with Buddhist figures stencilled upon them," together with "paper stencils and pounces."[4]

Some 400 miles from Turfan is Tun-huang, another center of the Central Asian silk route and a meeting place of the great cultures of the Far East; near it are the Caves of a Thousand Buddhas, caves cut into the rock of a cliff, which have served continuously as shrines from the time of their founding more than fifteen hundred years ago. The lively narrative of the excavation of the sealed manuscript room walled up nine hundred years ago and discovered by a mendicant priest in 1900 is told by Sir Aurel Stein in the second volume of his *Serindia*,[5] where he also describes the painted walls and passageways of these caves, which again show the "multiplication of Buddhas with which Buddhist piety, using the convenient means of the stencil, has covered the walls of so many shrines," and which as a religious performance brought the worshipper nearer to Nirvana. In one room "rows of stencilled Buddhas, dark brown, with white draperies, on a pale green ground" give their testimony of some ancient faith; while another room reveals seated Buddhas "in coloured robes, painted on a background of light greenish-blue by means of stencils." A fragment of a stucco wall recovered at Khā-dalik is striking in the character of its design and rich in color. Its horizontal rows of small images of

4. Quoted from *The Invention of Printing in China* (ed. 1931), by Thomas Francis Carter, who examined the contents of an unopened box brought back by this expedition and deposited in the Museum in Berlin. See pp. 29, 105, *et passim*.

5. *Op. cit.*, vol. II, pp. 795, 927, 930; vol. I, p. 166; vol. III, pp. 1111 ff.

the great teacher, each within a separate niche, sitting on lotus cushions and wearing robes of "red, dark brown, white or cream," were produced, Dr. Stein affirms, "without doubt by the convenient use of stencils." And they are mentioned as having a part in the mural paintings of the Grotto of Wan-fo-hsia, done several centuries later (c. 1341) when Europe was beginning to stencil image prints with brilliant color.

Again on Asiatic soil we find the stencil in the hands of Japanese craftsmen, producing designs on fabrics and paper. An early example of stencilled silk, a fragment of *aya* believed to date from the Nara period (710–794), is photographed in the Victoria and Albert Museum *Guide to Japanese Textiles*. Its stencilled pattern of the sacred wheel, with the eight spokes symbolic of the "teachings of Buddha," remains today sharp and bold in outline. In Japan at this time both stencilling in the ordinary sense of the term and a closely related process known as *kyotechi* were practiced. Among the textiles of the ancient and priceless Shōsōin Collection at Nara are fragments of silk gauze in soft colors done on pale grounds by this technique.[6] The silk to be patterned was clamped between two boards pierced by a design through which the dye was applied to the material. When a repeated pattern was required, the silk was folded for each duplication before it was fastened between the boards. No method could be much more primitive than this, but it gave decoration without a trace of elementary character, the outlines intentionally softened. One example dating somewhere between the sixth and eighth centuries, illusive and yellowed by time, has a design of floating blue tassels and birds with flowers in their beaks, executed with all the quality and freedom of pictorial composition. The details of the birds' feathers must have demanded the utmost cunning of the knife which cut the duplicate patterns in the two boards. If these fragments of early centuries, lacelike and frayed, show so much beauty, it is probable that there were masses of patterned textiles brought into being by the stencil.

Notable examples of gold stencilling of a later period and of an advanced technique may be seen on certain Japanese Nō robes. These brilliant stage costumes were a sort of field of honor for the nation's art, where the weaver's shuttle, the dyer's purple, the skill of the needle, the artist's brush, and the gilder's precision in the handling of leaf and powdered gold vied to outdo one another. The stencil was in this company. Into these costumes went not only the richest of brocaded weaves but also the genius of a race. For the most part there are no definite dates given to the Nō robes, but they may have originated in the fourteenth century and reached their highest development in the late sixteenth, when Kāno Eitoku set the fashion for the lavish use of gold in decoration, to which there was a wide response throughout Japan.

6. Some thirteen examples are reproduced in color and in their actual size in the four volumes of *Gomotsu Jodai Senshokumon* (dyed and textiled fabrics of the sixth, seventh and eighth centuries, A.D.), Japanese text by Kiyoski Inouye and English translation by Jiro Harada.

4

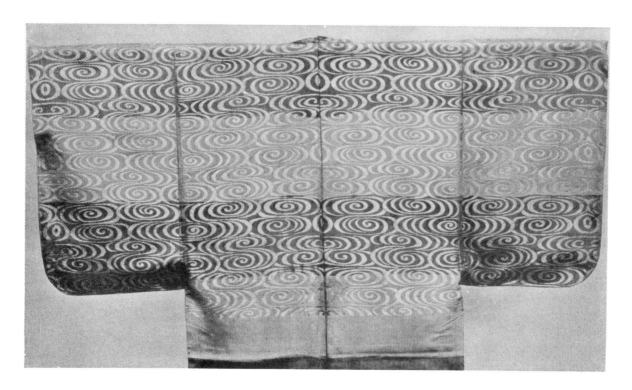

FIG. I. JAPANESE NŌ ROBES, OR STAGE COSTUMES

The seventeenth century example above is entirely stencilled on a banded background of yellow and powder blue. The lower robe of the sixteenth century has background motifs of conventionalized grasses and dewdrops stencilled in gold on lacquer-red satin. Flowers and outlines of flower beds are embroidery.

*From the collection of Miss Lucy T. Aldrich, courtesy of the Metropolitan Museum*

*Un Cartier.*      *Ein Kartenmacher*

FIG. 2. COSTUME ILLUSTRATING THE TRADE OF CARD MAKING

The original engraving, made about 1735 by Martin Engelbrecht, carries legends in French and German identifying the tools and finished products.

*Bibliothèque de l'Union Centrale des Arts Décoratifs*

For those who were not fortunate enough to see the 1935 exhibition at the Metropolitan Museum of Art of Nō robes and Buddhist vestments, including loans by both Japanese and American collectors, the catalogue[7] with its photographs of many of the exhibits will give an excellent idea of their types, although color and texture are lost in the reproductions. In a number of those described the stencil had a part, placing gold designs of bamboo on dark blue satin, pine tree fret on rich brown, trellises on black and terra cotta, or bell flowers and leaves on white satin, and chrysanthemums against yellow. These background motifs were generally combined with brilliantly colored embroidery. The two robes illustrated (fig. 1) contrast simplicity and intricacy. Even the camera has caught the shimmer of the satin of the upper robe, banded in yellow and powder blue on which the stencil has laid the ripples of an all-over water motif in silver. On the lacquer-red robe below, grasses heavy with dewdrops bend to the ground in rhythmic recurrence, their gold forming the patterned background for flower beds brilliant with peonies, camellias, pinks, and bell flowers, embroidered in silk floss. The stencil was pliant and sure in the hands of these master craftsmen.

The gentleman in Japan wore garments of silk, but cottons, so frequently stencilled in shades of blue, familiar to us all, have for long clothed the common man. Fragile stencils cut from mulberry fiber paper and waterproofed with the juice of persimmons have been the chief tools of this great industry of cotton printing. The complicated cut-outs are as a rule made in duplicate sheets of paper between which are laid threads of wild silk or a network of hair. These threads take the place of the ties, necessary parts of every stencil pattern, which hold together the form of the design. The pattern may be made in one stencil or two, and sometimes even four separate stencils in succession are used to complete it.

Another form of Japanese stencil which we must not overlook is the hidden technique used for stencilled pictures, which is often indistinguishable from hand painting. William Anderson in his book, *Pictorial Arts in Japan*, illustrates "The Hawk and the Wild Goose," done on silk (1779), as an example of this craft. This method so completely disguises the means which made the picture that, as Professor Anderson remarks, it would be difficult for any but an expert to distinguish between the reproduction done at a trifling cost by an almost purely mechanical process and the sketch of a skilled artist. Pictures of this sort decorate hanging scrolls in the guest rooms of Japanese houses.[8] Certainly the stencil in Japan has been developed in the hands of artisans to a point of high excellence. We wonder whether Japan imported the stencil from China or perhaps Korea; she was always a borrower we know, but whatever she borrowed she transmuted into beauty of her own.

7. *Japanese Costume;* the introduction by Alan Priest gives a historical sketch.

8. Some excellent examples may be seen in the British Museum collection.

Europe as well as the East early knew the convenience of the stencil. It may seem surprising that the first documents on the subject do not take us to Greece, that inspiration of European art, but most Greek decoration in paints and dyes has been destroyed by time, leaving only her sculpture and pottery. Lacroix reminds us, however, that the learned antiquary, de Caylus, believed that the patterns on Etruscan vases "were applied by no other method"[9] than by stencils cut from thin, pliant sheets of copper which conformed readily to the contour of the vase and produced designs of clean-cut outline, but scholars have left largely unexplored this aspect of the ancient craft.

Records tell us that in the first century Quintilian,[10] the great Roman preceptor, is recommending the stencil as a means of teaching boys to write, for their inexperienced hands could more rapidly learn to guide the stylus with the aid of perforated letters. In 403 Saint Jerome "confined far from man's turmoil in a tiny cell," where he laments "past sins" and tries to "avoid present temptations," writes to Laeta regarding the first lessons of her daughter Paula. He suggests that she be given a set of letters made of boxwood or of ivory and that she be told their names and be allowed to play with them, making play a road to learning. "When she first begins to push a stylus through wax with her faltering hand," he continues, "either guide her untrained fingers with your own hand, or else have the alphabet cut in a plate, so that she can follow the pattern between the edges of the slits without slipping outside."[11] Theodoric, King of the Barbarian Ostrogoths (454–526), whose hand was trained to the sword, had passed ten years of his childhood in Constantinople and commonly traced the first four letters of his name through a stencil cut in a plate of gold. Procopius, the historian, also tells us (527) that the signature of Justinian, Emperor of the East and the great lawgiver, was guided by a piece of wood perforated by the letters J U S T, and that the same device formed the monogram with which Charlemagne, Europe's great patron of learning, signed his documents of state. Throughout medieval Europe the sacred monogram I. H. S., stencilled on the rafters and walls of churches, was a favorite decoration in combination with freehand floral and symbolic patterns, and manuscripts are bright with ornamental capitals often in part or entirely the work of the stencil.

There are times when a familiar method takes on new meaning, and it was the advent of paper into Europe—China's greatest gift to the world—that brought the stencil into expanded usefulness. Throughout the Middle Ages secular and ecclesiastical masters had demanded the skills of artist and artisan alike. On castle and cathedral, manor house and monastery were lavished tapestries and embroideries, carvings and metal work, glass and ivories; but the houses of bourgeois, peasant, and serf were for the

9. Lacroix, Paul: *Histoire de l'imprimerie,* "Le livre d'or des métiers," p. 56.

10. Quintilian: *Institutio Oratoria,* libr. 1, cap. 1.

11. See *Select Letters of Saint Jerome,* Loeb Classical Library, epistles 4, 107, 117.

Faiseuse de Cartes.     Eine Kartenmacherin.

### FIG. 3. ANOTHER CARD MAKER

The legend of this engraving also by Engelbrecht identifies: 1. tub with color to moisten paper, 2. brush for sprinkling, 3. stencils, 4. face and point cards, 5. pestle, 6. glue brush, 7. sheet of paper, 8. stencil brush, 9. round palette, 10. moistener, 11. polishing stone, 12. cards to be polished.

*Bibliothèque de l'Union Centrale des Arts Décoratifs*

FIG. 4. IMAGE PRINT

The "Virgin and Child with Saint Anne" (c. 1500) has the simplicity and directness
characteristic of many prints on which the stencil laid the color.

*British Museum*

most part somber shelters, brightened only by some chance bit of handiwork, some token from a pilgrimage to a local shrine or nearby fair. But closer relations between East and West, brought about by commerce, crusades and conquests, added two new possessions to enrich the life of the common man. Into his drab world came playing cards for a spare hour's entertainment and the bright image print to hang on wall or from ceiling, and with these things came the block print and the stencil, precursors of the printed pages of Gutenberg. Perhaps the desire for some sacred picture or "little saint," as the image print was often called, some charm for protection that could be secured at small expense, was the outcome of the same universal need and impulse that had left those fragments in the Caves of a Thousand Buddhas and in the ruins of Turfan.

Whether the production of playing cards antedates that of image prints is not definitely known. Dr. Thomas Carter was inclined to place the cards first. It is certain, however, that they were made in Germany, Spain, Italy, and France when the fifteenth century was well under way and that the stencil was a tool in their making. The earliest existing cards, many of which have been found in the covers or boards of old books, are painted by hand, colored by stencil, or printed in simple black outline. Among the oldest, considered by experts as prior to 1440, the crude archaic figures show numerous breaks in the outlines, which point to the stencil rather than the woodblock. The block print, however, was the usual means of printing, and almost always formed the basis on which color was applied. This method produced not only playing cards and religious prints but decorative sheets, an industry which broadened into wallpaper and broadsides, and with little change in the details of technique covered the period from the fifteenth to the middle of the nineteenth century.

Breitkopf, writing in 1784, gives the following account of laying the paint with stencils:

Their method of enlivening their woodcuts was extremely simple. It was not done singly figure by figure, and stroke by stroke with small pencils [brushes] but the whole sheet was covered at once with colour by means of large flat brushes. They took pasteboard, pasted the impression of their print upon it, and cut out all the parts which were to receive the same colour. Thus they formed as many pierced pieces of pasteboard, called "patronen" [stencils], as there were colours in the painting or design.[12]

This method of production, further removed from today than the count of years would warrant, is portrayed in an unusual manner by two card makers (figs. 2 and 3). They come from the series of prints made by Martin Engelbrecht[13] of Augsburg about 1735,

12. Quoted by H. T. Morley in *Old and Curious Playing Cards*.

13. M. Paul Marteau of Maison B. P. Grimaud, conceded to be a final authority on playing cards and small prints, says the man and woman card makers are from the series of costumes of *métiers* or trades first engraved by Hermissin and later reproduced by Martin Engelbrecht.

7

in which he personifies the trades of the day by figures dressed in the tools and products of their craft.[14] According to René Colas this whole series was originally intended as models for costumes of the ballet.

Although throughout Europe the histories of the playing card and the image print parallel each other in much of their development and spread, for both were often the work of the same person and shop, the image print was to have a wider scope and to lead to different endeavors. The earliest image prints, from the fifteenth century, were sacred in character, scenes from the Bible or from the lives of the saints. They naturally had the sanction of the Church and were spread among the people to fortify their faith as "images of preservation" and "bringers of good luck." We may be sure that mendicant friars and itinerant vendors carried them to every fair, and that they found willing purchasers at each shrine of pilgrimage. They were an art for and of the people, primitive in both drawing and coloring. Although most of the first image prints appear to have been tinted by hand, the stencil has added the color to many. An early Italian woodcut, "Calvary" at Prato, and a French "Saint Roc" colored in red, green, blue, maroon, and violet, at the Albertina Museum in Vienna, besides numerous others, indicate that the method was widely distributed. In the Virgin and Child with the young Saint Anne (fig. 4), a French work of 1500, the red and green robes and the yellow seat bring that touch of brightness which appealed to noble and peasant alike.

That the coloring of block prints by means of stencils had become a traditional method by the beginning of the sixteenth century is confirmed by an old woodcut called the Briefmaler (fig. 5), designed by Jost Amman, born in Zurich in 1535. It shows a painter at work in his shop stencilling image prints, with his brushes and colors at his side. More supplies, or the finished papers, are piled on a chest in the rear. What we can distinguish of his patterns suggests that his subjects are not religious. From the German version of the legend the painter appears not to be happy in his branch of art, nor with his pay:

> A Briefmaler am I. With the brush I support myself. . . . I am not partial
> to stencils with which poor work is done and for which the pay is poor.[15]

A literal translation of the Latin legend reads:

> I decorate with various colors all the faces which the printer gave me in

14. Duhamel de Monceau in his *Art du cartier*, Paris, 1762, throws further light on the craft depicted by these prints. To make the stencils of the "point" cards, punches shaped as hearts, diamonds, clubs, and spades were driven through the oiled sheets with a single blow of the mallet. Those for the face cards had a pattern printed in outline which was fastened securely to a sheet of stencil paper by "pin-pegs," and with a sharp pointed knife that pierced the two papers all parts of the figures colored yellow, for

example, were cut out. This operation completed the "yellow stencil," and was repeated with the different colors. The painter passed the brush back and forth in wide motions across the stencil, and the uncolored sheet or *carton* beneath received the color through the openings or "windows."

15. Acknowledgment is made to the Prints Division of the New York Public Library for the translation.

simpler dress. Here the dutiful brush aids me in every part and decorates my work with flowing garments. To each one I give his own color which he ought to have. In all matters I augment his own splendor.

EFfigies varijs diftinguo coloribus omnes,
Quas habitu pictor fimpliciore dedit.
Hic me peniculus iuuat officiofus in omni
Parte, meumĝ vagis veftibus ornat opus.

Cuiĝ fuum tribuo quem debet habere colorem,
Materijs cultus omnibus addo fuos.

FIG. 5. "DER BRIEFMALER"
This woodcut by Jost Amman is one of a series executed for Schopper's *Panoplia Omnium Artium*, 1558.

In France the wood engravers and the colorists of these painted sheets (*papiers peints*) were known as *dominotiers* and their bright papers as *dominos*,[16] terms with no English equivalent. From the end of the fifteenth century to 1850 a list of uses of this popular art included religious pictures, of early production as well as of the nineteenth century; banners in imitation of draperies to be carried on poles by the devout in their pilgrimages; sheets of songs, popular and religious; ballads and short tales to pass away a winter's evening; political squibs and bits of local history, which served as the illus-

16. The *Encyclopédie ou dictionnaire raisonné* (des sciences, des arts, et des métiers), 1765, defines the *domino* sheet: A paper on which the tracing, designs, or figures are first printed with clumsy wooden blocks. The colors are put on afterwards by means of a *patron* or stencil.

trated news sheets of the day; grotesques and caricatures; military posters from Orléans and Epinal to incite a lagging patriotism in those bitter days of the Revolution; and papers for wall hangings which gave the illusion of rich textiles. There were decorative colored prints for the homes of the peasant and bourgeois to be bought for a few pennies; papers to be pasted on cardboards for games of *loto, dames,* and *tarots;* bright squares for lining boxes and clothes presses. And this same peasant could stop at a stall in the market place to buy a box of these sheets, twenty-five of them 12 by 16½ inches, to be placed end to end to dress his fireplace or to make a border for his wall.

Just a hint of the designs may be had from another print by Engelbrecht, which shows a maker of these bright papers as a spirited figure in fancy dress, representing her trade (fig. 6). *La Dominotière's* costume is composed of her tools—stencils and brushes —and "illuminated" papers patterned with flowering branches. In the background we can see her companions preparing the sheets, one holding the brush straight to avoid letting the color slip under the edge of the stencil and blotch the outline. The other essentials of production complete the picture and tell the story of these "painted papers," valued today for their charm of design and clear color.

About 1688 the stencil found itself destined to color the wallpapers of Jean Papillon, the famous master *dominotier.* Known in his own France as the "father of wallpaper," it was he who saw in the single sheets the future development of wallpaper as we know it today. By matching *domino* sheets he produced not only patterns in which motifs repeat but also those in which each sheet is different, making possible large designs imitative of tapestry, scenes, or architectural ornament. The *atelier, "Au Papillon,"* on the rue Saint Jacques was a busy center as we see it from a sketch (fig. 7) made by the son, J. M. Papillon, in 1738. Here we watch the craftsmen and women stirring the dye in the caldrons, coloring the papers by stencils, drying and doing up the finished sheets into packets. We see even the walls being cleaned and the cracks in the plaster being filled before the new decoration can be completed.[17] Sometimes the single sheets were pasted end to end and sold in rolls instead of the usual quires.

In his Treatise on Wood Engraving, written in 1766, J. M. Papillon describes the making of these papers:

> The only thing printed on this sort of paper is the outline of the design, which is engraved on wood. This means of putting on colors by stencil with a brush always produces a certain untidy result.

There may have been difficulties in placing the colors, as Papillon notes, but they were always fresh and gay, and the drawings strong and simple without excess of ornament.

17. The original drawings made in 1738 were found in Langres in the house of Diderot's sister by M. Violle, l'Intendant général de l'armée.

FIG. 6. "UNE DOMINOTIÈRE"

This maker of *domino* papers, showing her craft by her tools and dress,
was also engraved by Martin Engelbrecht about 1735.

*Bibliothèque de l'Union Centrale des Arts Décoratifs*

FIG. 7. MAKING "DOMINO" PAPERS

These *domino* paper makers are reproduced from a wash drawing by J. M. Papillon made in 1738. The women are applying colors through stencils.

*Reproduced through the courtesy of MM. l'Intendant général Violle and Henri Clouzot from "Histoire du papier peint en France"*

In 1723 Savary des Bruslons gives a contemporary tribute when he writes of this paper, used for so long only by the people of the country or the "lesser people of Paris," that it was "brought to such a point of perfection and good taste that beside many shipments to foreign countries and to the larger French cities, there was scarcely a house in Paris, no matter how important, that had not some of it."[18] And for our day M. Clouzot has written, "It is not necessary to be much enlightened in order to prefer a *domino* paper of the seventeenth and eighteenth century, awkwardly colored with a brush, to a roll of paper printed in twelve or fourteen colors by one of the perfected machines of the nineteenth century."[19]

Before leaving France let us examine another early aspect of stencilling, for applying pattern directly to walls antedates the use of the *domino* prints in bringing ornament and color into interiors. In central France churches and other buildings were not only ornamented with the sacred letters I. H. S., as we have already observed, but simple motifs *au pochoir* (by stencil) were early repeated in borders or on vaultings.[20] An example of the characteristic quatrefoil, dating from the fourteenth century, is still visible in the refectory of the Abbaye de l'Epau. The next two centuries give more abundant and more typical illustrations of the stencil's accomplishments in defining architectural divisions with borders and single motifs, in imitating elaborately patterned fabrics, in starring or, to use the French expression, "sowing" backgrounds with simple units, and, in more ambitious undertakings placing single figures or groups, sometimes in combination with other types of painting.

The church at Biozat has an effective early sixteenth century wall stencil of the martyrdom of Saint Sebastian, in which the pale young saint languishes between his tormentors, who are clad in hunting costumes of red, blue, and ochre, against a pale ochre ground with red stars. Contemporary and of equal charm are angels in the compartments of a vaulted ceiling in the crypt of the church at Iseure. On a pale gray ground starred with black and red the half figures, partially hidden behind well-defined clouds, have red dresses slightly modeled in darker red, halos and wings of ochre, and scrolls of white, where the legends have now been erased by time. In this ceiling, as in the Saint Sebastian, stencils were used for the entire composition except for obvious details.

The imitation of fabrics by repeating single designs on a ground was, however,

18. *Dictionnaire universel de commerce.*

19. *Historic Wall-Papers* by Nancy McClelland; introduction by Henri Clouzot, p. 8.

20. For information of the use in borders and patterns on walls and vaultings from the fourteenth to the sixteenth centuries I am indebted to the two volumes of *La peinture décorative en France du XIe au XVIe siècle*, P. Gélis-Didot and H. Laffillée; and *La peinture décorative en France du XVIe au XVIIIe siècle*, Gélis-Didot. In this extensive record of ornament the examples of early stencilling are illustrated by colored plates and by cuts, with detailed descriptions, which we value the more because Viollet-le-Duc, to whom was given the restoration of many medieval buildings and to whom we should naturally turn for comments, does not seem to have mentioned this method, which so often solved the problem of placing decoration on roofs and walls.

the most frequent use of the stencil in this period (fig. 8).[21] Many of these motifs are clearly derived from vestments illustrated in contemporary paintings in Sienna and Pisa, which in turn had borrowed their patterns from the Orient, for the spell of Eastern stuffs so dominated the taste of Europe that their traces are universal. These examples show a striking likeness to the motifs found in two contemporary Florentine panels (fig. 9), the backgrounds of which are stencilled in blue on white. A church of the early fifteenth century at Chateloy has decorations with leaf forms which are especially noteworthy for their design and charm.

Stencilled decoration of the late fifteenth century was not confined to interiors, but was even placed on the outer walls of houses. Naturally most of this ornament has perished, but three examples still survive at Montferrand. It is not to be thought, however, to quote the opinion of Gélis-Didot, that these were isolated instances of their time, because it would be out of character for dwellers in provincial France to venture decoration not generally accepted and in use in their own section. The best preserved house is in the rue Cordelier, where the entire façade is covered with repetitions of two designs, one producing borders in black and orange ochre, the other interlacing the spaces between with compositions in black, terra cotta, and pale ochre (fig. 8b).

From these few illustrations we can see how much the stencil could and did contribute to the decorative art of the Middle Ages. It was one means of simplifying the execution of certain types of ornament, and in the hands of a careful worker produced distinctive decoration.

We should expect to find in England the same decorative methods as on the Continent, for in many respects her artistic history is but another phase of that of her neighbor across the Channel. To the Norman love of color was added that of the Saxons. James K. Colling, writing on decoration in England,[22] reminds us that long before the Battle of Hastings in all probability early wooden churches had been painted both inside and out in vivid hues. But if these structures are only ruins or tradition, illustrations of the stencilled work of the fifteenth century remain, where the wooden roofs and rafters, sometimes richly decorated in color, frequently bear the sacred monogram alternating with that of the Virgin. One instance of this type, dating from 1420–1440, may be found on the nave roof of Holy Trinity Church, Blythburgh, Suffolk. Mr. Philip M. Johnston, who examined the rafters when some reparation was being done under his care, deposited

21. The English term "stencil" may have come from this process of starring or laying in of backgrounds by this technique, since it is apparently derived from the Old French *estenceler*, to sparkle or cover with stars, which in turn comes from the Latin *stincella* or *scintilla*, a spark. Seventeenth and eighteenth century France, however, used other terms, *patron, moule*; while the Modern French is generally *pochoir, poncif*, and *modèles découpés*.

22. *English Mediaeval Foliage and Coloured Decoration Taken from Buildings of the 12th to the 15th Century*, London, 1874.

FIG. 8. FIFTEENTH CENTURY FRENCH WALL STENCIL MOTIFS

These units were reproduced from small stencils cut by Miss Alice S. Erskine. *A* and *D* are from a church at Chatelroy, the background unit *C* came from Chateladrun, *E* is from Cunot, *F* is from an abandoned church at Saint-Pierre-le-Moutier, and the two units of *B* cover the façade of a house at Montferrand.

*"La peinture décorative en France du XI<sup>e</sup> au XVI<sup>e</sup> siècle,"*
*by P. Gélis-Didot and H. Laffillée*

FIG. 9. FIFTEENTH CENTURY FLORENTINE WALL PANELS
The backgrounds are stencilled in imitation of a textile.
*Staats Museum, Berlin*

FIG. 10. DETAIL OF AN ENGLISH ROOD SCREEN
The screen, from Ranworth Church, Norfolk, has this stencilled unit as a background for saints on
alternating panels. The stencil applied an adhesive which was overlaid with gold.
*Courtesy of Dr. Joan Evans*

in the Victoria and Albert Museum tracings of the designs with notes on the handling. Both the monogram I. H. S. and the floral motifs are stencilled on a white ground with scrolled traceries freehand, in shades of green. In fact, from his observations Mr. Johnston is inclined to carry the use of the stencil "in England further back than the fifteenth century examples in Norfolk, Suffolk, etc. to the fourteenth century, even to the thirteenth, as in the wall-paintings of pure pattern work in West Walton Church, Norfolk."[23]

Stencilling, however, seems not to have been practiced to any large extent in England before the fifteenth century. Norfolk and Suffolk have left perhaps some of the best examples of this medieval work. The churches of this section in the same century and the next contribute in the ornamentation of their rood screens some extremely interesting examples of stencilling. Because there was a great scarcity of good building stone in East Anglia, the churches were built principally of flint; but oak abounded in the dense forest, and the fine interior decoration in these eastern counties is perhaps due to the more common use of wood. Wood, together with the plastered wall, suggested more than did stone the perfect surface for ornament in color. Moreover, during the reign of Edward III (1327–1377), owing to the active trade in cloth and wool between the east coast of England and Flanders, East Anglia was a prosperous province, and tempted Flemish painters and weavers as well as artisans from the south of Europe. It was undoubtedly the competition between these artisans and English craftsmen which stirred the native colorists to exert their utmost skill. Many of the rood screens are richly patterned in red, yellow, blue, green, black, white, and gold, with both pictorial paintings by hand and designs by the stencil.

In the fifteenth century, to repeat the comments of Professor Tristram, the stencil was used principally for gold diaper on backgrounds, for gold motifs on the garments of saints and other sacred figures, and for background units in color. Sometimes the outline was disguised by adding brush work. Patterned and brocaded textiles often furnished more elaborate types of design, like those on the screens at Saxthorpe, Norfolk, where the brush has also given final touches.

Many instances of this early decoration, obscured since the Reformation by whitewash or paint, have been rescued by careful removal of the outer coat. Such was the case with a portion of paneling of an oak screen from West Stow Church, Suffolk, which dates from the first quarter of the fifteenth century (fig. 11). On its arrival at the Victoria and Albert Museum it was found covered with white paint, the removal of which left the stencilled decoration uninjured. The fragment is divided into eight panels painted alternately red and green, with floral patterns in white, now toned to a deep ivory. Touches of green and yellow are seen on the large flowers which suggest the lily con-

23. Quoted from a letter in reply to an inquiry by the author as to the period when stencilling was first used in England.

ventionalized; the floral motifs in the cusped arches above the panels appear to be conventionalized thistles. The design has the character of the stencil, the broad veinings acting as ties for the bold formal pattern so suitable to the structure of the screenwork of this "Golden Age" of English woodwork. Glimpses of the oak appear throughout the panels where the paint is worn, giving a warmth to the broken color. Only one narrow buttress of the screen remains, but it too bears a tracery by the stencil.

One of the most colorful and spirited screens is the sixteenth century example at Ranworth, on which Professor Tristram considers there is an outstanding illustration of stencilled ornament. Many artists using various decorative methods have obviously contributed to its beauty. One of the motifs of most frequent occurrence (fig. 10) is used as a background for saints as well as in separate panels. Although the three small blossoms are handwork, the remainder is stencilled in burnished gold against a deep green ground, for the slight flattening of the unit of design remains constant. One of the thirteen or more panels on which the ornament occurs has as many as eighty units, so that the stencil must have been a welcome aid in the long task.[24]

These examples are only a few of the many that might be gathered, and it would seem that stencilled decoration on ecclesiastical furniture in this period is deserving of more careful study and of a more complete record of forms and colors; such details add to our exact historical knowledge. The descriptive museum label on one piece of woodwork from a Suffolk church, obviously stencilled, merely designated the design as "painted," without a mention of the method, nor does the most comprehensive study of the English rood screen even use the term.

During the sixteenth and seventeenth centuries the uses to which the stencil was put in England multiplied many times. The late Charles Sayle, writing on the finding in 1911 of some early fragments of English stamped wallpaper (1509) at Christ Church College, Cambridge, notes that "the earlier custom for applying decoration to walls was to use a stencilled pattern on the surface itself," and cites the example found at St. Cross, Winchester, as the work of Cardinal Beaufort (c. 1500), as well as similar designs on plaster done in the late sixteenth century and discovered at Trinity College by Dr. W. Morley Fletcher. An old manor house in Hertfordshire has a room with stencilled walls in soft reds on a cream ground. Though the present work was done only fifty years ago, it is a copy of a very old wall in the neighborhood, which no longer exists. Tudor roses appear with other designs in an all-over pattern. If this room conveys in any way the character of the early stencilled wall, we should wish to see it revived more often.

Although careful research has been made only recently in England for examples of early paper, fragments colored by the stencil like those on the Continent have been

24. I am indebted to Mr. F. S. Smith for identifying this special pattern as an example where the adhesive was applied by the stencil; also for tracings and measurements of the unit.

FIG. 11. PANELS OF AN ENGLISH ROOD SCREEN

On this screen, from a church at West Stow, Suffolk, there is fifteenth century stencilling.

*Victoria and Albert Museum*

FIG. 13. DETAIL OF ENGLISH WALLPAPER

This example was printed from a woodblock and stencilled in two tones of blue on a white ground (c. 1740).

*Victoria and Albert Museum*

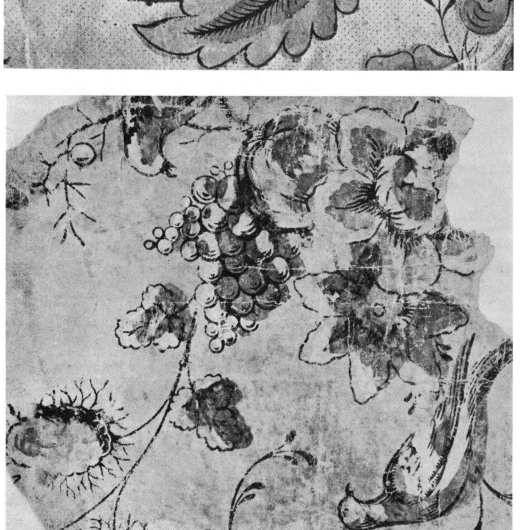

FIG. 12. FRAGMENT OF ENGLISH WALLPAPER

Found at the Old Bell Inn, Sawbridgeworth, Hertfordshire, this paper has
a pale blue ground, a black outline and stencilled colors (c. 1700).

*Victoria and Albert Museum*

found dating back to 1600, the date given a paper from a fifteenth century timber house in the village of Borden, Kent. How widely wallpaper was favored in London cannot be determined, for the great fire of 1668 destroyed whatever hangings were in use before that time. It is often only a chance occurrence which brings to notice some bit of paper, such as that found at the Old Bell Inn, Sawbridgeworth, during the alteration of a window. The collection at the Victoria and Albert Museum includes many examples of recent accession. Flower sprays, birds, and conventional designs in clear tones pattern these fragments, and even if the colors overlap and fail to meet, it does not matter. The black outlines of the woodblock in many instances are indistinct, and on some it is obvious that the color was applied before the outline was printed. In fact, this practice was advised by Dossie, whose directions were to stencil all parts of each color in the design and then to give an outline to the whole by printing it brown or black.

In a fragment of English wallpaper (fig. 13) which is in two tones of blue on a black and white ground, the register is fairly accurate, but in the one from the Old Bell Inn (fig. 12) it is a matter of seeming indifference to the worker whether or not the stencil guides the color to the proper spot, but the result has its own charm for the eye, and there is always satisfaction in the grace of design and color. The background of this latter paper is a dull blue against which green leaves, red flowers, sometimes overlaid with brown by a second stencil, and birds of blue and red show distinctly the marks of the brush. The tempera has left an outline less blurred than when water color was used.

Sometimes the stencil alone designed and colored these decorative papers. A portion of an English wallpaper from The Holy Trees, a house in Colchester (fig. 14), is an excellent example on which the stencil creates its own pattern without the aid of woodblocked outlines. On a gray-white ground the shades of dulled blues and browns have touches of yellow. At the base the soil is broken with small hillocks from which serpentine tree trunks with branching leaves and flowers, designed with great boldness, rise at regular intervals. The four blues overlap one another as they form the flower and define the detail, and the whole bears a striking resemblance to contemporary English needlework.

By the seventeenth century there had come into fashion a type of paper known in England as flock and in France as *tontisse* (shorn), made in imitation of brocade and velvet hangings. Flock, consisting of finely ground wool gathered from the clothmaker's shearings, was applied to a ground by an adhesive. The method was an early one, and some small flock prints in imitation of textiles date from the fifteenth century. In France records indicate that the adhesive for the flock papers was impressed upon them by means of engraved woodblocks only, but in England these papers were produced not only with the aid of woodblocks but also with stencils of leather or oilcloth, as described in 1758 by the often quoted Robert Dossie. The process was simple. A design was wood-

15

blocked or stencilled upon the paper or canvas with glue, varnish, or heavy oil, and the powdered wool was scattered over the entire surface. When it was dry, the loose flock was removed, leaving a counterfeit textile whose texture satisfied both eye and touch, the whole produced at no great cost. In an example from the office of His Majesty's Privy Council (fig. 15), dating from 1735, the bold pattern, large in scale, is red on a pale rose ground. These English papers were as a rule limited to two colors, one for the ground and another for the flock, and their beauty lies largely in the breadth and vigor of their design.

One more use of the stencil should be added to these references, one only recently brought into the field of scholarly research by Miss Eva Judd O'Meara in her "Notes on Stencilled Choir-Books."[25] Although stencils during the Middle Ages placed signatures, sacred monograms, and ornamental capitals in manuscripts, it was apparently not until long after the invention of printing that they were used in the making of those glorious seventeenth and eighteenth century books of music, where stencils were employed not only for notes and ornamental initials but even for the words of the text. Many of these choir books, done by individual scribes, are of such merit that they bear comparison with fine printing.

It was the chance finding of a stencilled Graduale among some volumes of music at Yale University which prompted the article on this neglected subject. This service book of the Gregorian chant, made in 1755 for the Augustinian Abbey of Loo, Flanders, by "U. Boddaert," was prefaced with a letter to his abbot describing the process of stencilling. It is a large volume of 332 pages of heavy, watermarked paper, bound in leather with metal clasps, and showing the signs of much handling. The pages are of fine and finished workmanship. Ornamental initials with medallions stencilled in red, black, green, blue, or yellow mark the greater festivals of the year, while religious symbols and other small paintings such as that of the Three Kings at Epiphany seem to have the outlines traced "with a stencil and the color filled in free-hand," but the extraordinary "beauty of the book lies entirely in the treatment of the text and music." All of the letters of the four alphabets used are slender and effective, well designed, and well cut, and the notes throughout are finished with serifs. The page reproduced (fig. 16) shows the balanced proportion of the notes and letters and gives proof of a perfected craft.

The chief source of information on stencilled books and their makers was a collection of notes gathered together more than a century and a quarter ago into a chapter of a book by Fischer von Waldheim,[26] the learned librarian of the University of Mainz, who was apparently an enthusiastic believer in the worth of the stencil in the hands of an able artificer. He collected the names of many expert workers of the seventeenth and eight-

25. *Gutenberg-Jahrbuch*, 1933, pp. 169 ff.
26. *Beschreibung einiger typographischen Seltenheiten* *nebst Beyträgen zur Erfindungsgeschichte der Buchdruckerkunst*, 1800–1804.

16

FIG. 14. DETAIL FROM ENGLISH STENCILLED WALLPAPER

Produced entirely by stencils without the customary woodblocked outline, this paper comes from "The Holy Trees," Colchester. The complete panels are 6 ft. 4 in. high and date from about 1750.

*Victoria and Albert Museum*

FIG. 15. PANEL OF ENGLISH FLOCK PAPER

On this wall covering the adhesive for holding the flock was applied by
the stencil. The date is approximately 1735.

*Victoria and Albert Museum*

semper, & in sæcula

A Lle lu ia

℣ Ascendit De-

tio ne,& Dominus

FIG. 16. PAGE FROM A STENCILLED GRADUALE

The Graduale or book of the Mass was stencilled in red and black for the Augustinian
monastery at Loo, Flanders, by U. Boddaert, 1755.

*Library of the School of Music, Yale University*

eenth centuries who were practiced in using stencils for printing and ornament, and for painting flowers, altar hangings and other objects; he describes the stencil cutters in Paris who made alphabets, flowers, and other decorations, and he reports that he had himself seen alphabets offered for sale by street vendors on the Pont Neuf. No reference to the stencil can awaken more interest than the observations of Fischer, shedding light as they do on individual workers, creative in the love of their work.

We often have facts relating to the lives of the great masters of art which make them real for us, but in the minor crafts such details are all too often lacking. What sort of man, we ask, was Claude Renard of Liège, who in 1736 came to Mainz, and who received a public testimonial praising his skill for making stencilled designs and alphabets better even than those obtained by print, and for willingly teaching his craft to others? For his skill he was later exempted from the payment of taxes by the town council. Fischer shared in this admiration for his fellow-townsman, for he devotes three pages to a description of the patterns: asters, pinks, roses, tulips, some of which required several stencils. And there was Peter Thomas Bauer, a monk of the Carthusian Monastery near Mainz, who in 1760 stencilled a choir book of 252 parchment pages. The title page, with its flowers, vases, a crown with golden rays above the monogram I. H. S., and a pair of birds holding blossoms in their beaks, was so tempting that someone, unable to resist the longing to possess it, cut the page from the volume.

Yet if we have little information about the craftsmen themselves, we know them from their work—work extending down the ages and across many lands. We see them with their stencils bordering the bark cloth of Fiji; repeating the image of the great Buddha on paper, silk, and temple walls; in Japan, patterning satin and serving the large industry of cotton printing. In Europe we can trace them as they ornament church and monastery, walls and rood screens, apply color to image prints and playing cards, and later advance to *domino* sheets and wallpaper. The story is only partially told, for as we turn to America with her stencilled walls and furniture, we shall recall these antecedents and notice still others which bear directly on her development of the tool. But there is perhaps no better summary of the method, its history and its achievements than that of Gélis-Didot—a "process known to everyone, and as old as the need to which it responds."

# PART ONE: STENCILLED WALLS

THE stencilled walls of America, like so many things which have been closest to the daily living of its early settlers, have passed with them, and too frequently we unearth these and other intimate records only by chance, and almost always in fragmentary form. Fine furniture has remained, a treasured heirloom, but the common things, the four walls which have surrounded everyday comings and goings, have crumbled away or been buried beneath layers of paint and paper by new generations who thought the decoration crude and out of fashion. Yet along country roads, often in deserted by-ways left by changing currents of transportation and industry, and sometimes on main thoroughfares which still link the first settlements as they did in the early days, there is a sufficient number of stencilled walls to tell of their popularity, to enable us to reconstruct the story of their simple patterns and clear color, and to renew an appreciation of their beauty.

The walls which have been recorded in this volume give in no way a complete history of the subject, even as we are able to know it after the lapse of over a century; for the ground which I have covered is a relatively small one and includes only a limited portion of the countryside in Connecticut, Massachusetts, Vermont, New Hampshire, Maine, Rhode Island, New York, and Ohio. Even in that section there are undoubtedly many examples still hidden behind paper, paint, or plaster; and other localities may add different treatments as well as new designs. It is a search that leads into quiet villages and over grass-grown roads, for to my knowledge no early stencilled walls have been found in the larger centers of life. Urban development with its rapid growth does not preserve for us the handiwork of the past as does the slower moving rural district, for the constant demolishing of old houses in the city and their replacement by other buildings would naturally obliterate all traces of this work.

Just when our forefathers began to ornament the walls of their dwellings by the stencil we do not know, but, in the area indicated, the earliest date which I have found for the use of stencilling as a wall decoration is 1778. Most stencilled rooms appear to belong to the first quarter of the nineteenth century, when their presence in such quantity throughout New England proves their favor. It was a favor honestly won, for these walls, even as we see them today, show forms of ornament bold in conception and stripped of the trivial—decorative in the essential qualities. In execution, however, they show great range of skill; some marked by a primitive hand, childlike and naïve in character and treatment, others the work of trained artists with a knowledge of arrangement and design.

Although we can probably never gather all the facts that went into the making of this chapter in the decorative arts of this young nation, the outline of its development is not difficult to trace. After the log cabin of the settlers had given place to the square, well-balanced house so typical of New England and rough-hewn surfaces to plastered walls, there was need of ornament and color to satisfy the feeling of achievement which had come with material progress, and a wish to carry on the traditions of distant home-lands, a desire to keep the culture that linked this new world with the old.

Existence for the settler on the land or in the small colonial community had been, for the most part, a hard fight for food and shelter with little assurance of security. To meet the needs of each day had been a full task; the house, the farm, the many duties to be performed for the welfare of the community were the first demands. There had been little time to think of bringing color into the home, nor had bright walls been encouraged by the Puritan outlook. But by eighteen hundred more tolerance had come with the greater religious and political freedom, while, harbored by peace, the material progress of the centers of industry was carried to the villages by the rapid expansion of transportation. Waterways and new roads were being opened, and by boat and by stage-coach wares and fashions were reaching the remote and outlying districts. With these changes even the farmer was able to plan the adornment of house and wall to satisfy his inherited sense of design and love of color.

One means of fulfilling this wish for color in daily living was already at hand, for among those wares which passed along the routes of commerce were sheets and rolls of wallpaper approved by fashion both at home and across the sea, for wallpaper had come early to the Colonies from France and England. "Painted papers," colored by the stencil, were found in the inventory of Michael Perry of Boston, who died in 1700, and Daniel Henchman records their sale from 1712 to 1714.[1] A fragment of one *domino* paper treasured at the Historical Society in Nantucket carries the title, a "Peep at the Moon," printed in capitals across the heavens.[2] The popularity of wallpapers together with the obviously higher cost of imported ones soon encouraged American reproduction. Apparently the first Colonial manufacturer was Plunket Fleeson of Philadelphia in 1739, where he sold his product in a shop with blankets, goose feathers, and buttons. By the end of the century the industry had greatly increased, with changes in design reflecting the shifting modes from abroad.

Geometric and floral motifs, borders and all-over patterns had their turn, but borders and stripes were especially in favor. An advertisement during the time of William and Mary (1688–1702) of the Blue Paper Warehouse, Aldermanbury, London, gives the practical reason for their first use with the *domino* papers in its instructions:

> First Cutt your Breadths to your intended heights, then tack them at the
> top and bottom . . . leave a vacancy of about an inch for the borders to
> Cover, then cut out the borders into the same lengths and tack them strait

1. McClelland, Nancy: *Historic Wall-Papers*, p. 238.
2. Originally on the walls of the Jonathan Paddock
house, Pearl Street, Nantucket, and referred to by Kate Sanborn in *Old Time Wallpapers*, p. 96.

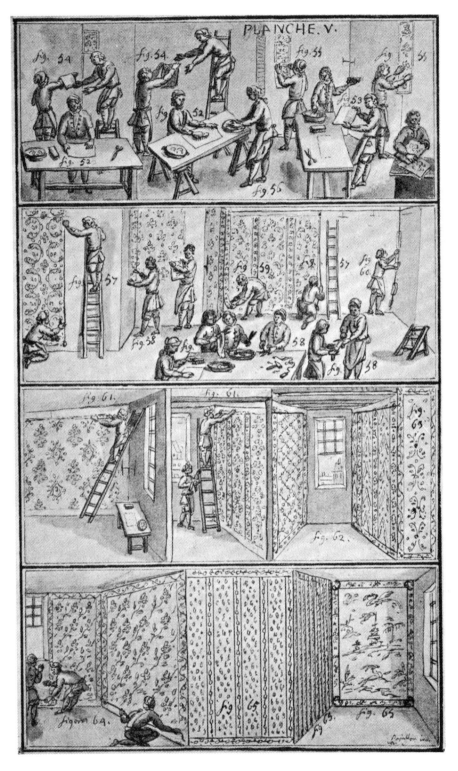

FIG. 17. HANGING "DOMINO" WALLPAPERS

The original is another wash drawing made by J. M. Papillon in 1735.

*Reproduced through the courtesy of MM. l'Intendant général Violle and Henri Clouzot from "Histoire du papier peint en France"*

FIG. 18. ORIGINAL KIT OF WALL STENCILS

These stencils and brushes were used by Moses Eaton (1796–1886) of Hancock and Dublin, New
Hampshire, and probably also by his father, Moses Eaton (1753–1833).

*Owned by the author*

down over the Edges of the Breadths and likewise at the top of the room in imitation of a Cornish and the same . . . at the bottom.[3]

Perhaps they owed some measure of their continued reputation to J. M. Papillon, son of the great *dominotier* who had been the first to combine single sheets into continuous pattern. But we know that this liking for borders was shared by those of taste in our own communities, for in 1771 a letter from the painter John Singleton Copley, relating to the papering of his house on Beacon Hill, Boston, directs: "Get the next low prised papers, carry them to the Sealing and with the Border the Rooms will look well."[4] The newspapers of Boston, New York, and Philadelphia carried numerous advertisements of borders in particular, and they were even advertised in some of the smaller centers. An announcement of Thomas S. Webbe in the *Albany Gazette* for June 5, 1795, specifies a great variety of borders among his stock. A bill rendered the previous year by William Poyntell contains the items "120 yards elegant narrow rose border" and "8 yards festoon."[5] Both were used with plain or with all-over pattern papers. Borders still found a place at the top or bottom of a wall even after 1817 when scenic papers, so much the rage in France, had crossed the ocean in trading vessels to find equal favor in America, especially Dufour's "Bay of Naples" and the "Monuments of Paris." Yet despite domestic production, wallpaper, in its wide variety, was still a luxury which many might desire but few could afford.

One has only to compare a group of these papers with stencilled walls to see that wallpapers were an important influence on the actual placement of the stencilled patterns which so frequently were used to bring into the country house and tavern the same strong color. The treatment of frieze and border, the division of wall space into panels, and the grouping of designs indicate clearly that there was more than a chance relationship between the two. In one of Papillon's wash drawings (fig. 17) made for the encyclopedia of Diderot and d'Alembert, but for some reason not included in the work, we see the borders used at the base of the wall and as a frieze. They also define the corners of the room, while stripes divide the wall surfaces into vertical panels. The sprays in their placement suggest many arrangements on the stencilled wall.

Although stencilling as wall decoration met in its own way the demand created by the mode of wallpaper, and followed in treatment many of its decorative arrangements, it imitated the actual designs only in a very limited way and consequently has a singular integrity of pattern and a tradition of its own, as we shall see when we consider the motifs in detail.

3. Photographed from a handbill in the British Museum, and reproduced in *A History of English Wallpaper*, by Alan Victor Sugden and John Ludlam Edmondson, plate 33.

4. Quoted in *Old-Time New England*, publication of the Society for the Preservation of New England Antiquities, January, 1935, p. 91.

5. McClelland, Nancy: *Historic Wall-Papers*, p. 256.

The origin of stencilling in America has awakened little interest, but we do find a few references to early stencilled walls which attribute their origin to the Pennsylvania German settlers from the Rhine Valley. Yet these pioneers from the Palatinate, like those from other localities, brought the skill of their home arts with them, and, had the stencilled room been a significant part of their tradition, they would also have developed it, to some extent at least, in America. I have as yet been unable to find any stencilled walls in Pennsylvania, although I have asked many who are familiar with local arts and the history of the period. Such evidence for their non-existence is, of course, not conclusive, for they may have escaped even the most searching eye. In this region painted patterns adorn the exterior of large barns, but I know of no stencilled rooms of early date in William Penn's country. Stencilling has also been ascribed to itinerant Hessian soldiers who earned a living by this craft after the close of the Revolution. Though I have succeeded in finding only a few of the names of the actual artisans, there has been among them no trace that would suggest these antecedents, and the tradition of the Hessian soldier appears to be unverified.

A majority of the settlers in the section where stencilled walls remain were of English ancestry, and their memories and cultural traditions reached back to the shires of England, and especially to East Anglia. Even if the story of the stencilled decoration in Britain has not yet been written, we have already seen that there and on the Continent, in both ecclesiastical and domestic building, this humble tool had a very real part. As a simple means of bringing strong, clear color into dark interiors it was probably as familiar to the painter as was his brush or his rule. Even if no craftsman brought to America the recollection of some particular wall in a far-off homeland, the use of the stencil in putting the color on the printed outline of wallpaper could easily suggest to some ingenious worker its direct application on the wall. Coloring through a stencil did not wholly pass with the *domino* papers, for Robert Dossie is still advising it in *The Handmaid to the Arts* (1764),[6] that manual of practical directions, which was sufficiently popular to go into a second edition at a time when first printings usually sufficed. He advocates the use of the stencil for the coloring of the less expensive papers because it is a cheaper method than "print," and "can be done by the common workman." Interestingly enough he defines the limitations of the stencil as a tool not only for paper but also for wall ornamentation when he adds:

> This is nevertheless only practical . . . where there are only detached masses or spots of colours; for where there are small continued lines, or parts that run one into another, it is difficult to preserve the connection or continuity.

6. *Op. cit.*, vol. II, pp. 455, 456.

22

We may be sure that along with the itinerants who carried so many products of the national industries to outlying neighborhoods went journeyman artists, singly or in pairs, seeking patronage. Rumors were abroad from New England's coast and hill towns of the building of new houses and the enlargement of old ones. Instead of carrying rolls of expensive wallpaper with which to tempt his clients, the painter had but to open his kit and unroll his own talent upon the walls. His outfit was modest, consisting of some dry colors, brushes, a supply of stencils cut from thick paper, some measuring tools, a builder's cord, and a piece of chalk. With them he was prepared at no great cost to the owner of the house to transform the walls of white plaster to tones of ochre, red, and green, and given a supply of skimmed milk, a much used medium in mixing the color, he gave good measure in exchange for a small wage and "his board and lodging."

The arrival of a journeyman artist was an event of importance to the village; a welcome would be waiting for him by those eager to refurbish the old house, and an audience at hand to spur him on while he mixed his colors. We can see the family gathered to choose the backgrounds, pale pink, ochre, or gray. The north parlor should have yellow. How would they plan the patterns? Would a vine be used to divide the wall into vertical panels? What borders would they choose? Would they have the heart and the frieze with bells? The rooms would be done at some inconvenience to the family, but the reward would be worth it. This picture is not one drawn from imagination; it is what happened over and over again in every state of New England.

Besides itinerants there were many local artisans following other trades and occupations who could turn painter on demand, for it required no outstanding skill to stencil a simple wall. Some workers may have returned to farm or shop from the active life of the road and plied their trade as opportunity offered in nearby towns and villages. Such, no doubt, was Moses Eaton of Hancock, New Hampshire, probably a journeyman in his youth, for a single neighborhood could hardly have worn down the bristles of his brush or piled the green paint so high upon his stencils. On the other hand, in the case of Lydia Eldredge Williams, it was "home talent" which stencilled the two rooms of an old house in Ashfield, Massachusetts.

To realize the range in ability of these early craftsmen, one need only turn to the illustrations to see how individual painters have imprinted their skill in design and color. We find a variety of forms among these strong patterns; borders of flowering stems, roses, acorns, and conventionalized leaves resembling laurel competed for favor with a multiplicity of geometric figures. Borders outlined the windows, mantels, and doors, and the corners of the rooms, while deep friezes edged the ceilings. There were swags with bells and heavy tassels, conventionalized maple leaves, designs of scattered flowers, pine trees and crossed boughs, classic patterns, and deep festoons with cords and pendants in which French influence is apparent. The overmantel carried the elaborate pattern of the room, where birds, weeping willows, spirals, the Federal eagle, woven baskets or urns filled with flowers were placed in varied arrangements. Quarter-fans filled the corners of plain wall surfaces, framed by narrow borders of geometric design or by graceful vines and flowers. On the broad wall spaces, frequently divided by stripes, single motifs were used: floral sprays, oak leaves, the pineapple, stars, diamonds, sunbursts, and other forms derived from the circle. Small and large discs as well as hearts frequently supplied strong accents of contrasting color at the center of some motifs. The swastika, an emblem universal in its use, is seen in southern Berkshire County, Massachusetts, and in Connecticut. All-over designs of continuous pattern were also included in the wide scale of stencil ornament. We find different elements of design combined; a motif from the classic revival will be artlessly grafted onto a design which is primitive both in origin and execution. It is such unschooled treatments that make us unconsciously apply the term "folk art"; but when the same elements are handled by better-trained artisans, the result acquires a sophistication that raises it above the primitive into the field of skilled endeavor.

Many of the designs were repeated or used with variations from 1778 to the end of the first quarter of the nineteenth century. The same motifs are found from Connecticut to Ohio and from New York to Maine, but this community of design need not surprise us, for itinerants would naturally have copied from one another. It was the spirit of the day to lend willingly a possession, and patterns were readily borrowed from a friendly neighbor. Although I have found no evidence that stencils had a common source of distribution or were sold by itinerant vendors, some facts may come to light indicating such a practice. The wall stencils of Moses Eaton, cut from heavy paper of different makes and qualities, do not suggest quantity production. The unschooled artisan usually lacked the ability or interest to make his own patterns, so, when one motif was found successful, it was easier to copy and repeat it than create less successful ones, especially as the technique of the stencil, being controlled by the placement of the ties, presents a rather specialized problem in design.

In cutting stencils a sharp knife was the essential tool. Nothing intricate in structure could be cut from stout paper saturated and toughened by applications of oil and paint to prepare it for hard use. Stencils were often destined to be rolled into a pack and carried on long journeys. When in 1820 an unnamed itinerant went on horseback from Boston to Hollis, Maine, he obviously took in his bundle the frieze which he stencilled at "Quillcote"[7] to border his freehand painting. We do not know on how many other occasions this border of festoons and dots was placed on walls along the one hundred mile route, but, even if it did not do other service, the trip alone would test any paper pattern. The original stencils which I have seen from three old outfits were all cut from heavy

7. Home of the late Kate Douglas Wiggin.

paper on which coats of oil, paint, and sometimes shellac had been applied, although in the case of the rooms in the Capt. John Coolidge house, Plymouth, Vermont, the stencils were made of leather. In Moses Eaton's kit there is a beveled edge on many of the patterns to render a sharper outline to the motifs. A sufficient margin was left surrounding the cut-outs to protect the walls from the careless handling of the paintbrush. The brushes themselves were round with long handles, smaller ones being used for accents of color. Borders of repeating forms were cut in strips about twenty inches long, individual units being reproduced as many as six or eight times in one stencil. For some separate motifs a single stencil produced the completed pattern, while others required the combination of two, three, and sometimes four stencils (one for each color), making elaborate ornaments. Large friezes of bold pattern were usually composed of two stencils and two colors; the green would be put on first and carried around the top of the four walls to allow sufficient time for the paint to dry before the red pattern was superimposed. No register marks appear on the old patterns, although in the friezes a straight edge was gained by placing the top of the stencil against the ceiling. For vertical bands and single motifs the careful worker used a chalked cord in the same manner as did the busy artisans illustrated in Papillon's drawings.

Once designs are chosen and the patterns cut, stencilling a wall is a simple process. Few directions are needed except to use a flat color, to keep the stencils free from paint on the under side which touches the wall surface, to use the paint sparingly on the brush (a little is better than too much), and to mix enough paint to complete the work in order to insure uniformity of color. A scale drawing of the room to be patterned may be made and the wall treatment planned inch by inch, as perhaps the artisan did in the case of the Hickox house in Washington, Connecticut, although more probably he worked, as many another, without a detailed plan. Moderate care in the arrangement and placement of the designs is the prime requisite for good results. The stenciller has none of the problems that confront the paperhanger; there is no need of having a smooth wall or of applying size, no matching of figures, no cutting or measuring of long rolls of paper into lengths, and no question of mixing paste to hold it flat and fast.

The colors of these early painters were for the most part strong and enduring. From the wreck of fallen buildings I have gathered fragments of old plaster which still show sharp pattern and pure color. A flat paint was used, and whatever broken color we see today is the result of fading and exposure, for the designs were never shaded. Black, greens, yellows, pinks and reds predominate, although there was an occasional red-brown, and rarely blue. Green seems to have been the most fugitive, for in many instances the blue in its mixture has disappeared leaving only yellow. Besides the original plaster, the backgrounds were limited to yellow and red ochres, blue, and shades of rose which can be described in no better way than that they are the tones of Joe-Pye weed.

By way of comparison, the primitive artist's paintbox was not so different in its color combinations from that of an itinerant. Black, white, and yellow and red ochre have an age-long tradition and are among the first pigments used. We find them in the earliest existing frescos in the caves of Spain and France. Yellow and red earth, chalk and charcoal need little or no preparation. In Egypt from 8000 to 5800 B.C. tomb frescos show the use of the same natural earths with the additional red of cinnabar and the blue of copper; in Crete there are later examples in the frescos of Knossos, 1500 B.C., where charcoal as well as yellow and red ochre was again used. Slate palettes still exist on which the colors have clung these many centuries.

Although the colors of stencilled walls lead our imagination back through the centuries to the scenes of man's first wall paintings, the pigments of our period were not the natural earths. Numerous advertisements from contemporary newspapers show that dry colors were to be had at an early date in the Colonies. By 1724 "all sorts of colors ground in oil, fit for painting, by Wholesale or Retail, at Reasonable rates" were advertised in the *Boston News-Letter* (June 4–11). These dry colors were mixed with various mediums, skimmed milk being frequently used. A chemical analysis was unable to determine whether the paint on certain fragments of plaster gathered in Vermont was tempera or oil. On the wall of Moses Eaton's house it is evident that oil was the solvent.

The name of Moses Eaton has already been frequent in these pages, but justly so, since much of my knowledge of stencilled walls has come through the possession of the old work kit (fig. 18) of this artisan from Hancock and Dublin, New Hampshire. For many years his outfit stood in the attic of his farmhouse in Dublin, where he perhaps put it himself after the last wall by his hand had been completed. His patterns are to become familiar to us through the following illustrations. The stencils themselves, with paint caked upon them, give the reds and greens which Eaton used, and the clean underside of the thick cut-outs indicates how neat-handed an artisan he was. The much used kit makes us feel almost a partaker in his day's work.

## MASSACHUSETTS

The first date given me for a wall decorated by the stencil in America is 1778, when the old Goodale homestead (fig. 19) at Marlborough, Massachusetts, was remodeled by Abner Goodale against the coming of his future wife, Molly Howe, whose father, Ezekiel Howe, was owner of the Redhorse Tavern (now known as the Wayside Inn) at Sudbury two miles away. The original house, a one room dwelling, was built in 1702 by John Goodale, grandson of the immigrant, but seven generations added to the old house until it numbered nine rooms, as it stands today. Recent work of restoration by

FIG. 19. STENCILLED WALL, GOODALE HOUSE, MARLBOROUGH
The patterns were stencilled in 1778 when Abner Goodale "redded up the
homestead for his bride."
*Owned by Dr. and Mrs. Arthur M. Greenwood*

*(Reproduced in color following page 80)*

the present owners has brought to light the original pine sheathing, the floor and ceiling boards, two enormous fireplaces, and what for us has special significance, five rooms with walls of plaster "stencilled in gorgeous design and color, done in 1778 when Abner Goodale 'redded up the homestead' for his bride."[8] All of the stencilling was found under paper except a wall surface back of a large cupboard, where the pattern was preserved in almost perfect condition.

Abner Goodale had been wounded in the battle of White Plains, and during the time he was invalided at home the old house was enlarged. Five stencilled rooms were part of the embellishment of the new second story, though whether they are the work of Abner's hand or that of another is not known. The walls are today very much as they were in 1778; a minimum of reparation has been done, whole sections of wall surface remaining untouched; against this brilliant background stands contemporary furniture. The dull yellow of the ochre walls with their bright and vigorous patterns, the glow of the pine floor and furniture, and the bronze of old chintz give a true picture of rooms of this period. It is more than a picture, for these are actually rooms of 1778 with no discord of electric fixture or heating device to mar wall or floor. On the white and ochre walls of five bedrooms are patterns stencilled in shades of green, red, pale rose, and blue-black, some of which we shall find in other houses. In one room is the frieze of swags and wedding bells. What more appropriate decoration could Abner Goodale have chosen for his young wife?

At Upton on the Mendon road, not far to the southwest, in a house whose age has been completely disguised by recent alterations, four motifs remain in a built-in bedroom closet which are identical with those at Marlborough. Here is the same border of heavy leaves with rounded edges (which we are also to see in Rhode Island), the upright of diamonds, and two single wall patterns, one a variant of the well-known circular design, the other a nine-petaled flower. The illustration (fig. 20) shows a section of the stencilling which adhered to the back of the wallpaper torn from the wall by the owner so that I might see the original. The tempera paint made an interesting transfer, one way of recording the pattern.

The walls in the Willard house at Still River, Massachusetts, which adjoins the town of Harvard, repeat in the parlor the upright vine with berries and leaves found in the Goodale homestead, with variations as may occur in any hand copy, and in two other rooms some patterns are also identical. No record exists by which we may date the first stencilling. Ever since the grant in 1659, this property in Still River has remained in the Willard family. The fine house is distinguished by a handsome pediment over the front door with a carved pineapple, the emblem of hospitality, as its central ornament.

8. *The New York Historical Society Quarterly Bulletin*, April, 1936, p. 41.

FIG. 20. PATTERNS IMPRINTED ON BACK OF WALLPAPER, UPTON

These typical patterns were found on the back of a piece of paper torn from the wall of a built-in closet. Stencilled designs have often been preserved in this way.

FIG. 21. PARLOR, WILLARD HOUSE, STILL RIVER
The decoration is a faithful restoration of patterns dating about 1800.

*Owner, Mrs. E. W. Merrifield*

The bad condition of both plaster and decoration made it necessary to restencil the walls. In such reproductions we always miss the softened colors of the old surfaces, where, after a hundred years or more, the faded pigments have taken on other shades; but when walls have become blackened by age and old plaster starts to fall, we must renew them if we are to live with them. When the work is faithfully done, we are grateful to have the patterns preserved for another century. In the Willard house restoration was carefully carried out. The patterns were traced and duplicated as only a lover of the old house would have done them, the parlor and one bedroom being restencilled by the owner herself. How well the task was performed the illustrations show. The walls had first to be painted, then stencils cut with "embroidery scissors," before the actual work of stencilling could begin. Only one who has seen a wall in the course of such enrichment can guess how often the stepladder must be moved and mounted.

The principle emphasized by modern design, which teaches the value of picking out a motif and repeating it elsewhere in the composition, was not unpracticed by these craftsmen, for on many walls we find a single detail of one pattern reappearing in another design, as with the flower unit of the parlor wall spray (fig. 21) which, in a larger scale, is carried into the frieze. The center of the same spray is also seen in the frieze, between the arches made of small triangles. Four variants of the thistle in shades of green, yellow, and blue are used on the walls of the bedroom (fig. 22); in the decorative frieze, the large and small motifs, and the upright which divides the wall space. At the ceiling the thistle alternates with a pattern of ovals, placed above the uprights. In a second bedroom the motifs are dark green on a white ground (fig. 23). The vine used in the parlor now follows the surbase, for the same designs were often adapted to different arrangements. The light structure of the deep border at the top of the wall is in contrast with the usual sturdy type, while the stripe of alternating diamonds and petals was a favorite pattern. As we see it here, it required two stencils; but in its most elaborate form, as it appears in the Sage house, South Sandisfield, three colors resulted from three stencils.

In Marblehead, Massachusetts, the town adjoining Salem, there is a room, dating from 1791, of very different character from those at Marlborough and Still River. Instead of stripes and single motifs in all-over patterns, the old Peter Jayne house, which stands on what was known as "New Meeting House Lane," has a stencilled border in black defining ochre walls in broad panels as it follows along the framework of doors and windows and the top of the wainscoting (figs. 24 and 25). The unit of design is a six-pointed star or flower inscribed in a circle, the spaces between the petals being filled with small triangles, while the outside of the geometric border is a broken line of bars separated by small diamonds. We shall see a similar treatment of paneling by means of borders in the Governor Pierce house, Hillsborough, New Hampshire, and in the ballroom of a tavern at West Townsend, Massachusetts, but this banding is more elemental and bold in its decorative effect. The fine woodwork of the house, the paneling over the fireplace, the double cornice surmounting the high walls, the soft and mellow shades of ochre in contrast to the striking border make a room of distinction and dignity.

The date of the stencilling involves a bit of local history which brings added interest to the house. Built in 1724 by a noted schoolmaster of Marblehead, it was a frequent meeting place for the followers of John Wesley, and it was here in 1791 that the Methodist Church was organized in the "upper hall where about the fireplace may still be seen the old tiles with scenes from the Bible, placed there by members to commemorate the organization."[9] The walls are said to have been done also at this time as part of the decoration of the hall. In 1825, when certain structural changes were made in the old house, the room was divided into two; the new partition, which lacks the stencilled bands, can be seen at the left of the fireplace in the illustration. We owe the present excellent condition of the walls to the covering of paper which was only recently removed, and we appreciate them especially in this house notable for its many associations with the years preceding the Revolution. They enable us to reconstruct the scene of those tense hours when the Committee of Safety, which numbered among its members the patriots John Hancock, John Adams, and Elbridge Gerry, held its secret meetings in the same upper hall.

The dates recorded for the stencils at Marlborough and Marblehead, 1778 and 1791, are important and have special value because in other cases there is little reliable information by which we can determine the exact year any wall was done. Illustrations and references to other examples in Massachusetts are scattered over the state, not confined to any single area. On leaving Still River and moving westward, one finds traces of the stencil at West Sutton, at Fitchburg, West Townsend, Ashfield, and throughout Berkshire County—Pittsfield, Sheffield, Tyringham, Otis, New Marlborough, Southfield, Sandisfield, and New Boston. In discussing them, consequently, we shall be largely influenced by their geographical relations or by indications of work attributable to the same hand.

At Ashfield, sixty miles west of Still River, are walls where there can be no doubt as to the identity of the artist, even if no precise dating of the painting is now possible, although a member of the family[10] suggests 1820 to 1830 as the approximate time. Entering Ashfield from the direction of Cummington, one goes down a steep grade where on the hillside to the left of the road is the farm of a pioneer settler, Ephraim Williams, the first of his name to come to Ashfield. In this old house five rooms painted about a hundred years ago by Lydia Eldredge Williams tell of her liking for decoration and of her perseverance in a monumental task.

9. Fearey, R.: *Old Marblehead*, p. 23.

10. I am indebted for these facts to the great-great-granddaughter of the painter.

Lydia, born in 1793, was the daughter of Levi and Thankful (Sears) Eldredge, who came to Ashfield from Yarmouth on Cape Cod, Massachusetts. She lived in the old house from 1812, the year of her marriage to Abel Williams, son of the pioneer and a colonel in the militia, until his death in 1854 when the property was sold. How much she loved its generous proportions and its sense of well-being can be guessed by the effort she bestowed in adorning its walls. Three painted rooms on the second story and two on the attic floor are said to be her work; two are a combination of the stencil and brush, while the three smaller rooms are entirely hand work.

If we know the person who has painted a wall, it gives added living interest; we surround the work with questions which can never be answered. Why, we ask, did Lydia depict over and over again the small motif of red flames rising from little piles of firewood? What did it signify? Again we ask, with even more interest, what was the connection between the stencilled tulip she used and an identical pattern still dimly seen on the floor of a small bedroom adjoining the Lafayette room at the Wayside Inn, Sudbury? Over the stencilled pattern in the tavern I placed a tracing taken directly from the walls done by Lydia Williams, and in scale and design they were practically alike. Did she, on some momentous visit to Sudbury, copy it (the distance was a drive of eighty miles), did she merely spend a night at the inn on her way to Boston with Abel, or was the drawing brought to her by some "traveled friend," who knew her fondness for ornament? Perhaps the pattern came to Ashfield by the medium of an itinerant peddler; if this were the case, the floor at Sudbury and the walls at Ashfield could easily be contemporary.

To return to the rooms themselves (fig. 26), one is a large bedroom extending the depth of the house. On a gray ground the tulip stencilled in black divides the wall into narrow panels, and a freehand border in black, white, and scarlet outlines the top of the walls, the door and window frames, the chair-rail, and the surbase. Small red flames spot the background at regular intervals. The unusual freehand work of the borders was done with a round paint brush of stout bristles and with dryish paint, the bands being placed with such accuracy as to suggest the timely help of a chalked cord. In the bedroom on the floor above (fig. 26, bottom) the yellow wall has the same graceful tulip alternating with a new freehand pattern, a bold and novel feature of decoration, a sort of Maypole composed of a sturdy post around which winds a heavy ropelike vine. The border in black, white, and red is a slight variant of that in the room below. Again there are the flames, though much smaller than those in the first room, which appear to be but irregular spots in the illustration. The three smaller rooms were painted by the same hand method as the bandings, but in all-over patterns, one of which was made up of rows of festoons pendent one from another. Apparently there was no lack of creative spirit on the part of the painter when once the brush was in her hand.

31

In Massachusetts, Berkshire County, near the Connecticut border, has given us the most abundant and characteristic examples of the stencilled wall, yet even this series of illustrations is the result of long search. Information which led to the finding of practically every house came only after persistent questionings, for a stencilled wall excites little interest and, if remembered at all, is commonly characterized only as "painted."

In the northwestern part of the county there is a wall, unrelated in design to those farther south, which has probably escaped being demolished because of its location on the outskirts of Pittsfield. The property on which the building stands was part of the original "settlement lot" in the northwest corner of Pittsfield, close to the Hancock town line. As I looked for the authentic date of the house, the town records disclosed the sale of one hundred acres of this tract in 1792 to Joshua Robbins. From 1800 to 1820 the house appears to have belonged to Oliver Robbins and later to his daughter, Elizabeth French. No date was able to establish the year it was built, but the broad maple boards used in its construction, the excellent woodwork, and the type of door moldings suggest 1800.

Three stencilled walls were found by the present owner. Through a covering of blue kalsomine in the parlor appeared the outlines of an elaborate design, recalled by one who had seen it as "garlands surmounting upright posts." An effort was made to restore the stencilling but was abandoned when the decoration came off with the blue wash. There seemed nothing to do but to paper the walls, but perhaps when the paper is removed, the pattern will be revealed as it was in the house of Moses Eaton, Sr., at Hancock, New Hampshire, where the kalsomine adhered to the paper, leaving the original design clearly defined on the plaster.

In a small upstairs bedroom (fig. 27) the stencil definitely imitates wallpaper in an all-over continuous pattern. Stripes in black and white composed of leaves and buds alternating with bars and diamonds appear against a dull pink ground, where the brush marks are still visible in the thin pigment. The lovely shade of bluish rose is elusive; one to whom it appealed very much traveled many miles to ask me if I thought it could have been produced by a vegetable dye made from the beet. A frieze around the room imitates reeds, bound together with leaves and banderoles which have scarlet and black markings. The reeding has undoubtedly been done with a straightedge rule and lining brush; the whole is the work of a skilled and original artisan (fig. 28). The marbleized floor was a common treatment of the period. With the exception of the Hickox house no wall that I know shows more cunning in the use of the stencil, for it was a serious art to this painter. Such accomplishment is the result only of long practice and indicates that many walls must have served an apprenticeship for this skill.

In the connecting bedroom there is an elaborate frieze in white, red, black, and two shades of blue, representing festoons with a tied fringe and tassels. Four stencils have

FIG. 22. BEDROOM, WILLARD HOUSE
Variants of the thistle have been restencilled
by the owner.

FIG. 23. ANOTHER BEDROOM, WILLARD
HOUSE
The color is green on a white ground.

FIG. 24. BEDROOM, PETER JAYNE HOUSE, MARBLEHEAD

The stencilling dates from 1791 and suggests that the motif may have been copied from a tile.

*Owner, Mrs. M. E. Williams*

FIG. 25. ANOTHER VIEW OF SAME ROOM

FIG. 26. TWO BEDROOMS, EPHRAIM WILLIAMS HOUSE, ASHFIELD

Done about 1820 by Lydia Eldredge Williams, these walls are a combination of stencilling and handwork. The stencilled tulip uprights are identical in design with a border on the floor of a room at the Wayside Inn, Sudbury.

*Owner, Mrs. Clarence Hall*

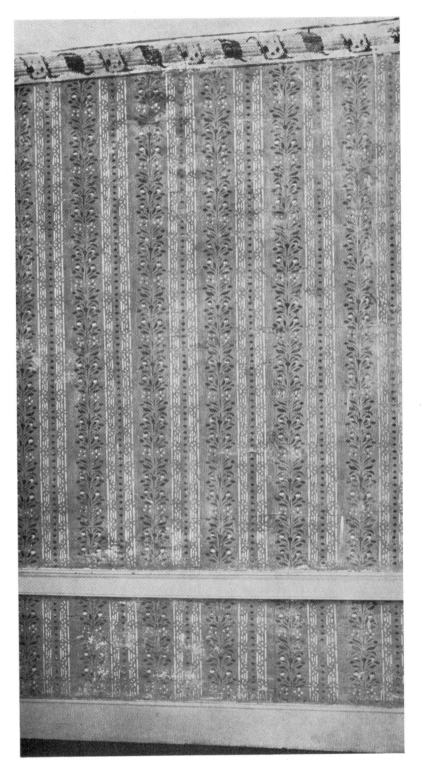

FIG. 27. BEDROOM, ROBBINS HOUSE, PITTSFIELD

This all-over stencilled pattern closely resembles a matched
wallpaper design.

*Owner, Miss Gertrude Watson*

FIG. 28. BORDER DETAIL, ROBBINS HOUSE
The handling of leaves and banderoles is interesting and unusual.

FIG. 29. ANOTHER BORDER, ROBBINS HOUSE
Running above the mantel and chair-rail in a bedroom, this pineapple and leaf border
is effective in black and yellow.

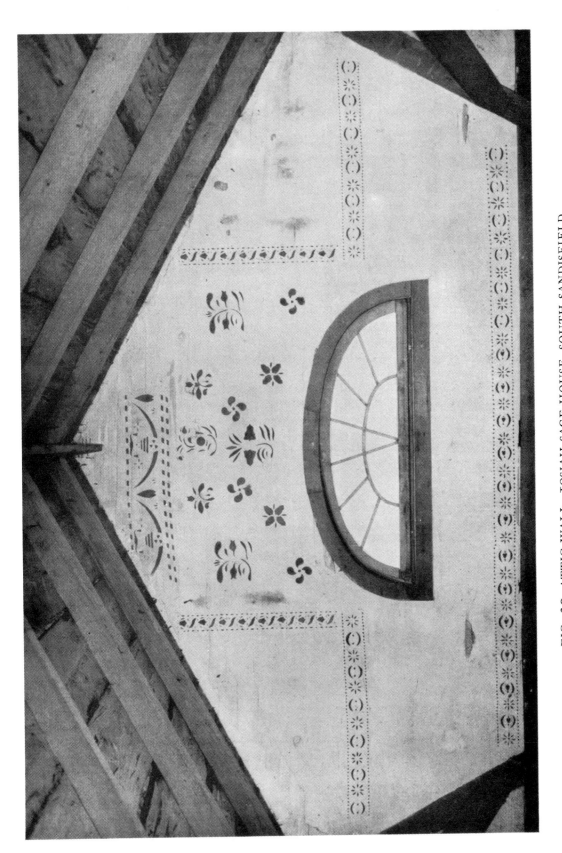

FIG. 30. ATTIC WALL, JOSIAH SAGE HOUSE, SOUTH SANDISFIELD

This wall of the house, built in 1803, offered the itinerant a surface on which to show the variety of his "wares." For the sake of clarity the faded motifs have been retouched on the photograph.

*Owner, Alfred A. Carter*

FIG. 31. PARLOR OVERMANTEL, JOSIAH SAGE HOUSE
One of the flower filled vases may be seen in its original colors on the plate
immediately following page 80.

been used to produce it, but its overdone detail lacks the charm of design which characterizes the first room. Above the chair-rail and mantel runs a striking black border (fig. 29) of conventionalized pineapples, leaves, and buds, all veined and dotted with ochre repeating the yellow of the wall. Under the chair-rail and above the surbase, traces still remain of black bands which continue the bold contrast of black against ochre.

In the southern part of the county there are definite traces of the work of an itinerant who industriously painted his way through this section about the year 1815. Certain motifs are characteristic of his hand, among them a deep pineapple frieze, a stripe composed of diamonds and flower petals (a pattern familiar in other localities as well, but unique in its marked elaboration by his hand), and a very ornamental treatment of a vase filled with large flowers, buds, and leaves.

My first view of a stencilled wall, to me a momentous occasion, was the work of this itinerant in the parlor of the Josiah Sage house, South Sandisfield, caught sight of through a front window one late October afternoon.[11] A curtain partly obscured the room, but the glimpse of two red vases of flowers over the mantel rewarded me for many miles of rough road along which only occasional houses were left to tell the glories of old Sandisfield. This section was formerly prosperous country, whose rich farmers were the money-lenders of Berkshire County. Sandisfield village early became the active center of the district and for three-quarters of a century remained the market for its dairy products. No landmarks of the town are left today; the church, noted for its graceful spire, has been destroyed by fire, and the fine old houses once facing the village green have fallen to ruin, or have been pillaged for the sake of doors and rafters. Even the huge doorstones have been carried away by motor truck or ox team and now mark the thresholds of modern houses. Today woodlands and overgrown pastures, cover for partridge and quail, replace the fertile fields of this once settled region.

The Sage house, with its reeded door moldings, well-designed eaves, and semioval gable windows, has the character of numerous dwellings of this date, which a stone in the chimney records as 1803. We can be sure there was much definite planning to be done before undertaking the stencilling of five or more rooms. The plaster in the gabled end of the attic (fig. 30) proved a convenient place for the painter to show his designs to the eager household, but the date 1824 scratched above the window frame may or may not indicate the year the stencilling was done. The resources of his kit, however, were far richer than his sampler, as the walls of the house reveal.

This worker had both a sense of the creative value of the stencil and the needed patience and precision to cut and combine individual units. The red urns which I had glimpsed through the window on my first visit are found over the mantel in both front

11. I am especially indebted to Mr. Julius D. Miner for telling me of the existence of the stencilled walls in this house.

rooms on the ground floor. In the right parlor (fig. 31) against a wall of pale gray the decoration does not have the quality of a set pattern, for the arrangement of the flowers suggests that some careful hand has placed them one by one in the well-proportioned vase, skillfully massing them against the delicate tracery of stems and leaves. An analysis of the way the design has been applied shows that the urns are done with two stencils, one giving the form of the vase in red, and the other outlining and dotting it in chrome. The heavy leaves and the delicate ones are cut separately in two sprays, and each flower and bud is placed at will on the end of a stem to give variety in the grouping. The larger blossoms seem to weigh down their stems, while the others stand erect in the feathery foliage. The walls of the room are divided into panels. The details of the heavier vertical stripe, not clearly seen in the photograph, are green, red, and yellow, and were made with three stencils, one for each color. The center of the diamond pattern is chrome, and its green border has small diamonds superimposed in yellow, while the petaled motif in red also has a yellow center. The alternating stripe at the extreme right in the illustration is again made up of diamonds obliquely "reeded" in red and green, and petaled forms of the same colors link the heavier figures. Vertical stripes serve also to frame the doorways and to define the small cupboard. The bells of the frieze have a sense of rhythm which is carried into the swag and tassel, while the treatment of the tongue and the petaled star gives lightness and balance to the border edged by broken lines and diamonds. A corn-flower in the lower border at the bottom of the wall is carried over into the lacy texture of the motif centered with four hearts and is repeated in the panels and over the mantel-piece, while flower sprays from the vases have been skillfully used again in two other wall motifs. Much of the original charm and character of the room has survived, and the impression it leaves with us today is one of lightness and delicacy.

A second parlor, badly disfigured by time, still shows on its pale yellow walls the same alternating stripes, although the omission of the intervening motifs gives a quite different effect, characteristic of the artisan. In placing the same pots of flowers over the mantelpiece no attempt was made to center them against the striped background. The pineapples of the top border we shall find repeated in the frieze of a second floor bed-room to the left of the stairway (figs. 32 and 33), this time done on a grayed ground. A graceful vine with red berries follows along the corners, windows, and doors of the room, while an acorn border, tried out in the attic, edges the baseboard. The frieze appears to be a pineapple, which is red spotted with ochre, but more interesting is the heavy green stem which binds the whole into a unit and contrasts with the tracery of the flowers and leaves. Twisted bands in red and green give the effect of roping the frieze in place. This unit together with the cornflower, the two formal flower sprays and the starlike motif repeating the leaf of the border, make up well-spaced patterns which all show precision and fineness.

34

FIG. 32. DETAIL OF BEDROOM PATTERNS, JOSIAH SAGE HOUSE

*(Reproduced in color following page 80)*

In one of the two remaining rooms the covering of hard white paint had been removed in very small sections and showed a new floral border, light in quality. On gray and yellow walls the color scheme of the three rooms was originally a usual combination, green, red, and yellow, but exposed to sunlight through many years, the fugitive pigments of the greens have changed to innumerable shades of yellow, and those of the reds, to pink and salmon, giving, as far as color is concerned, a very different impression from the original. Fortunately not a single brush stroke has revived the faded color.

The Sage house stands on a side road, a short quarter mile from what was known as the Sandy Brook Turnpike. To the south the road goes to the Connecticut line; and in 1803, to quote an early history of Berkshire County, it "offered a favorable communication with Hartford." To the northwest the road leads to New Marlborough and Southfield, and we have only to follow it to reach another house, where we shall find this craftsman again at work. In the Southfield section of the town of New Marlborough, only five or six miles from the Sage house, I traveled a dirt road to the untenanted farmhouse, built by David Baldwin (1753–1822), who had come from Wallingford to settle here. This locality, formerly one of well-tilled farms and not far from the village of Southfield, is now marked by deserted houses and cellar holes. It was during the lifetime of the son, Nathaniel (1782–1858) that the stencilling was done. A member of the family, who often returned to Southfield to renew the contacts of his early days, recalled the sturdy house of the past, with its rafters of solid oak, the cupboards, the fine mantelpieces, the notably good door latches and hinges, and especially the stencilled walls both downstairs and on the second floor. Today, only the hallway and upper bedroom show the original designs. Perhaps red urns of flowers once occupied the space above the mantel in the parlor, but we may only guess. Carpenters had already begun renovation when the photographs of the gray and faded walls were taken.

The stencilling of the bedroom (fig. 34) is admirable with its bold stripes in the patterns so very typical of this journeyman, and found in the left parlor of the Sage house. In this low-ceilinged room the border used above the reeded baseboard is effective as it replaces the customary elaborate frieze. The craftsman laid his frieze first and then carefully measured the uprights, but at the bottom the stripes and border merge in casual freedom. Yet this room, empty of furniture as it was, had a special charm of symmetry and dignity; against the grayish ground (perhaps a wash of milk-paint) the tones of ochres and mulberries had a color quality that could never have been present in the first strong red and green, a glimpse of which was disclosed under a loosened board pulled away from the plaster it protected. The hallway had suffered much with the wear of years, but on pale gray walls the large flower spray and uprights with their reeded ovals and petaled motifs (fig. 35) were combined with the pineapple border familiar also from

FIG. 33. BEDROOM, JOSIAH SAGE HOUSE

The placing of the green vine with its red berries shows how the stencil could be deliberately
adapted to the structural details of a room.

FIG. 35. DETAIL OF HALL, DAVID BALDWIN HOUSE
These two graceful single designs have already been
seen in the Josiah Sage house.

FIG. 34. BEDROOM, DAVID BALDWIN HOUSE, SOUTHFIELD
The two uprights are the same as those in the Josiah Sage parlor.

*Owner, Frederick Beers*

South Sandisfield. The once brilliant red and green had here again turned to mulberry of many shades and an even richer chrome.

From David Baldwin's the artisan had not far to go to reach New Marlborough by way of the same Sandy Brook Turnpike. We can take it for granted that on one occasion at least he went in this direction, for in a house on the outskirts of the town are the same patterns, colors, and treatments which we have just noted in Sandisfield and Southfield. In a list of physicians of New Marlborough in a history of Berkshire County, written in 1829 by "Gentlemen, Clergymen, and Laymen," Edmund Peet is included, and the date of his death given as May 6, 1828. This reference is all we know of the first owner of the small remodeled farmhouse which as it appears today gives no promise of anything relating to the past. The difficulty of securing information about these stencilled walls, even from the occupant of the house itself, is often astonishing. In this particular instance, when I asked the tenant if the stencils could be seen, he answered, "There are none, only some marks left on the walls from old wallpaper." These "marks" in three rooms and the small hall proved to be the original stencilling.

In its day it was doubtless a good house. When I saw it, the roof of a small porch over the original front door, now no longer used, still had a deeply cut frieze ornamented by reeded bands, although the columns had long since disappeared. One mantel also showed the same type of reeded carvings. In the rooms on the right and left of this discarded doorway the paper was torn off, leaving uncovered large portions of the original walls, "soon to be repapered" we were told. Above the mantels were the familiar arrangements of large flowers in red pots. There were also the friezes of festoons and bells and of the conventionalized pineapples, the acorn border, the same diamond uprights, and the pattern which outlined the baseboard in the Baldwin bedroom. The colors of the two rooms combined black and red on a white ground, and green and red on yellow. In the small hall and in a bedroom on the second floor was the narrow border of the star and crescent shown by the itinerant in the garret of Josiah Sage. The swastika was used in a new treatment with four hearts at the center, clustered about a small diamond. In the bedroom the paper, only recently removed, had preserved the walls in better condition than in the other rooms, but they were all dim reflections of former days and may be valued only as indications that they were by the same worker whom we have followed from Sandisfield.

Other walls, less elaborate than those of the Sage house, are scattered throughout the southern part of the county. Vague rumors reached me of a room in the southeastern part of Sandisfield, close to Seymour Mountain and to the south of Hanging Mountain. It was difficult to gather any definite information relating to the house or its history, past or present, except that lumbermen were cutting timber on the property and that the road

37

was in such bad condition it was doubtful if a car could climb the grade. Entering West New Boston by the Beech Plain road and crossing Clam River, we began the ascent of a succession of hills, each one steeper than the last. It was a forsaken neighborhood but for the ruts of heavy truck wheels. We left the car when the road became too difficult and walked the last mile to the derelict and half-ruined house which appeared on a rise of ground back from the road. The glass and even the sash had gone from its well-designed Palladian window centered over the doorway, but the deep cornice, carved with festoons and tassels, being sheltered by the eaves, was still in good condition. The floor plan of the house was similar to others of this period: a small square hall with the stairs rising at a steep pitch, a room on either side, and at the rear a large kitchen which ran the width of the house. All three rooms hugged a huge central chimney which provided them with fireplaces. The one remaining mantel carved with diamonds and squares and similar to others we have seen suggests that some experienced local carpenter must have built these houses scattered throughout this section, which in so many ways resemble one another.

The lumbermen were in full possession of the house as well as of the road. In one of the upstairs rooms a temporary roof made of planks and sheets of tin had been put up over the bed to keep summer rains from the occupant, but in a room on the first floor fragments of stencilling still could be seen where the whitewash and paper had fallen. On plaster which had originally been white were traces in black and red of the frieze of festoons and bells; the acorn border outlined the window frames; two large flower motifs and two very small conventional figures completed the simple wall plan of this well-proportioned room. On the chimney-breast enough pattern was left dimly to distinguish two urns filled by using one of the flower stencils of the walls, and perched on each spray sat a pair of small love birds with a heart suspended between them. But the wrecked walls, broken windows, and litter still spoke of a once orderly existence, and brought to mind the vivid contrast between the first clearing of this pine forest to provide the location for the dwelling and this second clearing, a rough leveling of young and old growth, which in the careless march of another age spread havoc over the whole hillside.

Perhaps our same itinerant before climbing Seymour Mountain had at one time journeyed to the top of Smith Hill in Tyringham, in the northern part of the county, and from Tyringham had taken the road, long since discontinued, over Dry Hill, to New Marlborough and Sandisfield. In any case, at Tyringham we find the same sort of wall decorations, the motifs all widely placed, and the identical flower patterns in the house built by Aaron Canfield in 1799. Tradition says that it was "too much of a dwelling for him to maintain," and it came into the possession of Oliver Smith in 1815; the stencilling was on the walls when the house was transferred to the new owner. A bit of local history which I have not traced to its source relates that the State of Connecticut at this time was investing school funds in mortgages in Berkshire County, and that the Canfield house

38

was one to which a loan had been granted. The date of the stencilling is probably closer to 1799 than to 1815, for the painting would naturally have been done soon after the house was completed rather than when holding the property had become a burden to the owners.

The story of the decoration of the house on Smith Hill is as fragmentary as are the stencils themselves. The two halls, though faded and crumbling, in places clearly hold their tempera patterns of chrome, black, and scarlet on plaster thinly washed with white. In the frieze of the upper hall (fig. 36) the use of the heart with the bell and the small spray is a new combination. The floral motifs and the swastika (fig. 37) are broadly spaced on the walls outlined by the acorn border, and are shown also in the "sampler" in the garret at South Sandisfield—in fact, most of the designs of this house appear there even to the small spray centered with the red heart. The running vine of single leaves above the baseboard is also used beneath the chair-rail. In a large room on the ground floor a coat of paint and sections of new plaster almost blot out the patterns, leaving only traces of the vine seen in the hall, the frieze of bells, and a new border of buds and petals along the doors and corners.

Although the wallpaper on one of the two bedrooms upstairs partially obscures the pattern, I picked up from the floor a dislodged piece on which there is a perfect impression in color and outline of an extremely decorative design made with two stencils, the red forming slender leaves and a center stem; the green, three plums with clean-cut serrated leaves curving from narrow stems. This pattern is again placed over the small mantel to fill a red vase, while throughout the house the frieze of bells is used with the tassels hung from hearts. Nowhere is the wall surface divided into narrow panels.

Wherever there is a group of these walls we are sure to find the bells and tassels. In every state of New England they are repeated with variations. When more than a single stencilled room occurs in any house, it is almost certain one will have the pattern. In Eaton's outfit the design is childlike in its drawing, but in the Smith house much more detailed. The use of this frequent border may have been more than a random choice, perhaps a symbol of some specific happiness which had come to the house. In earlier days marriage meant an actual house, a permanent dwelling, not a temporary shelter. In another old house in the first settlement of Tyringham are two hearts cut in the upper panels of the parlor door, which are definitely recorded as having marked the coming of a bride. When red hearts appear, as they do so often in single stencil patterns and in borders, their significance may have been more than mere accents of color.

In the village of Tyringham a former tavern, opposite Marshall Stedman's rake shop, has an upstairs room with motifs similar to those on Smith Hill. There were many other stencilled walls in this section, if the numbers that have come to my attention can serve as an indication. Two rooms in the old Deacon James Freeman dwelling on Beech

Plain road, north from West New Boston, have been described as having had "stripes in red and green and borders of half moons." In Montville the third oldest building in the village, built by a man named Colton and later known as the Robinson house, still preserves on a single wall six designs of the Josiah Sage rooms and is without question the work of the same man. In what was formerly the small parlor the plastered wall has the pineapple frieze, the border of arcades, the uprights of diamonds, and two wall motifs, the large red blossoms and the pattern centered with four hearts. An urn is filled with flowers and is placed above the imitation marble mantel, which shows bold veinings in gray and black with reeded medallions in deep red. North from New Boston in the Pomeroy house at Otis, once kept as a tavern, fragments of borders in the parlor to the right of the door continued to show their indistinct outlines until the building was demolished about twenty years ago. And again in Otis, near what was known as the West Center road, a deserted farmhouse has in one room the familiar frieze of swags and bells in very faded green and red; and a new banding of fluted discs edged by half circles runs along the baseboard and at the corners of the ochre walls.

Returning to New Marlborough by way of Hartsville, one passes an almost unnoticed gateway which opens into a grass-grown lane leading down to a vacant house built by Nathan Chapin before 1800. It is completely hidden from the road by the steep hill sheltering it to the north. The lane was once a county road which crossed the Konkapot and connected with a road to Mill River. It took a very discerning eye to find the stencilling in the two rooms. In the larger one the hard lime washes which covered it could be chipped away only in a few places, just enough to enable one to see dark olive green and deep red patterns on yellow ochre. Practically the only figures traceable were an acorn border more primitive than those we have yet found and a banding of conventionalized maple leaves. The smaller room had walls of a deep rose-salmon on which all the designs were in dark green with uprights similar to those of the Southfield house, but in one color. Over the baseboard the border was formed of alternating large and small leaves with cut edges, like the one which we shall see at the bottom of the wall in the Clark house in Washington, Connecticut. There was a new spray of four flowers whose pointed outlines indicated many petals. The coloring was altogether different from any combination we have seen, the effect of the rich ochres, reds, and greens being subdued in contrast to the customary bright tones.

At Sheffield in the old dwelling sold by Jared Canfield to Ephraim Dixon in the year 1835, designated in the deed as "lying on the east side of Massachusetts Turnpike road number twelve," the black and red stencilled walls of the narrow two-storied hall were found some years ago under their many layers of paper by the owners. Below the frieze of bells and loops on smooth white plaster there are two wall motifs which were already noted in the hallway of the Smith house in Tyringham. The small vine of the

40

FIG. 36. UPPER HALL, OLIVER SMITH HOUSE, TYRINGHAM

Stencilled before 1815, these patterns in black, chrome and bright red were found under layers of wallpaper (photograph retouched for clarity).

*Owner, Marshall Stedman*

FIG. 37. DETAIL OF HALL, OLIVER SMITH HOUSE
Broad spacing of motifs characterizes the placement of the units in this house.

FIG. 38. OVERMANTEL AND SECTION OF PARLOR WALL, BELDEN HOUSE, NEW BOSTON
The patterns are in apple green and red on a gray-white ground.

*Owner, Mrs. Goddard Du Bois*

FIG. 39. PARLOR, CURTIS HICKOX HOUSE, WASHINGTON

The parlor of this house, built in 1797, is one of the finest existing examples of wall stencilling.

*Owner, Russell C. Jones*

Smith house also runs around the front door, but there are no borders to follow the base-board or mark the corners. The two houses may therefore be by the same brush, although the one in Sheffield has the appearance of less experienced workmanship. The walls in southern Berkshire County resemble one another very definitely. Some are simple, as are those on Smith Hill, Seymour Mountain, and in Sheffield, while others like those in the Sage and Baldwin houses have greater sophistication. The two groups, however, show many identical patterns, and if they are by the same artisan, it may indicate that a more practiced handling developed later when he attained greater maturity in his craft.

As one leaves this district by the New Boston road on the Massachusetts side of the Connecticut State line, not far from Riverton there is a spacious old house formerly belonging to a family of Beldens. Only one bedroom (fig. 38) remains to show its sten-cilled decoration, where a fireplace is again the focus for elaborate design. The two red vases are again filled by placing a flowering stem at different angles, while two crisp birds perched on willow trees introduce a vivid note. Stars and sunbursts give lightness to the walls in contrast with the massive vine which borders the mantel and panels the room. What might be termed the "carnation spray" is more detailed than in the Sage house, and the frieze shows new variations, notably in the bow-knots of red which tie the tassels hanging from the diamonds. On a grayish white background the soft green, still showing brush strokes, is accentuated by its complementary red, making an agreeable whole. With artistic freedom the craftsman places two red discs against the stem of the carnation with-out botanical precedent, but he gains an effective note of color. Such are the naïve and quaint touches of the brush which we often find on these walls.

### CONNECTICUT

Examples of stencilling in Connecticut come from but a small section of the state, including only Washington and Milton in Litchfield County besides Middle Had-dam on the bank of the Connecticut River, but no walls that I know deserve our admira-tion more than those of the parlor in the Hickox house at Washington. Although the property has recently passed to other owners, four generations in direct descent lived there and identified themselves with the growth of the town—citizens active and well established in the community, some of them men of rank in the Colonial army and in the judicial life of the county. In 1797 Curtis Hickox built the house in which his great-grandson not long ago found hidden and forgotten stencilling when the opening between two rooms was enlarged to admit additional heat. The parlor at the time was covered with a fine old French paper, green and black on white, that had been on the walls for at least a century. This date helps to place the stencilling as of the early nineteen hundreds, for in all probability New England thrift would not permit an elaborate wall painting to be immediately replaced by an expensive paper. In cutting away the necessary plaster, parts of this paper were also removed, and on the back of the fragments were clear colored impressions of a stencilled pattern whose existence until then was unknown to members of the family.

We cannot but admire the resourcefulness of the owner of the house when he faced the problem of removing the frail and valuable paper by a method which would preserve it and also safeguard the painting beneath, whose character, whether sturdy or perishable, as yet could not be guessed. With sound sense and Yankee ingenuity he waited for a heavy penetrating fog, a day characteristic of New England, then opened the windows and at intervals tested the paper until he could peel it off in long unbroken strips. Later, when the fragile French paper was used in another room, the right method was again cleverly selected. He found that paste applied directly to these delicate sheets dissolved them, but if the application was made on the plaster itself, the damage was avoided. This quick method of work offers an amusing comparison with the laborious process followed recently in Italy in lifting a certain valuable wallpaper. Heavy wet sheets were hung near the surface for long hours and repeatedly dampened until at last the paper came away without resistance. Our process was a matter of a single afternoon.

The room today (fig. 39) is one of singular beauty and taste. There is intricacy yet a classic simplicity in the reeding of the columns and the background of the border. The tasseled festoons break any feeling of severity that might come from the formal treatment of the uprights, while the curve of the climbing vine carries a quality of lightness into the well-balanced spacing of the decoration. Conscious variation in the placing of the columns below the chair-rail shows the same unerring sense of form that marks the whole. The etched tracery and the beading on the background of the oval discs in the frieze appear more distinctly in the narrow border following the chair-rail and the baseboard.

Warmth and austerity contrast in the coloring of this room. Against dull ochre thinly brushed on the wall (fig. 40) the black of the reeding is emphasized by small white diamonds and white leaves binding the columns. Any heaviness in the black tassels is relieved by highlights of white, but black accents pick out the veining of the leaves and stems. The frieze, with its dark gray background and slender reedings of black and white, gains balance by the carrying of the same gray to the lower borders. A paler gray softens the vine and gives it delicacy. The coral red flowers on the vines and columns as well as the hearts centering the fluted white ovals in the frieze contribute a contrasting brightness and vitality. In design, color, and masterful handling of the stencil this unidentified artisan has no peer.

We have more definite knowledge of the man who stencilled the walls in the

FIG. 40. DETAIL OF PARLOR, CURTIS HICKOX HOUSE

(*Reproduced in color following page 80*)

Hartwell house between Washington Green and the town line of Roxbury, but as to his name we know nothing more than that in the community he was called "Stimp" (perhaps short for Stimpson). Tradition records that he "drifted into the village" when he was past middle age, that his background was obscure, and that other capacities not so pleasing as the painting of walls are responsible for immortalizing even this partial name. The childhood memory of a small boy passed on to the next generation tells of a certain fearful day in 1834 when this artisan, crazed by strong drink, came to the house of his chief benefactor with intent to kill. Only the timely intervention of the neighbors prevented a tragedy, for, responding to cries of distress, they overpowered the drunken man and tied him to the whipping-post near the green until he could be carted away to the Litchfield jail. He returned to Washington, at least for a time, for in the Hartwell house there are still the heavy iron staples and window bars which were added as a measure of security against a recurrence of the visit.

The parlor in this house, stencilled by "Stimp" about 1830, was found under five layers of paper, but the walls were in such bad condition that complete restoration by a local painter was necessary before the room could be used. Although in this process the sharp outlines of the original decorations have been lost, one can count against a ground of warm buff many of the motifs seen in the southern part of Berkshire County, among them the urn holding a spray of flowers with two red birds sitting on the top twigs. A new design of serrated leaves, massive in form and linked together by quarter moons, defines the corners of the room and edges the baseboard, a pattern which, as we shall see, links these walls with the Clark house on Church Hill and with a house at Dover Plains, New York, and carries out the tradition that this obstreperous itinerant did "other houses in the neighborhood."

In the dwelling on Church Hill built by Samuel Clark, who settled there from Milford, "Stimp's" stout leaf border (fig. 41) frames the door and follows the corners of the walls. The frieze, another leaf variant, is incomplete as we see it, the top of the design evidently having been covered when a new ceiling was placed at a level lower than the original. The effect of this heavy design is striking, even if we cannot recapture the former height of the room. The border at the floor suggests the top band in smaller scale. The colors are apple-green and rose on white plaster of rough texture. The deep indentations of the leaves in the frieze, in the uprights, and over the baseboard, though lost in the photograph, have a decorative value which adds to the charm of the room. If we consider the state of collapse the building had reached before it was restored, the stencilling was found in excellent condition and little retouching was needed.

On the same hill there are unmistakable traces of this painter in the Titus house, built in 1760, where three rooms are known to have been stencilled, and possibly a fourth,

44

FIG. 41. BEDROOM, SAMUEL CLARK HOUSE, WASHINGTON
This work was done by a painter known as "Stimp," who "drifted into town" before 1830.

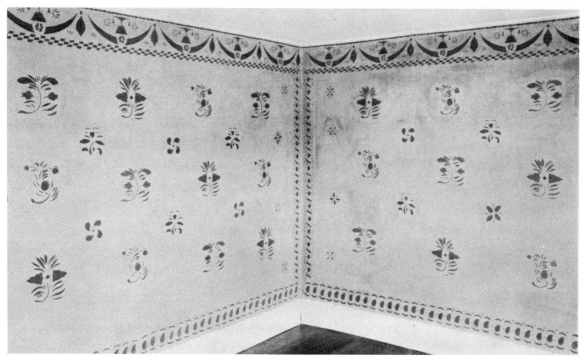

FIG. 42. BEDROOM, PERRY HOUSE, DOVER PLAINS (N.Y.)
Probably also the work of "Stimp," little retouching was done to these designs in
green and red on light yellow ochre.

*Owner, Mrs. William Morgan*

FIG. 43. HALL, IRA BUEL HOUSE, MILTON

These patterns were found under the usual many layers of wallpaper. On a dull yellow ground the motifs combine red and green, except for the uprights in solid green and the stars in red.

*Owner, Joseph J. West*

but only a part of one wall has been rescued from under a coat of hard lime wash. In removing this brittle covering, the paint was in no way disturbed, and a small sample of original work was revealed, where the upright vine which divides the wall into panels is identical with the one above the baseboard in the hall of the Smith house at Tyringham.

That the indomitable "Stimp" left Connecticut and crossed the border to Dover Plains, New York, we can be very sure, judging from the similar patterns found in a house on Perry Hill, a journey of thirty miles from Washington. Perhaps he covered the distance on horseback, or was given a lift, since a century ago this was the custom of the road. In this locality tradition says that for safety the first houses were built on the hillsides with the valley and Ten Mile River well in view, since its shores were hunting grounds of the Indians, not always the most dependable of neighbors. In the old part of the house, built about 1793, previous to the settlement of Dover Plains, a stencilled room was discovered when a local painter was removing wallpaper to make some needed repairs. A few hours after the work had started the owner came to the room and to his amazement found completed what he had thought would be a long day's task. The four walls so quickly stripped of their old covering showed a glowing ochre ground with designs in soft greens and touches of red (fig. 42). The workman, who possessed a vast store of quaint and practical knowledge of paints and all that pertained to them, said that a rye-flour paste had been used in applying the paper, a fact which explained why it had lifted so easily.

The walls needed little retouching, and no new stencils were cut with which to sharpen the outlines. Difficulty in matching the red was finally solved by the same knowing painter, who mixed a pigment from the juice of poke berries. To guide us in dating the stencilling we have only the statement made some years ago by a ninety-six-year-old woman that as a child she had often visited the farm and remembered counting the bright wall figures as a favorite game. The exact border of heavy leaves which defines the corners in the Clark and Hartwell rooms runs along the base of this wall. There is little doubt that the same artisan was responsible for this group of walls in Connecticut, but whether he was responsible for walls elsewhere in Connecticut, in Berkshire County, or in other regions, or where he spent the years before he "drifted" into Washington, we shall probably never know. Though many of his motifs and treatments are the same as those we have seen in Massachusetts, we miss in Connecticut many characteristic patterns of Berkshire County, such as the large and important grouping of flowers over the mantels, the three color diamond-shaped uprights, and the pineapple frieze.

A stencilled hallway found recently at Milton adds a new group of designs to those in Litchfield County. This town, near the west branch of the Shepaug River and known to its first settlers as "Blue Swamps" from the gentians which grew in its fields and along its river banks, was once a small industrial community which developed around the excellent waterpower. The old town then boasted seventeen mills and six schools, but, when the railroad passed it by, the industries moved to more convenient points of distribution. In this quiet village, in pleasant rolling country, stands a house built in 1774, which at the death of Ira Buel went to his widow Prudence, and was used for a time as a tavern, where, tradition likes to relate, Lafayette once "spent the night." There is no date to mark the stencilling; indeed, only by dint of hard labor were the patterns rescued at all, for many layers of paper had been applied with so strong an adhesive that in removing them the walls were badly marred. The best way to preserve the delightful patterns was to trace the units and reproduce them on another wall. The photograph of this reproduction (fig. 43) gives the motifs and the general manner in which they originally appeared but fails to convey the richness of the deep green and Venetian red of the patterns on their pale yellow ground. These two colors are combined in all the designs except in the vertical vine, which is green, and in the small sunburst, which is red. The well-designed frieze, though harmonizing with the single motifs, lacks sufficient mass to balance the unusual border above the baseboard. The relationship of details creates the impression of a well-formed plan carried out by one who had an instinct for composition.

A wall painting in a room in Washington, Connecticut, where the stencil appears to have silhouetted certain figures before they were accented by brush touches, has special interest as a combination of handwork with the stencil. This technique has a long history. According to Gélis-Didot it was practiced in France in the fifteenth and sixteenth centuries. It was also referred to by Vaudoyer in connection with a room done in the second half of the eighteenth century by Fragonard in his house at Grasse, where the hand strokes almost completely disguised the effect of the stencil. Moreover we have the authority of Professor Tristram that this same use of the stencil was also practiced in England.

With these antecedents it is not surprising to see indications of this old method in the "painted room" of the Red House at Washington, built in 1772, which has frequently been cited for the unique decoration of its walls and their historic past. The Red House was the home of two brothers, Joel and Leman Stone, one a hot Tory, and the other an equally ardent Whig. An entry in Joel's diary indicates the fervor of his partisanship:

> I was firm in my resolve rather to forego all I could call my property in the world than flinch from my duty as a subject of the best of sovereigns. Sooner to perish in the general calamity than abet in the least degree the enemies of the British Constitution.[12]

12. Smith, Mary M.: "Story of the Old Red House" (in ms.), Gunn Memorial Library, Washington, Connecticut.

46

The patriotism of the other brother is equally evident from his conspicuous choice of the Federal eagle, the emblem of the new Confederacy, to adorn the walls of his room.

In spite of the differences in their political opinions the two brothers lived in the same house, but it was not until the uncovering of the "painted chamber" some years ago that there was a record of the exact division of the dwelling. Legend records that the "west chamber," belonging to Joel, was decorated with British warships and other devices symbolic of his allegiance, but no trace of them remains; perhaps they were destroyed when his property was confiscated by the victorious Federalists. The date of the uncovered walls of Leman's room must be placed after 1781, judging by the thirteen stars surrounding the head of an eagle. The decoration is well preserved, and on buff walls vertical rows of large medallions formed by delicate vines enclose alternating white figures of a stag and a Federal eagle, with heavy markings of black and red defining the details and outlines. In the stag a keen eye can easily trace the use of the stencil in the exact repeat of the lift of the head, the curve of the back, and the planting of the feet, but in the eagle its use is obscured by the many superimposed brush strokes of black.

Fragments of a frieze which once adorned the ballroom walls of an old tavern in Connecticut give us another example of a stencilled design embellished by brush strokes. This old building, which for seven generations has remained in the Whitmore family, stands on sloping ground at a bend of the Connecticut River at Middle Haddam, at one time an active ship-building and shipping center, whose celebrated ship-yards were adjacent to the inn. The tavern was part of the life of the river, the great artery of a growing commerce, and from its landing is seen a wide sweep of water to north and south. As one of the changes which were made in 1800 the gambrel roof was altered to give additional depth on the front of the house and to provide space on the second story for a large ballroom. Though much of the house is unchanged, the ballroom has been divided, and a glimpse of the old stencils may be had only from a vantage point on top of a huge chest of drawers which now occupies most of a closet cut from one corner of the room. Yet we can picture the dome-shaped ceiling, the walls of clear ochre banded by a frieze of festoons and tassels, the seats at the two ends of the room, cushioned with green rep, renovations which in their day brought fresh life to the old house. Of special interest for us is the deep frieze, with its fringed festoons of palest rose from which fat tassels swing on pink cords. The tassels are bound at the top and tied at the side by bows of the same deep rose, which also edges the top of each scallop, and black brush marks added by hand etch the fringe and the threads in the tassels.[13]

Again I should like to emphasize the incompleteness of this recording of Connecticut rooms, for both stencilled and frescoed walls were far more numerous than these few

13. One further example may be seen in the hall of a house near Portland, Maine, where stencilling is combined with freehand markings in the wide curve of a climbing grapevine, while the trellis is obviously handwork.

pages would indicate.[14] In an early advertisement running in *The Connecticut Herald* in 1804, D. Bartling and S. Hall "respectfully inform the ladies and gentlemen of New Haven" that they will execute directly on the walls of rooms "that much admired imitation of stamped [printed] paper" in a way "far superior to the manner commonly practiced in this state." And they hope to "meet with that encouragement which the inhabitants of this city are ever ready to accord to native talents when endeavoring to introduce cheaply into use the knowledge of arts which combine utility and elegance," and in which one of the advertisers has already given "general satisfaction" in "different parts of the United States . . ."

## NEW YORK AND OHIO

The walls of the William L. Gardiner house, not far from New Lebanon, New York, in Garfield, formerly Stephentown, are also linked in design with those of Massachusetts and Connecticut, though the crude work in no way resembles the excellent craftsmanship of New England examples. The house, lived in by three generations of Gardiners before it came into the possession of its present owner, is large, substantial, and spacious in its proportions. Today only two upper bedrooms and the upper and lower hall remain of the rooms stencilled by an ambitious workman in the early years of the last century. His name is not remembered, but we know of his coming from Canada to the door of the house one autumn day, hungry, penniless, and asking for work. We can almost hear his pleadings and his reply to the queries as to what he could do. He was a painter, perhaps a wall painter, by trade. Here was the owner's chance to have the rooms and the two broad hallways ornamented during the winter months. A bargain was made, in all probability for little more than room and board. Designs were gathered either in the neighborhood or perhaps over the Massachusetts line in the form of rough tracings by some member of the family or by the artisan himself, who then cut the stencils from these poorly-sketched copies.

We must judge his skill of execution, however, by his accomplishments. He was very evidently not afraid of the brush and seems to have liked the solid quality of design, for his stencils are heavy, and he has multiplied his lines until they have a massive, compact quality. He had little feeling for well-placed decoration and no use for the yardstick to align his patterns, since his walls are crowded and poorly arranged; yet we must credit him with a sense of movement and vitality in the tight swirl of his patterns and in his

14. In 1936 an interesting contribution to the records of walls, both stencilled and freehand, existing in Connecticut was begun under the direction of Mr. William L. Warren, State Director of the Index of American Design, Federal Art Project.

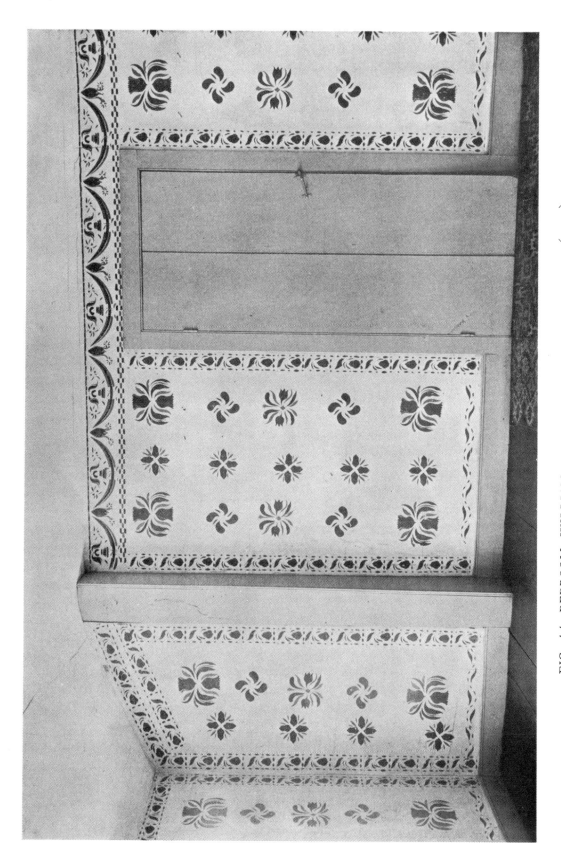

FIG. 44. BEDROOM, WILLIAM L. GARDINER HOUSE, GARFIELD (N.Y.)

Garfield, formerly known as Stephentown, is in Rensselaer County, New York. The stencilling was done, tradition says, by a Canadian in payment for food and lodging.

*Owner, T. A. Straight*

FIG. 45. BEDROOM, FERRIS HOUSE, HAMILTON COUNTY (OHIO)

Built about 1820 in the Lower Little Miami Valley, the house had original stencilling which has been reproduced. The patterns were all traceable except some details of the festoons and vases. Note the similarity of
the uprights to those in fig. 41 and to the surbase border in fig. 42.

*The Thomas J. Emery Memorial, Mariemont, Ohio*

elaboration of familiar motifs, such as the bell with a broader treatment of the swag. The neat running vine and the bold rendering of the acorn border are effectively used in the corners of a bedroom (fig. 44) and at either side of the half-pilasters. The patterns and colors (black with touches of red on a thin whitewash over gray plaster) are kept fairly uniform in all the surviving rooms, but familiar as these basic designs are, one feels on entering this house that he has come upon an entirely different use of the stencil, one touched by a heavy hand, but not without its quaintness.

As the colonists from over the seas brought the traditions of their homelands with them to the new world and made the fashions of England and the Continent their own, so the men who pushed the frontiers westward took with them the backgrounds and ideals of their first homes. Among these pioneers who went into the Northwest Territory in 1799 and joined a small group already settled in the Lower Little Miami Valley, in Columbia township (Ohio), were Joseph Ferris and his wife, Priscilla Knapp Ferris, from Fairfield County, Connecticut. There is reason to believe that about 1812 they built the one-room structure of brick with its peaked roof as their first permanent home. This room later became the kitchen, when in the days of their prosperity the family enlarged the house, using brick made in the vicinity and hand-hewn native timber. Although the Ferris family was numerous and important in the community, we have few facts about Joseph except that he owned many acres, and was miller, distiller, and farmer, taking "his produce to New Orleans by flat-boat." He also built a frame structure as a schoolhouse for his eight children and "any others who cared to attend," hiring and paying the teachers himself. In a second floor bedroom with a fine fireplace and built-in cupboards original stencilled walls were found in 1928 when the whitewash on the walls was being removed by workmen.[15]

Although the patterns were too indistinct to be left without restoration, they were sufficiently clear for precise tracing, only the vases above the mantel and the swags being partly obliterated. Below the chair-rail was a border of small leaves and dots, and above the baseboard was the same design which was similarly used in the Clark house, Washington, Connecticut. In repainting (fig. 45) it was decided to keep this lower wall space without pattern. Three floral sprays and a sprig of "cherries" break the panels formed by the columns. Their ornamental base is a new treatment, but their leaf design edged with half discs appears to be identical with "Stimp's" upright band in the Hartwell and Clark houses, in Washington, Connecticut, and with a border at Dover Plains, New York. We do not know who did the stencilling in Ohio; the designs may have been traced and sent by post from Connecticut, or some itinerant may have taken his kit and jour-

15. These stencils were found and reproduced by Miss Marion Bridgeman at the time the house was being restored under the direction of the late Richard Henry Dana of New York, as a historical museum for the town of Mariemont, a part of the Thomas J. Emery Memorial, Hamilton County.

neyed "West," but no other examples of the craft have been found in the vicinity of the Ferris house.

In that part of the Western Reserve Territory known today as Summit County, Ohio, a region settled by pioneers from Groton, Connecticut, another stencilled wall has left a memory of upright columns of conventionalized designs, not leaves and flowers, against a gray plaster. The house, built by Moses Smith of Groton, one of those who broke the trail by ox cart sometime between 1800 and 1810, stood in the settlement of Middlebury, named after the Connecticut town, now a part of Akron. Although the house has long been destroyed, sections of the old walls were salvaged, which accounts for the vivid recollections of another generation.

We can only record these rooms as we see them, making such comparisons or inferences of kinship as appear reasonable, remembering always that the natural impulse and habit of these journeymen would have been to copy designs from one another. As we go to New Hampshire, Vermont, and Maine, we shall lose sight of some of these familiar motifs and shall find new groups of ornament and new arrangements, indicating that certain patterns were more or less "locally" used.

### NEW HAMPSHIRE

New Hampshire has yielded many stencilled walls, for in a few months' time, spread out over several summers, I found some thirty-odd houses which bore this type of decoration in all stages of repair, from ruin to restoration. Within the bounds of a little over two counties there are two distinct groups of design: one includes the type of pattern so well illustrated by Eaton's outfit and shows the same general treatment of walls already familiar from Massachusetts; the other, marked by a greater refinement of line and proportion, is found in Bleak House at Peterborough, in the Governor Pierce house at Hillsborough, and elsewhere, all apparently being the work of one hand.

Let us first stop at the Wilson Tavern in Peterborough, New Hampshire, as did the old market wagons or "pog teams" which carried the farmers and their produce to the Boston market, for here we shall find our first definite date for stencilling in this state. The early history of the tavern has been provided by Miss Jenny Scott, who in 1892 sold this property, which had been in the family four generations. Robert Wilson, her great-grandfather, owned some three hundred acres of land in the pioneer settlement of Peterborough, but her grandfather, William Wilson, built the tavern in 1797, when the original stencilling was part of the "finish of the house." The ell was added by him in 1807, enlarging the tavern to seventeen rooms.

In these early days the hostel was the center of the community and the meeting

FIG. 46. PINK ROOM, THE MANSE, PETERBOROUGH

Built in 1797 and known today as Bleak House, the Manse introduces a group of patterns which
are distinguished by their simplicity and grace.

*Owned by the Society for the Preservation of New England Antiquities*

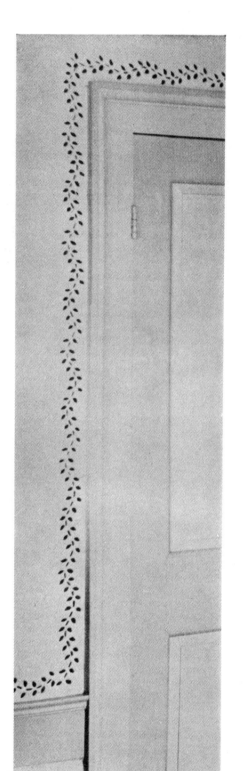

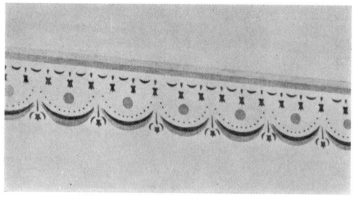
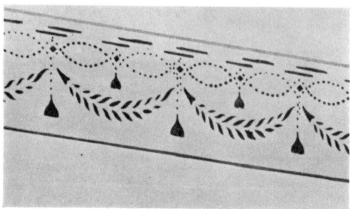

FIG. 47. DETAILS FROM THE MANSE

At the left is shown a running vine from the blue bedroom which follows the door, windows, wainscoting, and mantel. Right, at top, is a deep chrome and black frieze from the same room. The center frieze is from the dining room. The bottom frieze, from a second bedroom, is also set off by a line from the lower wall.

place where all important town affairs were transacted. Old and young gathered to dance in the spacious ballroom with its two fireplaces and the swinging partition that served to divide it into two rooms, which could be used for bedrooms when the inn was crowded. Today the fireplaces and partition remain, but the stencilling has disappeared from the walls. The former owner recalls that as a child she "admired the frieze" at the top of the walls, the uprights spaced at intervals, and the flower motifs making an "all-over" pattern in greens, reds, and touches of blue against a white ground. If the present covering of white paint is ever removed we shall be able to date definitely another wall pattern. Miss Scott remembered also a "yellow room" on the east side of the second floor, with a black frieze and a border which ran around the doors, windows, and moldings in contrast to the warm tone of the ochre background.

Near the Wilson Tavern is a house known today as Bleak House, built by the same carpenter-builder in 1797 for the first parson called to the community. One who for many years had been familiar with the history of the "Manse" gave me the following facts relating to its decoration.[16] The walls of five rooms and the two small hallways in the original building were stencilled. Those in the present dining room had evidently been subjected to hard use, for they emerged only in fragments from under fourteen layers of paper. From a section found in good condition back of a large old cupboard, a local painter took his pattern for reproduction. No pains were wanting to insure accuracy in tracing the designs, with the result that this reproduction is close to the original. On cream walls a looped and tasseled frieze in black and rich yellow-brown was placed just below the molding at the ceiling, while a delicate border in black followed the narrow woodwork in the corners and along the top of wainscoting, door, and mantel.

The walls of the parlor (fig. 46), known as the "pink room," kept their freshness much longer, probably because they were found under only two layers of paper, and we now see them in almost "their original stencilling," so little retouching was required. Walls of palest pink are divided by a black line from the light gray background of a frieze on which the draped festoons and tassels, pendent from starred medallions, are in two shades of light blue with markings of blue-black. The narrow vine above is also in blue-black. Inspired no doubt by French form and color, there is a spaciousness and feeling for design in this dignified room as well as a mature conception of the use of a simple but effective tool.

Other rooms in the house display corresponding subtlety in their decorative details (fig. 47). In the "blue bedroom" the walls and ceiling are the same soft tone, but the ground of the frieze is warm buff, separated from the plain wall space by a black line, done with the straightedge and a lining brush. A deeper chrome alternates with black in the leaf arrangement of graceful festoons and in the rays of the sunbursts, while a

16. The late Mrs. Blanche Fowler Post, West Peterborough, New Hampshire.

fernlike vine in black, running around the door and above the chair-rail, completes the pattern and color harmony of this pleasing arrangement. We are told that "this stencilling was only retouched in places," and that "no new stencil was cut." The frieze will reappear in the Wood house at Hancock, where the design is visible today only in a closet. Another bedroom on the second floor has a border of black upon a warm gray ground, combined with deep cream walls, which is effectively defined by the dotted line frequently used in developing ornamental forms in both wall and furniture stencils. Small punches were the customary tools for cutting such holes, uniformity and clean-cut openings being essential to their decorative value. The frieze of garlands and cords in the hall was restored some twenty years ago by an old painter, Washington Greenwood, then aged eighty.

These rooms leave with us a sense of pleasure and an awareness of the taste of their designer, who liked the classic restraint of simply-placed ornament, the grace of the tied festoon and trailing vine, but who demanded variety within the limits of his chosen motifs. Advertisements in newspapers at the end of the eighteenth century which described wallpaper borders as patterned in "festoons," and as "narrow flat borders" remind us how much the taste of the day was being influenced by this type of decoration.

Many of the patterns in Bleak House are repeated at Hancock in the Salmon Wood house, built in 1801 to replace a small structure of earlier date. The new building was kept as a tavern by its industrious owner, who at the same time farmed several hundred acres, ran a sawmill, a blacksmith shop, held the office of selectman, and was enrolled on many local committees. The deep simple cornice, the half-pilasters, and the wainscoting of the parlor show how excellent a builder he was. The small hallway, painted a deep rose, has the frieze and tassels (fig. 48) used in the halls at Bleak House. The border which outlines the corners and door trim has been made with two stencils, an uncommon practice in so narrow a band, one producing the black detail and the other the crimson veining of the leaves and the dotted line at the edge.

The whitish wall of the parlor (fig. 49) has a frieze stencilled on a deep cream ground in the same blues as at Bleak House but with a different distribution of the three shades. The folds of the deep scallops caught up with medallions have the quality of fabric and show an able handling of light and shade. No retouching appears to have been done to mar in any way the original form or color. A careful craftsman fitted the blue-black border neatly around the chimney structure and picked from his patterns three big urns of flowers for the overmantel (fig. 50). Adornment for her chimney shelf need never again concern the housewife of this dwelling. Between the two windows the painter has taken his flowers and placed them below a mirror which occupied the upper section of the panel, and with discrimination centered one unit of his frieze above.

In the two bedrooms on the second floor, where corners have been partitioned off

FIG. 49. PARLOR, SALMON WOOD HOUSE
The frieze is stencilled in three shades of blue on a gray ground
in this house, built about 1801.

FIG. 48. FRONT HALL, SALMON WOOD HOUSE, HANCOCK
The garlands of the frieze are red and green.

*Owner, Louis B. Thacher*

FIG. 50. PARLOR OVERMANTEL AND PANEL, SALMON WOOD HOUSE

This economical artisan saved his patron the expense of the usual mantel ornaments by painting them on the wall. A panel between the windows in the same room (shown at right) had the undecorated space left for a mirror.

FIG. 51. PARLOR, PETER FARNUM HOUSE, FRANCESTOWN

The overmantel design in the Wood house is here used as a wall motif in deep blue against ochre.

*Owner, Arthur Starrett*

FIG. 52. BALLROOM, GOVERNOR PIERCE HOUSE, HILLSBOROUGH

The house, built about 1804, has a large ballroom, whose walls are deep rose with borders of black on white with additional touches of red.

for closets, bits of the two original friezes remain untouched, one repeating that of a bedroom at Bleak House. The artist had a very definite sense of the three dimensional, for his garlands have the quality of raised carvings, and his draperies the depth of folds. He has also studied highlights and shadows and skillfully cut his stencils to convey them.

On at least one occasion this journeyman painter repeated the overmantel arrangement of urns and flowers in the Wood house at Hancock, for we also find it as part of the decoration of a room at Francestown. Described in a village record as "at the crossing this side of Starrett's place," the property formerly belonged to Peter Farnum. From 1790 in a tannery standing near the house, two generations, father and son, diligently served the surrounding countryside. The house is "four-square," dignified and solid, and in what no doubt was the principal room (fig. 51), judging by the well-designed cornice, chair-rail and surbase, there are patterns similar to those at Salmon Wood's, but the painter has added new designs, making an elaborate composition. This work is today in poor condition, but a photograph taken years ago has preserved for us the decoration above the mantel shelf, now almost obliterated by the attempt of a former tenant to wash the wall. The photograph of even the best part of the room required careful retouching in order to define the details for reproduction. The faded pigments of the flower motifs between the stripes suggest that they too have been submitted to soap and water.

The painter was a skilled craftsman, willing to take the time to cut the finely-indented leaves of the rose medallions and to plan the compact frieze with its roped upper border and double wavy lines. According to his habit, the designs are placed on the wall with precision and judgment. He liked the softened effect of overlaying dark blue petaled rosettes and stars on circles of light blue and of setting the deep red sunbursts of the up-rights on blue ovals. His borders and the frieze in dark blue complement the warm ochre of the wall, an effect of contrast which is heightened by the red roses of the dado medallions with their accents of white. His frequent use of detailed borders, the upright, and the quarter-fan indicates the artisan's awareness of the Sheraton vogue in America at this time. The stencilling in the hall had been covered by wallpaper which was removed with no intent to save the original design, and although only faint traces of the frieze were left, enough remained to show its resemblance to one in the Benjamin Pierce house in Hillsborough.

The ballroom of the Governor Pierce house (figs. 52 and 53) is another tribute to the skill of the same artist and to the taste of its renowned master. A family legend recounts that when Benjamin Pierce built the dwelling in 1804, he himself chose, for their special significance, the patterns which were to decorate its main room of hospitality. His birthday fell on December twenty-fifth, and he selected for the frieze the "Christmas holly, the bent pine, and the lighted candles." His choice was a suitable one, for we have many records of this pioneer's generosity in welcoming both friends and strangers, especially at the holiday season. On one occasion he kept open house for the Revolutionary ex-soldiers in the state, and at another time, on reaching the age of sixty-seven, he invited to the birthday celebration his Hillsborough comrades-in-arms, for he had attained rank in the army of the Revolution and was Brigadier-General in the newly organized militia of the young Republic. The large ballroom must have overflowed with his guests, who ranged in years from fifty-nine to a patriarchal ninety. This spacious room, with its two large fireplaces, its fluted moldings, wainscoting, paneled doors and the fiddler's platform[17] was the scene of much of the social life in the county and state; quilting and spelling bees and dances were frequent, for its owner loved people, gaiety, and color. We are told that again and again he would call the boys and tell them to go yoke the oxen and bring the young people to his house for a dance which he always led with his wife. This governor of New Hampshire was a figure beloved in the community, where his connection traced back to 1786, when he was sent to survey the section of the state around Stoddard. Delighted with his first impressions of the fertile Contoocook valley, he decided to become a farmer. In two years he returned with a negro servant, and bought the tract of land from an Indian, who, family tradition records, planted a wild rose on the ground he had sold in memory of the one fair and honest white man he had known. The log cabin soon built in what is now Lower Village, Hillsborough, was replaced by the house which today carries on the memory of a man noted for his kindness and generosity of character, "a man of the people, whose natural qualities inevitably made him a leader among them," leadership which was carried on by his son Franklin, fourteenth President of the United States.

It is said that the stencilling of the rooms and halls was done soon after the completion of the house, antedating 1824, at least, for at this time a French hand-blocked paper, Dufour's "Bay of Naples," was put on the walls of the north parlor at a cost of five hundred dollars. Today glimpses of an ochre wall with a border stencilled in blue-green with a line of brilliant Chinese red at its inner edge is seen when the paper occasionally lifts from the plaster. In favor of dating the stencilling close to 1804 when the house was built, we again repeat the comment, made about the Hickox house, that the New England conscience would have found it unbecoming to place a French wallpaper over a wall recently ornamented by any method whatsoever.

A small piece of the original paint and stencilling now in a closet discloses the same coloring in the hall as in the parlor. The back hall has a frieze of black with touches of red against its pink wall. The sitting room is a deep rose with a border in black on a white ground. Venetian red in powdered form mixed with skimmed milk was a paint commonly applied both to barns and to interior work in New England a century or more

17. No trace of it or of the two partitions which were used to divide the room remains.

54

ago; sufficient quantity would be mixed in the morning to complete the job planned for the day. This old-time mixture was used in the restoration of these walls.[18]

Another link identifying the painter of this house as the one responsible for this group of New Hampshire walls is the similarity between the friezes in the hall and sitting room at the Pierce house (fig. 54) and two of those at Bleak House, Peterborough; in the former they are incomplete today, but close examination proves them to have been the same original patterns. The faithful hand and eye which restored the almost indistinguishable outlines remaining in the hall and sitting room of the Hillsborough house reproduced only those parts of the design which could be seen instead of rounding out the pattern by applying imaginary lines. Such fragmentary clues build up the evidence for attributing this group to a single worker.[19]

The Joslin Tavern, West Townsend, Massachusetts, built about 1790 just south of the New Hampshire line, was undoubtedly another stopping place of this itinerant, for the decoration of its ballroom (fig. 55) is very similar to that in the Benjamin Pierce house. The walls are laid out in the same panels, bordered by white bands patterned with black. The frieze is identical, and the quarter-fans are placed at the corners of the panels in keeping with the Sheraton spiral of the overmantel. A second room has the same simple treatment of panels, borders, and frieze (fig. 56). On these walls of cream and rose the fans of blue or black and orange make very lively rooms whose clear colors are the strong shades so typical of Empire wallpapers.

Perhaps this journeyman traveled inland from the seaboard town of Marblehead, just as in 1820 another painter is known to have ridden from Boston to Maine to fresco a landscape on the four walls of a room in Hollis. At least one dwelling in the old coast town of Marblehead suggests traces of his work, for his hand shows in the King Hooper house, built long before the Revolution by that noted ship-builder and merchant. Some say that he was called "King" because he was lavish in his hospitality and the dignitaries of the day thronged to his door; others, that the luxury of his princely living gained him the title; yet another version states that he earned it from the fishermen who valued the honor and integrity of his dealings with them. At any rate the spacious old house in the center of the town reflects taste in its fine paneling, delicate woodwork, and wide stairway with carved bannisters of varied designs. It is this stairway which leads to the large banquet hall or ballroom that runs the width of the house on the top floor. This room

18. Restored by Miss Rosina Dondero, Boston, Massachusetts.

19. As these pages are going to press, a wall in Guilford, Connecticut, which bears a close relation to those done by this New Hampshire artisan has come to my attention. In the course of demolishing a deserted house, built in 1752 by Samuel Robinson on the New Haven Post Road, a few patches of stencilling in a front room revealed the same frieze as that in the hall of the Governor Pierce house and in the dining room at Bleak House (figs. 54 and 47). The coloring was dark blue and deep red on a pale blue wall. Alterations made to the house in 1790 suggest a probable date for the stencilling.

may have been stencilled at one time, for in the two small ante-rooms leading from the hall we find on the ochre background a blue-green border (fig. 57), the same pattern and coloring that was used as an upright in the Starret house in Francestown. Tracings of the two are identical even to the curve of the small intersecting petals. Unfortunately time has defaced or obliterated much of the Marblehead work, but in one of the small rooms there is a narrow band of scrolls and a starflower outlining the door, window, and corners, which suffices to identify it as the exact border used in the parlor of the Wood house, Hancock, New Hampshire. The walls which enclose the broad flight of stairs leading to the ballroom also showed the same deep ochre where I lifted the paper, and above the wainscoting were traces of a stencilled band with indented leaves, while with the help of a stepladder it was possible to detect in the frieze the same blue-green with spots of red. The halls of the first and second floor had been painted a soft, rich red ochre, and again above the wainscoting were details of a black border, but whatever else these walls may reveal must wait until the paper is removed.

Two rooms in a house at Deering, New Hampshire, south of Hillsborough, again repeat the pattern and the treatment popular in this area. The band at the ceiling is the one seen in fragmentary form in the small back hall of the Benjamin Pierce house. This group of walls has a refinement in detail, line and proportion which makes them as distinctive as they are unusual.

A type of stencilling more common in New Hampshire is the all-over patterned wall exemplified by the work of Moses Eaton, who takes a conspicuous part in these pages both because of his extensive work and because more is known of him than of his compatriots. Such family background as we have indicates that his father, Moses, Sr. (1753–1833), who was descended from the early colonists of Dedham, Massachusetts, served in the Revolution, and in his fortieth year moved from Needham, Massachusetts, to Hancock, New Hampshire, where, in 1796, his son was born. The house (more recently known as the Washburn house) today stands on a grassy path which was once the "King's Highway" and a main road to Concord. Moses, Jr., later removed to the adjoining township of Dublin, settling in the old part of town now known as Harrisville, where until only a few years ago one stencilled wall stood up dramatically from an overgrown cellar hole to mark the spot. The younger Eaton in a few years acquired the adjoining land,[20] where four generations of descendants have continued to live. His young days as a painter were probably over by the time he settled here, for after his marriage he turned to farming. Testimony of his ability is found in the fact that his corn was rated the best in the countryside, and he had the reputation of being a shrewd trapper. One suspects that he never quite mastered his restless itinerant's blood, for tradition

20. The present Clifton Richardson farm.

FIG. 53. DETAIL OF BALLROOM WALL, GOVERNOR PIERCE HOUSE

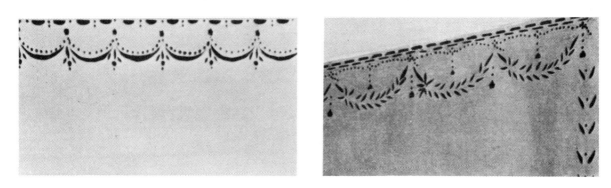

FIG. 54. TWO FRIEZE DETAILS, GOVERNOR PIERCE HOUSE

Compare these two restored friezes with those from the Manse (fig. 47, two lower right friezes).

FIG. 55. BALLROOM, JOSLIN TAVERN, WEST TOWNSEND (MASS.)

The tavern was built in 1789–1790, and the stencilling (reproduced by the owner, Dr. Henry B. Boynton) is similar to that of the ballroom in the Governor Pierce house.

FIG. 56. DETAIL OF ANOTHER ROOM, JOSLIN TAVERN

The upright and a fragment of the frieze show a treatment similar to that found in the ballroom.


FIG. 57. DETAIL OF BORDERS, KING HOOPER HOUSE, MARBLEHEAD (MASS.)

Among the few remaining traces of original stencilling in this fine old dwelling are these designs in blue-green on yellow ochre.

FIG. 58. WALL STENCILS OF MOSES EATON, 1796–1886
These stencils come from the kit of Moses Eaton, Jr.,
found in the attic of his house at Dublin.

states that the freedom and adventure of the road tempted him into an excursion "West." How much time the busy farm routine left him for stencilling is not known, but he did have time to decorate these two Dublin houses, and it was this knowledge that sent me on yearly visits to his home. My fifth visit was rewarded by success because of its timeliness, for plans were under way for repapering the parlor, and the sample book had already arrived. The actual operation was hastened by my unexpected call in order that I might at last see the stencils which Eaton had chosen for his own house. At the end of an hour the remains of three paperings lay heaped on the floor. To see the patterns Eaton had chosen to live with linked the painter vividly to the old work kit. At an earlier repapering the sight of these same walls by the artisan's eighty-year-old daughter Mary is said to have awakened poignant memories recalling the days of her childhood, when the Chelsea china was set out with blue Staffordshire and flowered teacups before the Franklin fireplace against the soft raspberry walls with their deep green and red decorations. The walls were divided by the upright of diamonds and petals into nineteen inch panels decorated with flowers with large red centers and geometric figures, while a band of roses and leaves ran along chair-rail and surbase. Between the two front windows was a flower-filled wicker basket in green and red. The frieze was the exact swag and bell with its characteristic tongue found in his work kit.

Examination of the kit found in his attic (fig. 18) disclosed, besides eight brushes, seventy-eight stencils which made forty complete designs varying in size from a large weeping willow to the small hearts, diamonds, and circles used at the center of motifs for spots of another color (figs. 58 and 59). No register marks for the accurate placing of one stencil upon another are found in any of these patterns, indicating that the artisan depended solely on his eye and on the upper straight edge of the stencil. Thick green, red, and yellow paint still adheres to these working patterns, showing the colors used. Vacant spaces in the box were filled by small pine woodblocks of much earlier date with designs cut at the two ends, originally used for printing linens, but showing traces of the same green paint. The designs are segments of circles, wreaths of leaves, flower petals, vines and stars. Of what use they could have been in connection with wall stencilling we do not know, for a woodblock would make a poor impression on a rough plastered surface.

Though Eaton's box contains some of the same motifs which we have seen in Berkshire County, his patterns have not the light rendering of detail or the intricacy of design. It is fascinating to see what a variety of ornament can be obtained with the different single units, combinations which seem endless. Eaton was an experienced and careful craftsman, as we have seen from the work in his own parlor, for he not only placed his patterns precisely but cut a beveled edge on the heavy paper to provide a sharper outline for the designs. The paint, thick on his stencils, indicates his favorites: the oak leaf, the large flower spray, the diagonal border, and the rose and leaf. Only one of all these patterns in his kit fails to appear on some wall which I have seen, though this stencil also has paint massed on it to show that it saw much use. Paints in dry form, red, green, and brown, stood for many years close to his tool box. On a recent visit to the house I learned that a hard lump of vermilion had come to light in a corner of the attic, but my hope of seeing it vanished when I heard that it had been put at the bottom of the winter woodpile away from young and mischievous hands. Any one who knows a New Hampshire woodpile can guess how long it would take for this chunk of red to come out of its hiding place. On the back of an old pine chest which stood in the Eaton house a spray of leaves was found stencilled in two shades of green from a pattern in the kit, but besides such mementos of his hand, his tools, and certain walls in the neighborhood, we have few facts which bear directly upon his work. Had the records collected by Luther Eaton been kept, we should perhaps have an answer to any questions. The eldest son of the artisan is remembered as "the antiquarian" of the family, but in order to rid the attic of the vast accumulation of his papers, two loads were given to a local peddler as the simplest way to dispose of them.

On my first visit to Dublin I learned that in Hancock there was a stencilled wall in the vacant house in which Eaton's father had lived, and here I hoped to find the same patterns as those in the old kit. When my guide, a young lad, took me into the parlor through the small entrance hall, I saw a large wall covered by musty paper. In one corner under a loose bit appeared the blue of a coat of kalsomine but only the closest scrutiny could detect under it the faint outlines of stencilled patterns. Spurred by my disappointment as well as by his own spirit of adventure, my youthful guide began vigorously to pull off the paper in long ribbons. The blue kalsomine came with it and left the stencils in clear outline, exactly the same patterns as those in Eaton's kit. In the center of the chimney-breast were two weeping willows, one above the other, with baskets of flowers on either side. Stripes divided the wall into panels, and the design of oak leaves and the flower spray were used over the walls. The frieze was the bell, swag, and pendant, and the rose and leaf border headed the chair-rail. The colors were green and red against a white wall. Life had come back into the old house.

Family tradition has it that Moses Eaton, Sr., also used these stencils, so the walls may have been the work of the older man, who perhaps had practiced this art even before he left Needham. He may have been familiar with the Goodale house at Marlborough, which is about twenty miles distant; of course we can only speculate, but both have the same frieze of bells and swags, and Eaton's kit also repeats other units, although in Marlborough the patterns are less solid in character and generally lighter in design. Since walls showing a similar treatment recur throughout New England, we cannot, even in the few adjacent counties in New Hampshire where Eaton, Jr., lived and worked, necessarily claim them for his hand, for we know of others who stencilled houses in this vicinity. Emery Rice, who appeared in Hancock much later than did Eaton, plied the same trade in the neighborhood. In a small house on the outskirts of the town, where the son of this artisan lived, a set of stencils was found, perhaps a dozen or more. One of them in my possession is a rather poorly cut imitation of the upright border of oblique lines found in Eaton's kit, probably copied from his pattern or from an earlier one, since this design is known to have been used before 1800. The stencilling in the Buchanan house in Antrim, built in 1808, is said to be the work of another craftsman, one Nathaniel Parker, born in North Weare in 1802.

In Hancock, on the road to Stoddard, stands a small, one and a half story house built near the turn of the century by Mansel Alcock in a clearing among virgin pines. It was a sturdy structure with solid carpentering, hand-wrought nails, and hewn lathing, disclosed where the broken plaster has fallen. In 1871 the building was moved across the road to make place for a more modern dwelling. In spite of this journey the one stencilled room is in fair condition. We have little question as to the probable artisan, for Hancock was at one time the home of the two Moses Eatons. Whether it was father or son who stencilled the room, he had only to walk a mile to Mansel Alcock's from the house on the King's Highway. The Eaton kit contains the identical patterns that appear on this wall (fig. 60); a detailed comparison of the motifs with the stencils themselves reveals no variations, even to the misfit of calyx and petals in the blossoms of the flower spray. Though in a state of dilapidation the room still keeps its original character, bright in its coloring of Chinese red and clear grass green on natural plaster. The bold design of oak leaves, the spray of flowers, and the circular forms are in scale with the robust tassels and loops, while the rose border above the paneling balances the vine at the top. The diamond upright encountered so often in Berkshire County has its simplest treatment here, made with a single stencil.

There is always the lure of adventure, and often its disappointments, in the hunt for stencilled walls. Eager with the anticipation of my first search in New Hampshire, I followed one morning a country road to the Charles Gibson house in Hillsborough, confident of seeing its century-old patterns still in their original condition. No welcome could have been warmer than the one I received from the new owner, who had recently purchased the property, untenanted for the preceding ten years, but when I explained the reason of my visit, I found that I had come six weeks too late. For over a month a painter had been diligently covering the patterned walls with solid washes of pink and yellow. Only one small bedroom had been left untouched, where there was a frieze of starflowers identical with the one in the Cooledge house, East Washington, and close-set uprights giving a pleasing effect of narrow striping. In the hall, the stencils which had covered both plastered walls and matched sheathing were still faintly visible under the coat of fresh paint.

In nearby Hancock, on a wooded road, in the old section of town, stands the empty shell of a clapboard house. No history tells when it was built, but we do know that it was occupied in 1792 by David Davis and at a later date by William Lakin. It must have been a good dwelling in its day, but only the four walls were standing when I made my visit, under the guidance of a young boy who had once poked through the debris for a bit of seasoned wood with which to make himself a violin. Without partitions, floor, or roof, the interior was still ablaze with color. The house was fairly large, perhaps four rooms on each floor in addition to the hall, and all seem to have been stencilled, though the patterns were sometimes too faded for identification. As I peered through a broken window frame into what remained of the structure, it looked like a rainbow of color under the open sky. One wall lay intact, face up on the ground, showing remnants of pale rose and clear ochre. In an upper room were the familiar bells, oak leaves, and a large floral spray. The reds were still bright in the hearts which centered the flower designs in the upper hall. Green had faded to yellow, except for a single leaf in a sheltered corner which still kept its freshness. Even in decay most of the units held their form, suggesting that the binder was a strong one, probably oil, but, since chemical analysis is futile when plaster has long been exposed to extreme weather, we cannot be sure.

A neighboring house on a parallel road also has a room of yellow walls with the same designs we have just seen in the Lakin house, bleached and weathered. Over the mantel is the basket of flowers which in this neighborhood takes the place of the vase of Berkshire County. The floor, painted black and white in imitation of marble, is a far-away echo of the current French fashion, which reached even the very small villages of New England.

Also comparatively near to the Moses Eaton home in Dublin was the Varnum house at Capers Corner in the oldest section of Peterborough, where some years ago stencils were found under eleven layers of paper. No pains were spared in restoring this small, one and a half storied house. An expert from Boston was imported to reclaim the battered and disfigured walls, and weeks were spent in the careful lifting of the paper alone. In the parlor and bedroom, where the walls are a deep rose and ochre, is the frieze of arcades and candles which in the Eaton box lacks the third stencil that produces the flame of the candle. The small flower spray with the large center is a unit that Eaton stencilled on the wall of his own "best" room. The wide and open spacing of the patterns is regular, and the heavy leafage of the border is well chosen for outlining the surbase and wainscoting. The work of reconstruction gives back two rooms which have not suffered in their retouching.

There is a singular charm in the room of another low-structured house at Antrim (fig. 61), also in Hillsborough County. On three sides of the room, stencilled designs

60

FIG. 59. WALL STENCILS OF MOSES EATON

Note how two or more cut-outs were combined to make a single pattern.

FIG. 60. WALL, MANSEL ALCOCK HOUSE, HANCOCK
These patterns are identical with Moses Eaton's stencils.

*Owner, Dr. L. Vernon Briggs*

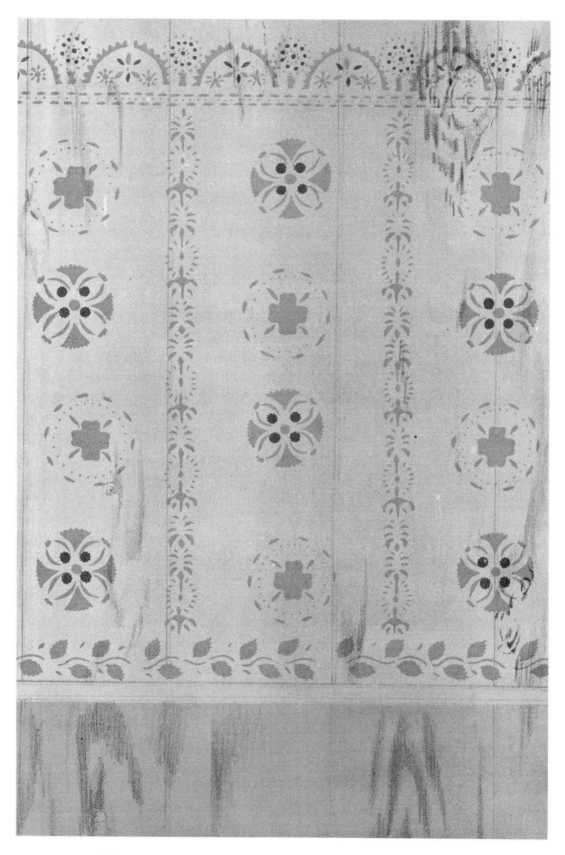

FIG. 61. STENCILLING ON MATCHED PINE SHEATHING, ANTRIM

*Owner, Miss Louise Q. Pierce*

(*Reproduced in color following page 80*)

were placed on beaded sheathing of close-grained "pumpkin pine," and were rescued by chance from under eight layers of paper. An ochre background is broken by the warm reddish undertones of the wood, adding richness to the color. Not a stroke of reparation has been done on the sharply defined patterns, which have been preserved in almost perfect condition on the sheathing, but are blurred on the one plastered wall. Even the delicate points that suggest the flame of the candle in the frieze have sharp outline and form. The harmony of the soft greens of the motifs has been carried into the gray-green paint on the wainscoting. In the circle centered with the four-lobed flower the second red stencil was used only once; the combination was evidently tried out near the door and the color scheme perhaps found not to the liking of the owner, because in the other units the contrasting red note is omitted. The stripe is of a type frequently used in Vermont. The room, as I recall it, was a very special one, small but glowing with life, its furniture of yellow pine in keeping with its brightness and vitality. At least three other rooms were stencilled. The north parlor, once guarded by drawn blinds except on special occasions, but now transformed into the kitchen, still clearly shows the original designs in olive green on pink behind the drawers of a new built-in cupboard. Roses and leaves above the baseboard and a scroll used as an upright completed the decoration of this "keeping" room. In an upstairs bedroom the paper had not yet been removed, but there were glimpses of an ochre background, and in the present sitting room the frieze of pine trees and crossed hemlock boughs on a deep rose background is visible in one small corner where the paper has been taken off.

In East Washington, north of Hillsborough, stand two fine old brick houses, built about 1808 by brothers, Lemuel and Isaac Cooledge, from brick made in their own kiln in the field back of the buildings. The oldest of the seven children of the present occupant of the Isaac Cooledge house proudly took me into the large parlor at the left of the entrance and showed me its "frescos," while all of the brothers and sisters tried to help me as I matched the rose pink of the walls from a box of colors (fig. 62). The stencils were in green and deep red. Moses Eaton's kit could have supplied all the patterns. The variety in the two sprays is gained by using in one instance the stencil which gave the green leaves only, and in the other by adding the red stencil which supplied the full-blown flower. It is good work, with the spacing well planned. In the hall (fig. 63) the stripe of turned buds is inverted for variety, and the heart has been placed in combination with the frieze. The baseboard is marbleized in shades of gray.

This section of New Hampshire can give many more examples scattered along back roads and main thoroughfares of town and village, for I have only touched the fringe of their number. One brief inquiry in the small village of Francestown added four houses. The nearby Gibson Tavern has a room of elaborate design, but restoration has

FIG. 63. HALL, ISAAC COOLEDGE HOUSE
Green motifs are on a rose ground.

FIG. 62. PARLOR, ISAAC COOLEDGE HOUSE,
EAST WASHINGTON
Again we find patterns which were in Moses Eaton's kit.

FIG. 64. PARLOR, PRESCOTT TAVERN, EAST JAFFREY

A wide stencilled frieze is combined with freehand scenes depicting Mt. Vesuvius, Deer Island, and Boston Harbor. The overmantel (below) is said to represent Dartmouth College.

failed to reproduce the original clear flat color so characteristic of this type of work. Another instance occurs in a fine brick-ended house with a white clapboard front and two arched doorways, on the main street of Hancock. On a strip of stencilled plaster saved in the hall, faint traces of a frieze suggest a starflower and leaf, but the sprays and uprights are clearly defined. At the "Fuller homestead" just beyond, rooms with stencils are remembered, though long since lost sight of. In a farmhouse at Marlborough (New Hampshire), adjacent to Dublin, a section of original work with the willow tree and overturned buds is preserved. And again on a country road in North Peterborough a very old house keeps the original stencilling in two halls, but in this instance it was either an inexperienced or a very hasty worker who placed the designs. Yet these rooms, whether well or crudely done, all tell of lives which were concerned with the pleasure of ornament, of tastes and interests which led to devising ways of bringing color into the house just as we plan for it today.

At East Jaffrey, south of Dublin, we find a New Hampshire example of stencilling in combination with freehand painting or "frescoing," indicating the versatility of some of the itinerants, who must have come equipped to practice either or both these arts as occasion offered. On the ground floor of the Prescott Tavern on the old post road from Boston to Keene is a landscape in freehand with a stencilled frieze. A metal sign over the fanlight of the front door of the hostel gives the date of its building as 1803. It is reasonable to suppose that these crude panoramic walls in the parlor were inspired by the fashionable imported wallpapers which were so much the vogue in America in the early eighteen hundreds. The self-taught itinerant painter could, like the celebrated Joseph Dufour, sketch scenes of other lands and take his clients on distant journeys, but his price was far less than that paid by the Governor of New Hampshire for the "Bay of Naples" on the parlor walls at Hillsborough. Perhaps the painter at East Jaffrey had in mind this very paper, first printed soon after 1815, when he included Mount Vesuvius in his fresco of Boston Harbor and Deer Island.

The painting was done in payment of a long overdue board bill. A stencilled frieze provides the color in the room (fig. 64) for the fresco is done in tones of gray and black. The red urns, the bright yellow uprights, the broad line of dark red at the base, the rich crimson of the roses, and the touches of soft olive green are vividly emphasized by the large black dots—an admirable bit of coloring. This color at the top of the room gives the frieze an importance in the decorative scheme which it would not otherwise have. The itinerant had imagination and courage in designing the fresco, and he evidently felt no hindering sense of proportion, for the enormous dog almost reaches the height of his master who, with beaver hat and ready gun, seems to have turned his back on the small and distant deer in favor of the overgrown squirrels scampering along the branches. A plume of smoke from Mount Vesuvius has a long sweep, curling above the door and floating into the next panel. Harbors and mountains occupy the other walls. Over the mantel is that important and early seat of learning, Dartmouth College (fig. 64, bottom), evidently an original conception of the painter, for it scarcely resembles an almost contemporary print of 1793. The sun appears above the main building, symbolic of the light of knowledge, and sun rays and large black stars break the wide expanse of sky. The technique of marbleizing was also part of this painter's skill, which he lavished upon the woodwork of the mantel where touches of red and blue were added to the grays and blacks. A turkey feather may have been the brush with which he produced these effects, since the tools of his kit were probably not elaborate. Perhaps a sponge was used for the foliage of the trees and for the heavy puffs of smoke from the volcano.

It is quite possible that this artisan may have used stencils for his stars and buildings, for this method was advocated by at least one wall painter, Rufus Porter, who was practicing this craft about 1820, and who later passed on to others many helpful hints regarding his own technique. To quote his words:

> The painting of houses, arbors, villages etc. is greatly facilitated by means of stencils. . . . For this purpose several stencils must be made to match each other; for example one piece may have the form of a front of a dwelling-house or other building cut through it; another piece may have the form of the end of the same house as viewed from an oblique direction; a third piece may be cut to represent the roof; and a fourth may be perforated for the windows. Then by placing them successively on the wall and painting the ground through the apertures with a large brush, and with such colors as the different parts require, the appearance of a house is readily produced in a nearly finished state.[21]

Certainly the draftsman who made a living by his art would welcome such devices to lighten the task. Porter allows a brief five hours for the four walls of a room done in "claro-obscuro" (tones of the same color) with "a variety of fancy scenery, palaces, villages, mills, vessels, . . . and a beautiful set of shade trees in the foreground."[22] With such efficiency, in which the stencil took a large part, he points out that painted walls could readily "supersede the use of paper-hangings," if for no other reason than that of economy.

21. "Wall Painting," *Scientific American*, vol. I, no. 26, 1845. Wall painting was only one of the many occupations of Rufus Porter, who contributed numerous inventions to the industrial development of the nation. He became editor of the *New York Mechanic* in 1840, and founder of the *Scientific American* in 1845. During the six months of his editorship he contributed a series of articles on various phases of ornamental painting. See *Dictionary of American Biography*, vol. 7.

22. *Ibid.*, vol. I, no. 30, 1846.

FIG. 65. PARLOR FRESCOS, JOSHUA EATON HOUSE, BRADFORD
Tradition has it that the work was done by "two young men" about 1818.

FIG. 66. BEDROOM, JOSHUA EATON HOUSE

The stencilling of this room was also done by the "two young men." Mottling, such as that on the fire board, was one type of brush work of the period.

Frequently these journeymen worked in pairs, perhaps one of them as apprentice to the craft. There is a definite record that "two young men" painted the frescos in the Joshua Eaton house at Bradford, some thirty miles north of East Jaffrey. They also stencilled a bedroom and marbleized the woodwork, adding by hand the ornamental roses and strawberries in the small medallions of the parlor mantel. That they were "young men" is all we can learn of their personal identity, but we can see that their skill excelled that of the nameless artisan who worked at the Prescott Tavern; nor were they confined to neutral tones of gray and black for their panorama of rolling fields and sheltered harbor. This house in Merrimack County which they decorated did not promise much of interest; modern frames had replaced the eighteen-paned window sashes, the old front door was gone, and a piazza disguised the well-proportioned lines, but, after I had entered and seen the bright wall paintings and admirable woodwork in the parlor, I wanted to remove the thick paint which covered the frescos in the halls, where the rising and setting sun had ornamented the east and west walls.

Joshua Eaton had come to Bradford after 1795 when there were only two houses in the neighborhood, traveling by bridle path since no roads existed at the time. His first shelter in this forest of New Hampshire was a small cabin, but in 1814 the large house was built. The owner soon became identified with the little frontier village. From captain of infantry in the Bradford militia he was promoted to the rank of major, and, when a Masonic lodge was formed in 1818, its meetings were occasionally held in his house. This fact gives us the approximate date of the painting (fig. 65), for the symbol of Masonic brotherhood seems to have been placed above the fireplace as part of the original decoration. The yellow rushes and foreground of the harbor scene stand out against the brown of the grass plot which surrounds the red house placed to overlook the tall-masted schooners. These artisans were conscious of perspective and knew how to brush in needed accents of yellow to indicate a flood of sunlight against the brown of the tree trunks and the black of shaded foliage. On another wall (fig. 65, bottom) they even noted the ripple that disturbed the reflection of the wooded islands. The young men had a sense of rhythm, and their handling of color is almost modern in its use of contrasts and clear tones. The blue, green, and buff of the marbleized baseboard are repeated in the closet at the right of the mantel—even the edges of the shelves are marbleized, for in this house details were handled with care.

Upstairs there remains one stencilled room (fig. 66) which has canary yellow walls and patterns of green and scarlet that show the same appreciation of color. The frieze includes a heart and a starflower which are also used to center the other two motifs, while a single leaf makes an effective running border above the wainscoting and mantel. The stenciller was not discouraged when he found that his frieze did not fit over the door; he picked a narrower border to take its place. Nor did he mind repeating a bit of swag to fill an awkward corner, for he was not hampered by careful calculations. The fireboard, typical of much of the crude graining in the country sections of New England, was obviously done with the brush and not the feather.

Leaving this section of New Hampshire, we find three centers of interest in the neighborhood of Deerfield, southeast of Concord. One is a tavern, one a house, and the other the attic of an abandoned farm in the Pawtuckaway Mountains. Journeying by stage many years ago along the "South Road," from Concord to Portsmouth, one would as a matter of course have stopped for a change of horses at the old Mack Tavern, supposed to have been named for the family that last occupied it. This hostel, now but a record of history, flourished as a roadside inn from 1820 until the coming of the railroad which traced new routes of travel. It not only offered accommodation to the traveler, but many a country dance took place in its large second-floor ballroom, which at other times could be converted into three rooms by partitions kept in a hall closet. A fiddler's seat (fig. 67) was built into the center of the side wall against a cream background stencilled with reeded uprights and a frieze of bold pattern suitable for the long wall space. By merest chance an old negative of the seat still in its original position has been preserved, for today the building has gone, after having been vacant for some thirty years before it fell to utter ruin.[23] The few facts that we have about the old tavern have been gathered and passed on from the memories of those who once knew it.[24] We learn that the upper and lower halls were stencilled in red and green on a gray ground, and, although the woodwork of the ballroom was unpainted, there is a recollection of touches of color on the sawed and carved reliefs of the fiddler's seat.

Whoever stencilled the walls of the Mack Tavern was undoubtedly the painter of a room and hall in the Freese house at Deerfield five miles away. From the time of its building, about 1805, by Andrew Freese, the house has remained in the same family. The walls of the large parlor (fig. 68) were discovered when the present owner started to repaste a section of old paper and found beneath it a clear ochre ground with patterns in red and green. There is a frieze of crossed boughs and trees, and motifs of oak leaves, flower sprays, and borders. The red veining on the green boughs, not revealed in the illustration, is a detail that has much decorative value on the original wall. Skillfully spaced wicker baskets and weeping willows cover the broad chimney-breast. When the paper was stripped from the hall (fig. 69), a frieze and uprights were uncovered, both of which are identical with those surrounding the fiddler's seat. Done in brilliant red and vivid green against the soft gray ground and untouched by the brush of restoration, these walls have kept their vitality.

23. I am indebted to Mr. Arthur J. Hammond for the use of the photograph.

24. For these facts I am indebted to Mr. William Lithgow Willey.

66

FIG. 67. BALLROOM WITH FIDDLER'S SEAT, MACK TAVERN, DEERFIELD

Before the tavern was destroyed the fiddler's seat was removed, and it is now at the Harrison Gray Otis house, Boston.

*Courtesy of Arthur J. Hammond*

FIG. 69. HALL, FREESE HOUSE
The upright and frieze are the same as those used in the Mack Tavern.

FIG. 68. PARLOR, FREESE HOUSE, DEERFIELD
The overmantel arrangement is well composed.

*Owner, Arthur J. Hammond*

FIG. 70. WALL STENCILS OF HENRY O. GOODRICH, 1814–1834

These stencils were found in the attic of an abandoned farmhouse in
Nottingham, near Deerfield.

*Owner, Arthur J. Hammond*

FIG. 71. STENCILLED SHEATHING, JESSE AYER HOUSE, HAMPSTEAD
This example of stencilling on matched pine boards was probably done about 1800.

In the Pawtuckaway Mountains the chance discovery of an old box of stencils in the attic of the Goodrich house at Nottingham, near Deerfield, adds one more name to our list of these early stencillers. The battered kit, which bore the name of its owner, Henry O. Goodrich, contained twenty-two patterns (fig. 70), one bearing the same signature which had identified the box. He could not have worked at this craft for long, since a stone in the overgrown family burying ground at the rear of the old house gives his dates, crudely cut—born August 26, 1814, died March 25, 1834. The patterns are casually cut; obviously no precise measuring and patient tracing took the time of this youthful artisan, whose knife was none too sharp, nor his eye too sure. The serrating for which he had a preference was seldom even, nor were the small incisions equal or the petals matched and regular, but he had a flair for effective design and liked symmetry and balance. Although there were no sprays of flowers, a hint of ornateness, such as we notice in the arcades or in the circular motifs, did not trouble him. His cut-outs all have rhythm and strength without complete originality, for we recognize as variants the willow, the sunburst, the turned buds, the seven-petaled flower, and the two versions of the arcade. The differences may be intentional, but they are more probably due to roughly sketched tracing or drawing, or to patterns seen on walls and half remembered.

As one goes south from Deerfield, the town of Hampstead, in the southeast corner of New Hampshire, has two examples of original stencilling. On the old Newburyport road along which the ox teams carried their loads of freight to Concord stands the Humphrey Cogswell Tavern, built in 1825. In a bedroom on the second floor the decoration has survived, although the walls are badly worn. A dark green vine with sharply indented leaves and red berries serves for the simple frieze, but there is no border edging the surbase. The background of very pale blue is a variation of the more usual grounds of rose or ochre. In one of the wall motifs the pale yellow petals of a large star alternate with green, while the second has a spray of three scarlet blossoms with a yellow-rayed center and green foliage. The coloring of the hall is the same, although the green and reds of the leaves on the murky blue wash are very indistinct.

The stencilling of one room in the ell of the nearby Jesse Ayer house is much earlier than that of the once popular tavern, if we may judge from the simplicity of treatment. On soft gray lightly brushed over matched boards of pine the two circular motifs are variants of one pattern (fig. 71). The variant with notched leaves is done in thin Chinese red in contrast to the other in green with pale yellow markings on the buds. The same treatment is continued on the three plastered walls of the room, but the green vine with its yellow flowers is so immature in its drawing that one can almost see the hand of some beginner curving his pencil in and out as he traces the crimped edges of the leaves. The house is one of five where this same border appears, the other four being the Goodale house, one at Upton, Massachusetts, and two houses in Smithfield, Rhode Island.

The simple treatment characteristic of the group and the date of 1778 given us for the Goodale stencilling suggest placing them all not later than 1800.

## RHODE ISLAND

At Stillwater, Rhode Island, in the township of Smithfield, on a large grant of land deeded to him in 1726, Elisha Smith built the house of oak-hewn frame which still remains in the family, its present owner being seventh in descent. Some of its rooms were finished in beaded and feather-edged sheathing, but, of the stencilling probably done near the close of the century, only one room and an attic wall have survived to the present day, while a third is remembered as having had an "all-over flower pattern." In the "parlor-chamber" (figs. 72 and 73) time has mellowed and softened the once bright walls to tones of yellowed green and dulled red, in some places completely obliterating the patterns. An uncommon treatment is found in a five-inch black strip painted along the bottom of the plaster wall, which takes the place of the usual wood surbase and sets off the green leaf border above. The four motifs are so closely spaced on a pale gray ground that the effect is almost one of horizontal banding unbroken by uprights. One must mount a few steps of the attic staircase to see the other original stencilling (fig. 74), where perhaps the craftsman did his sampling and at the same time tried out his substitute baseboard.. Above the five-inch strip of black he placed tiers of gray-green willow trees separated by a bold upright of diagonally turned leaves on which sharply serrated discs in black and Chinese red alternate in brilliant color contrast on a pure yellow ground, while the arcade and candle in green and red complete this delightful and original composition.

The Putnam turnpike, as one journeys south from Stillwater, brings the traveler to an old inn shaded by maple trees, whose fine paneled door with its fan woodwork above has not opened to the wayfarer for nearly a century. Built about 1790 the tavern in 1830 was sold by Thomas Paine to George W. Mowry who ran it as an inn for a few years more. All four rooms and the hall on the ground floor were originally stencilled, but even as early as 1830 the parlor was so worn that its new owner "reluctantly papered it because no one in the neighborhood could be found to restencil it." "Flowers" were remembered on its walls. Both paper and plaster are falling in the hall of the now vacant building, but there are traces on its yellow ground of the bell frieze and a very large petaled star. In the taproom only the edges of the leaves of a border are discernible under loosened paper. There are, however, two small bedrooms whose walls are yet bright, for the family was "choice of the stencilling," so tradition says, "and when the house was no longer a tavern and was rented to tenants, they were always cautioned not to wash the walls and blur the ornament, for it was 'milk paint.' " These rooms are rectangular, with

68

FIG. 72. PARLOR-CHAMBER, ELISHA SMITH HOUSE, STILLWATER

The wall has never been covered by paper and is probably an early example of stencilling.

*Owner, Miss M. C. Appleby*

FIG. 73 . DETAIL OF PATTERNS, PARLOR–CHAMBER, ELISHA SMITH HOUSE

The camera has even caught the marks of this artisan's brush.

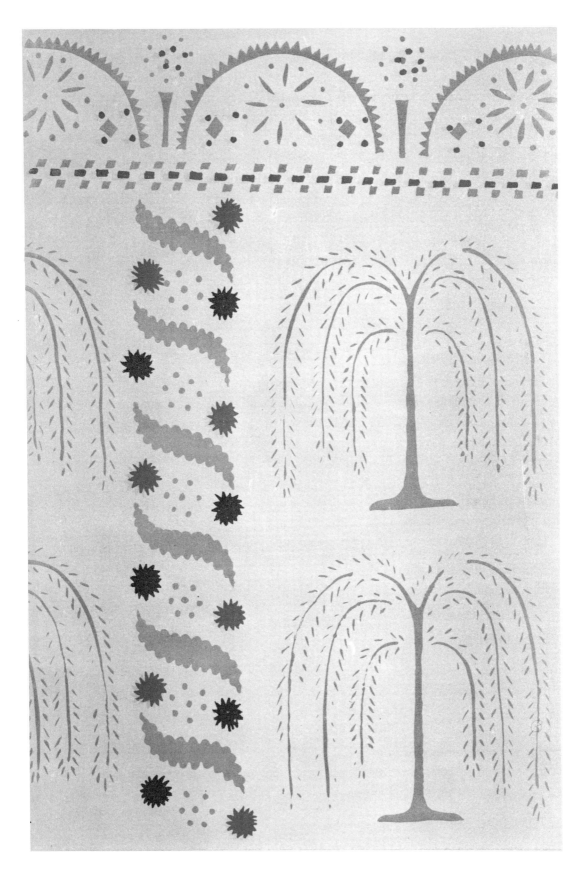

FIG. 74. WALL OF ATTIC STAIRWAY, ELISHA SMITH HOUSE

*(Reproduced in color following page 80)*

a single door and window, so that the walls have not been flooded with light. In one room (fig. 75) the ground is white with bold arcades at both top and bottom. The lower border is smaller in scale and identical with the frieze on the attic stairway of the Smith house. Green is used alone in the uprights which lack the usual color contrast. The parlor-bedroom (fig. 76) duplicates both the frieze and the vine of Elisha Smith's house, but the wall is divided into narrow panels broken by two flower sprays. The deep green of the upright is close to a rusty black, but the thin orange pigment of the flowers is brilliant in quality. These two buildings provide impressive testimony that one craftsman did them both, for the running vine of leaves with rounded edges, the frieze of bells with their heavy tongues, and the circular motif with the four serrated leaves are identical in both houses, even to the eccentricities of their cutting.

## VERMONT

In Vermont we find many of the same stencils which we have seen in New Hampshire and southern New England, but two rooms are notable as of very different design: one at South Reading, Windsor County, with an all-over pattern of leaves, and the other at Brookfield in Orange County with a flowering vine and distinctive uprights. Vermont has the further distinction of possessing an American eagle stencilled on a chimney-breast, surmounted by stars and fragments of a banner, and is, to my knowledge, the only state in which this patriotic emblem appears in stencilled form. My search centered in the neighborhood of Woodstock, and it was undertaken none too soon to gather the records of this fast disappearing art.

In order to take a picture of the Robinson house at South Reading it was necessary to make two long trips and on both occasions to empty the hall of a ton or more of hay and straw besides assorted farm tools and spare lumber. The stencilling was much worn and defaced from hard use, but even in its decay the house suggested something of its past. In 1792 Ebenezer Robinson, a soldier of the Revolution, chose a steep hill on the outskirts of South Reading in the shadow of Mt. Ascutney for the site of his log dwelling. But as this first home did not provide space enough for a growing family, a front section was added to the building about 1820, with fine mantels, a Palladian window and two fanlights. This progressive pioneer and his four sons became leaders in the near-by village as well as proprietors of the general store, the tavern, the starch factory, and the tannery. Some years previous to the enlarging of the house they had founded one of the first map-printing houses in America, employing, according to Thompson's *History of Vermont* (1820), a "copper-plate" printing press. Maps of the New England states, colored during the winter months by the women of South Reading, were pub-

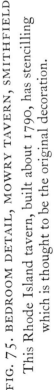

FIG. 76. PARLOR–BEDROOM DETAIL, MOWRY TAVERN
This wall has an upright and a vine border identical with those at the Elisha Smith house, Stillwater (fig. 72).

FIG. 75. BEDROOM DETAIL, MOWRY TAVERN, SMITHFIELD
This Rhode Island tavern, built about 1790, has stencilling which is thought to be the original decoration.

FIG. 77. HALL, EBENEZER ROBINSON HOUSE, SOUTH READING
These leaves are naturalistic rather than conventional in form.

*Owner, Mrs. H. M. Green*

lished, and when the rough roads hardened in the spring the maps were peddled in wagons throughout New England for money, or bartered for furs, dried apples, or miscellaneous objects, which were sold in turn at their store or passed on to Boston in exchange for other supplies. We owe many of these details to the contents of some letters which a great-grandson found "blowing around the attic" of the abandoned house.

This descendant of the builder, who loved the old house and often revisited it, tells of the discovery of the stencilled walls:

> On one of my trips after I had visited the house and was stopping in the village, the tenant requested me to return to the house. When I did so, I was told that the many thicknesses of wall paper which had covered the hall had fallen off during the night and that I might be interested in looking at the original wall decorations. Of course I was eager to do so, and much to my delight found the rather beautiful stencil decorations exposed, and on one of the leaves in the design, about three feet from the floor immediately to the left of the door, I found where my father had scratched his name with a sharp point, the white surface of the original wall showing through. He must have been a pupil in the early grades of the district school at that time. He was born in 1838, and his name must have been scratched perhaps eight years later.

This wall (fig. 77) stands unrelated and unique in pattern, suggesting that it may have been done by some member of the family whose skill and experience in the art of engraving gave him knowledge of design and a cunning hand. The naturalistic quality of the drawing is so striking that it almost looks as if five different branches of leaves, two small and three large, had been pressed and their outlines traced, but they did not come from the same tree or bush because one of the branches has leaves with cut edges. All of the sprays are green with the exception of two yellow plums with yellow stems, which tip the branches that form the frieze. A band of green diagonals and red discs is cleverly used to take the place of a chair-rail. The wind-swept willows above the baseboard, too faded to be photographed, have a character all their own as they rise from three small hillocks and bend to one side, and there is variety in the alternating leaf patterns separated by bandings of six-petaled stars and wedges inscribed within a circle. In a few years little will be left by which to trace these patterns.

My week at Woodstock brought a number of stencilled walls, some crumbling to pieces on remote hillsides and accessible only by foot, others more easily reached, surrounded by neat gardens and white fences. With the help of two kind persons who shared the interest of my search and who knew the turn of every wooded road for miles about, I was looking one day for a house near Plymouth Five Corners, where, according to rumor, there was a stencilled room. It was hard to picture this section of Plymouth as a once prosperous settlement of many houses, although its past glory at one time even included the digging of gold in sufficient quantities to be minted at "distant" Philadelphia. Only a few scattered buildings remain today. A steep narrow road brought us to the top of Slack Hill and to a comfortable farmhouse. It was a lonely spot, where during the winter a two mile walk to the letter box at the crossroads was the only link of communication with the outside world. Opposite us stood an unpromising little old house, the object of our search. We crossed the road to inspect it, more from a sense of duty than from anything else. The doors had been removed, the roof leaked, discarded tools filled one room, and all were free to pilfer in the wreckage. The door sill and part of the floor had caved in, making access difficult, but we measured the size of the opening, gauged the distance for our step and finally landed one by one knee-deep in the midst of shattered plaster. Before us was the spread eagle (fig. 78), centered above the fireplace. He was maimed and his talons were broken, for the wooden mantel had been pried out, but bits of the scroll still floated above his head in detached ribbons. Whether his claws ever held a sheaf of arrows or an olive branch, the remaining details did not indicate. We counted twenty-three stars between the eagle's outstretched wings, perhaps twenty-four, which would make the date 1820, when Maine was admitted to the Union, or 1821, the admission of Missouri. At the right and left of the eagle was a willow tree and above were single units of oak leaves in red and a flower of new design, characteristic of Vermont, in red and green. The green uprights were of the familiar overturned buds, while the frieze repeated the favorite bells and loops, stencilled on a gray background, the rest of the wall being unpainted plaster. A soft green rose leaf border ran above the baseboard.

The present owner of the property urged the removal of the eagle at once if we wanted to save him, for a government camp had lately come into the section, and the boys were finding the old house an excellent grab bag. We were assured that by cutting through the laths, the overmantel could be removed intact, without injury to the decoration. This Vermont lime plaster was as hard as brick and difficult to cut, but the eagle was rescued and, such as he is, is preserved today in Woodstock.

Some years ago at the post office in Plymouth I picked up a faded photograph showing the broken walls of a small hall where two eagles with outspread wings were stencilled. This picture and many others had been taken at the old Coolidge house three miles up the mountain when, because of Calvin Coolidge's election to the Presidency of the United States, the vacant and dilapidated house suddenly became an object of interest. Not many years later the structure was reduced to complete wreckage. By returning to Plymouth I hoped to find some trace of these eagles, but not a vestige of them could be found on the masses of plaster that filled the foundation and lay scattered over the ground. Comparing the photograph of this eagle with the one in that of the Slack house, one notices that the bodies of the two birds are alike, and that the spread of the wings and the lift of the head are the same, although details in both are lost. At Rochester, north of Woodstock, another eagle with stars above his head was recently discovered. At present the design is hidden under paper but perhaps some day it will give us the complete picture.

Although my hunt for the eagle among the ruins of the Capt. John Coolidge house in Plymouth was in vain, I later gathered information about the house and the artisan who had done the stencilling of its five rooms and two front halls.[25] The builder of the original dwelling, Capt. John Coolidge, was born at Bolton, Massachusetts, about 1756. At the outbreak of the Revolution he served on the Lexington Alarm in Artemus Howe's company and took part in the siege of Boston and the battle at Bunker Hill. The site of his house, on the Military Road which led from Charlestown on the Connecticut River to Crown Point, New York, was chosen at the time he was marching with his company to reinforce the northern army at Fort Ticonderoga in 1778–1779. It was his first sight of Plymouth, then called Saltash, and inspired by the deep wilderness and the reach of the Green Mountains, he declared that when the war was over he would return to this spot, clear the land, and adopt it as home. The first recorded town meeting of Plymouth tells that this spirited pioneer fulfilled his resolve, for his name appears among the list of town officers as selectman in 1789.

His upland farm is reached by a rough mountain road which ascends the steep hill from that part of Plymouth called in the early days "Frog City," a small settlement of houses in the lowland. On my visit to the house we went the first two miles by car, and the last mile on foot. Even then the way was not easy to find, for we climbed to a cellar hole only to discover we had gone too far. Retracing our steps and turning sharply to the left across a brook, we came upon the old Crown Point Trail, built at the time of the French and Indian War but today only a wooded path bordered by a stone wall where purple-fringed orchids were growing undisturbed. Before us was the abandoned dwelling among gnarled apple trees, overgrown grape vines, and worn-out lilac bushes. Part of the north wall was standing with remnants of its stencilled patterns, but, except for the brick chimney, the rest of the structure had fallen. Looking out across miles of unbroken timberland of pine and birch to Saltash Mountain, we must have viewed much the same scene which captivated the young soldier on his march to Crown Point, since pastures and fields of grain had returned to second growth.

The first dwelling of the pioneer was a log cabin, the usual type of shelter built by those who cleared the forest. A frame house, white plastered on the outside as was frequent in Vermont, replaced it some years later. The lime kiln a mile distant on the Military Road may easily have supplied the hard plaster. A third structure, a large clapboard house with eight or more comfortable rooms, was later attached to the plastered

25. I am indebted for these facts to the last member of the family who occupied the house, Mrs. M. B. Wilder, Sharon, Massachusetts.

73

house, which then became the ell. The new building has been attributed to Capt. John Coolidge, but it was built after his death in 1822, by his eldest son, Luther (1792–1856). It was called "the finest house in the county" when its walls were first stencilled in bright colors and the halls patterned with the spread eagle. Four members of the family tell us that it was Erastus Gates who did the stencilling when he was a "very young man," and that he also "painted other walls." Perhaps it was at this time he first met the daughter of Luther Coolidge whom he later married, for the stencilling of five rooms would have afforded ample opportunity for courtship. His stencils were cut out of old leather and must have made excellent tools with a coat or two of paint applied to keep them flat and stiff, recalling the fact that in *The Handmaid of the Arts* Robert Dossie mentions the leather stencils used in making the English flock papers of the eighteenth century.

How early Gates began to paint and stencil and from whom he learned his trade, no tradition tells. Perhaps as a boy he carried the ladder and held the chalked cord for the artisan who stencilled the room on Slack Hill, or he may have merely traced these patterns which appear on the Coolidge walls. We are probably safe in accepting the date of the Slack house as 1821 by the count of stars surrounding the eagle's head, but the stencilling of the Coolidge house was done later, for the new house was not completed much before 1830. Judging from the quality of his craftsmanship, we may be sure that Erastus Gates, though a youth of nineteen in 1830, had already served a period of apprenticeship, and had done other walls. We can only conjecture whether he adjusted the number of stars to correspond to the states in the Union, or whether he remained content with twenty-three, but stars there were, for they are still recalled by one of the family, despite the fact that as a child she was forbidden to use the front stairs "covered with carpet" except on "great occasions." Her memory also records the designs as green and yellow on a warm buff ground. It was a clever and even bold handling of design that spaced the eagle and sunburst at wide intervals on the walls of the hall (fig. 79) to prevent a sense of crowding in the narrow entry with its stairway cramped into three sets of steps, and we recognize at the outset the ability of the young painter.

At the time of my visit only the north wall of the "parlor-bedroom" (fig. 80) stood erect, but the frieze together with glimpses of the flower motif and the geometric figure were still green and vivid red on a gray background, while spots of the original red of the woodwork showed through a later coat of blue. One section of wall lay face down, braced against a rafter, leaving just enough space to crawl beneath it so that we could see a soft yellow background with uprights of turned buds centered with hearts in place of the more common diamonds (fig. 81). The dim impression of an ivy leaf was discernible, as well as the oak leaf and flower spray. Lying on the ground was a section

74

FIG. 78. OVERMANTEL, SLACK HOUSE, PLYMOUTH

This work may be dated about 1820 from the number of stars above the eagle's head. Details in the photograph have been sharpened for clarity.

FIG. 80. PARLOR-BEDROOM, CAPT. JOHN COOLIDGE HOUSE

These walls were the last to remain standing in the ruined building.

*Both photographs by courtesy of George E. Chalmers, Rutland, Vermont*

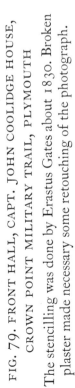

FIG. 79. FRONT HALL, CAPT. JOHN COOLIDGE HOUSE, CROWN POINT MILITARY TRAIL, PLYMOUTH

The stencilling was done by Erastus Gates about 1830. Broken plaster made necessary some retouching of the photograph.

of another wall covered with a hard lime wash, which had loosened in a few places, disclosing a pale green urn on a slender pedestal. The urn held sprays of flowers, now nearly indistinguishable. A narrow upright in one corner revealed green leaves placed at angles against a stem, and was unlike any design I had found before. We tried to dislodge the hard surface in order to see the other wall patterns, but it was impossible to make any impression upon it.

The southwest bedroom (fig. 82) on the second floor had a buff ground on which a single motif is combined with a double row of half discs in green and deep red. The east bedroom (fig. 83) on the second floor was the "guest chamber," and its walls must have been prized, for they had never been papered. New patterns are seen in the border of crescents and crosses above the surbase, in the band over the chair-rail, and in the upright which divides the wall, but the spray is that of the Slack house. Variety and excellent craftsmanship characterize all this work, which may well have been carried into other Plymouth houses.

The character of the painting would put the Alonzo Richmond house at South Barnard, north of Woodstock, at an earlier date, and it evidently was not stencilled by Gates, for the patterns betray a less experienced hand and in no way resemble his precision of manner. Ornamental eave troughs and leaders of heavy blocked tin add functional decoration to the building whose chimney bricks are laid diagonally in decorative patterns. Paper now covers a bedroom described as once having willow trees above the mantel shelf and a frieze composed of garlands and the "lamp of learning," but on the yellow background of the hall we find again the vertical overturned buds, and three variations of the green wreath and four-lobed flower of the Antrim house (fig. 61). Sometimes the leaves of the wreath appear without the stem, at others only the red stem is there, but in every instance a line of small green dots encircles the flower. Above the baseboard is a scroll with a small leaf repeated in the center of the circles. These walls where the painter carelessly placed his motifs often have a charm which the more knowing artisan did not achieve.

Approaching Twenty Mile Stream from the direction of Plymouth and passing through a district called "The Kingdom," now a kingdom of only five houses, one comes to the Belle Spaulding house, built shortly after 1800. Of the original stencilled walls only those of the hall and one small room remain. The room has long been used for storage, and gaps in the paper show rough yellow plaster with its frieze of crossed boughs and pine trees, the pattern of dots and reeded ovals over the baseboard, a flowering plant alternating with a petaled motif, and the uprights of the room at Antrim, New Hampshire. Pale pink and green stencilling has been carried from the low walls onto the slanting ceiling to give the effect of added height. The treads and risers of the stairs and the floor of the upper hall were marbleized in bold circular brush strokes of black, green, and blue on a gray ground. The walls of the hall are rough in texture, but the stencilling of red and yellow is sharp in its outline and particularly effective in the bold frieze with pendent balls, also used in the hall of the Freese house in Deerfield, New Hampshire (fig. 69).

Because of the dense spruce swamps of the lowlands in the region of Woodstock the earliest settlements were made upon the steep hillsides. From South Woodstock a road leads up a mountain to the land cleared by the pioneers of this section. Captain Noah Wood, one of the pioneer landowners, moved in 1807 from a small house into a new one of hand-hewn frame and low-studded first floor, closely resembling the type of home the colonists built in the new country. Moving the household possessions from the old building was distinctly recalled at eighty-five by a son, Otis Wood, who, though a child of two at the time, often related to his granddaughter the adventure of riding on top of the great load. Falling into the fireplace was a less happy recollection. We regret that he left no story of the stencilling, but his granddaughter recalls paying him visits and "loving the pictures on the walls." Broken plaster indicates where the chair-rail has been torn out (fig. 84), but if we could visualize this room in its newness, we should feel less conscious of the close spacing of the circle and leaf patterns and see them more as a single unit in accordance with the obvious intention of the artisan. On the other hand, the crowding over the mantel suggests the artisan's unwillingness to leave any pattern of his kit unused, with the result that a motif of eight hearts and circles, charming in itself, is lost in this all too abundant display. His willow tree, graceful in its sweep, is well cut with swift strokes of the knife, but it is overwhelmed by the central sunburst with its clearly indented half-discs and circles (fig. 85). The small green spray of the Slack house has here grown a new kind of blossom, and the heart now reappears upon a larger flower stem. Against a yellow wall the red and green frieze recalls the same variant of the bell that swung above the eagle in the Slack house. The red maple leaf, the sunburst, and the arcade and candle (used as a base border, not as the accustomed frieze) all have appeared in the John Coolidge house, undoubtedly of later date.

On another almost inaccessible hillside in Windsor County the Cady house at Hartland, near South Woodstock, repeats the same designs, but they were discovered by the merest chance when a hunter, passing the deserted buildings one day, heard the bleating of a sheep, and following the sound to the barn, opened the door to behold a woebegone, solitary lamb standing against a blurred and defaced stencilled wall. The ell of the house had been moved at some time and attached to the end of the barn, but its plaster retained the dim patterns which the hunter was to find still bright in several rooms of the crumbling house.

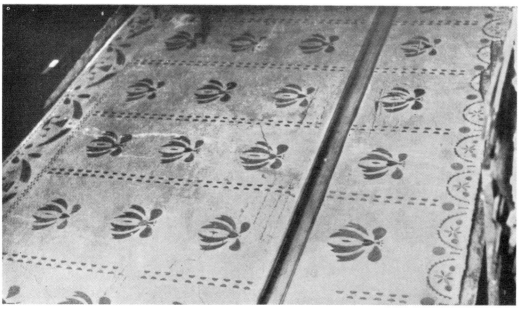

FIG. 82. SOUTHWEST BEDROOM, CAPT. JOHN
COOLIDGE HOUSE

The photograph reproduced is an enlargement of
a family snapshot.

FIG. 81. PARLOR, CAPT. JOHN COOLIDGE HOUSE

In this room the patterns were green on yellow walls. The photograph
has been retouched for details.

*Courtesy of George E. Chalmers, Rutland, Vermont*

FIG. 83. GUEST CHAMBER, CAPT. JOHN COOLIDGE HOUSE
The walls of this room were never papered.

*Courtesy of George E. Chalmers, Rutland, Vermont*

FIG. 84. WALL, WOOD HOUSE,
SOUTH WOODSTOCK

*Owner, Eugene C. Rhodes*

FIG. 85. OVERMANTEL, WOOD HOUSE
These excellent patterns seem dwarfed by the big sunburst in the center.

FIG. 86. HALL, SOUTH WOODSTOCK

The unusual frieze was restored by the owner, Mrs. E. Van L. Rhodes.

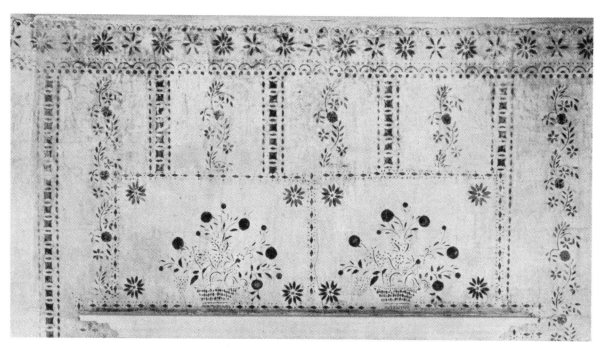

FIG. 87. OVERMANTEL, BROOKFIELD

Alterations in an old Brookfield house uncovered this attractive stencilling.

*Owner, Miss J. G. Fiske*

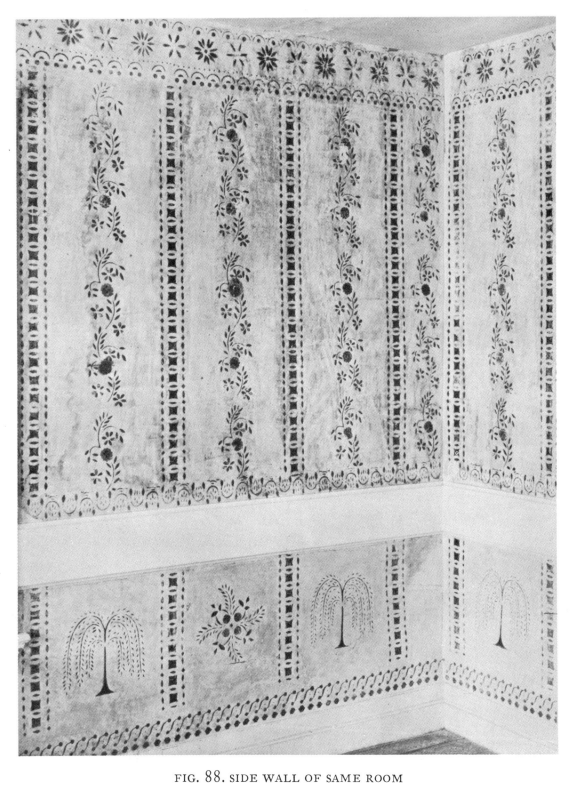

FIG. 88. SIDE WALL OF SAME ROOM

These patterns repeat the grass green and light brick red of the wicker baskets over the mantel.

A brick house with white trim surrounded by a low white picket fence on the principal road at South Woodstock has an example of painstaking reproduction of original stencilling.[26] The only way of restoring decoration which the wear of years and repeated pasting and removal of wall paper had reduced to a mere shadow was to trace and carefully recut the old designs. In the hall (fig. 86) green oak leaves combined with large red discs are seen for the first time as a frieze and have special character in this new treatment. The stripe of buds is centered with hearts, as in the Coolidge house at Plymouth, while the border which outlines the door frames was copied by the owner from the hall at South Reading, preserving an original design which is fast disappearing. Even the casual eye will recognize its decorative value as an addition to the sturdier designs, and the whole is an excellent example of restencilling.

A tradition of "red apples and green leaves," now under paper, in the fine old Joselyn house at Bridgewater Corners, with its two important doorways and its long shed with arched openings, completes this brief record of houses in Windsor County, the result of a search in only one limited section of Vermont.

In adjacent Orange County, on a stencilled wall at Brookfield, where alterations were being made on the ground floor of one of the oldest dwellings in the town, a new group of patterns appears. This property was deeded to Daniel Kingsbury in 1829 and continued in his possession for ten years, when he sold "all the land and buildings" which had been originally "conveyed" to him. Practically no retouching was done on the section of the walls where the photographs (figs. 87 and 88) were taken. Their resemblance to wallpaper is obvious. Although there are touches of a pale brick-red in the flowers of the sprays and in the wicker of the baskets, the green of the frieze, borders, and uprights against a white ground and the predominance of green in the panel motifs give a quality of peculiar freshness to this room. The designs themselves, though varied and detailed, combine so well that there is no feeling of an overlavish hand. Lightness marks the individual patterns, especially the floral spray, which seems almost an upright, the unit is so long and the spacing so close. The motif below the chair-rail and the branches that fill the baskets in their neat frames above the fireplace have equal delicacy. The slender border of curves and dots at the lower edge of the frieze is identical with one that follows a doorway in the Mather house at Marlboro, Vermont, suggesting that the work in the two houses may have been contemporary or even by the same itinerant. The willow tree is present in every section.

We need not dwell on the details of the old Mather house, built at Marlboro in about 1820 by Capt. Dan Mather, since it has already been described with care by Edward B. Allen in his *Early American Wall-Paintings*, but it provides another inter-

26. Restored by the owner, Mrs. E. Van L. Rhodes.

esting example of an artisan who was equipped both to fresco and to stencil. On a rise of ground two miles beyond the village the house stands facing the road, with the mill pond and the barn at one side. The frescos on the ground floor were painted, so tradition relates, in exchange for board and drink by a sailor who came to the door when the house was being built. Those parts done in the morning when the hand was steady show perspective and firm line, but by the end of the day when both head and hand had become uncertain, roofs began to take on new and strange angles. The stencilling done on the upper floor, however, indicates flawless sobriety in color, placement, and execution. The three bedrooms have a common background of pale pink, with designs in a dull, almost transparent, olive, and highlights in red. In one of the front rooms traces of earlier stencilling were faintly visible through the pink ground, probably a trial effort of the painter or perhaps the result of a change of mind on the part of his patron. Over the mantel the outline of the first pattern showed the same baskets of flowers used in the final decoration, but the upright of reeded diamonds in the under pattern was replaced by that of the turned buds. Around the entire room under the wash of pink there were glimpses of a frieze made up of a sunburst and a rectangular pattern, quite different from the present arcades and candles. Another design, peering through the pink on one part of the wall, was a swastika surrounded by a circle of half discs.

In the second lot of patterns of this same room we see for the first time, above each side of the mantel, a horse and rider, which would be a credit to any seafaring man. Over the door is a detailed pattern of dots and semicircles, which we have noted before as part of the frieze in a house at Brookfield. There is a slight divergence in the form and weaving of this artisan's wicker basket, which is filled with branches of cherries in place of flowers. These stencilled rooms have the soft quality of faded pigments, their mellowed tones of dusty pink, deep red, and olive blending without contrast. The same workman was undoubtedly responsible for marbleizing the woodwork of the upper hall and marking the door panels with fantastic brushings, and for placing on a fireboard the Federal eagle holding a bunch of arrows in his claws.

## MAINE

In the kit of Moses Eaton was a pineapple, lacking the leafage of the fruit, and for many months I had searched, hoping to find a completion for the design. From Saco, Maine, the Buxton road leads to the Grant house in North Saco, said to be the oldest dwelling in the neighborhood. The stencilled walls which I had come to see were among the first memories of the owner's grandfather, born in 1822, and are supposed to have

FIG. 89. HALL DETAIL, GRANT HOUSE, NORTH SACO

The pineapple motif, which is in Moses Eaton's kit, appears here for the first time.

*Owner, A. P. Grant*

FIG. 90. WALL SECTION AND OVERMANTEL, THOMPSON HOUSE, ALEWIVE, KENNEBUNK

A section of wall (left) with these vigorous patterns was removed and the overmantel (right) photographed before the house was destroyed.

*Courtesy of the National Society of Colonial Dames of America resident in the State of Maine*

FIG. 91. FRONT HALL, BARRY HOUSE, KENNEBUNK
The stencilling was discovered while a wall was being repaired.

*Owners, Miss Edith C. Barry and Charles W. Barry*

FIG. 92. HALL DETAILS, BARRY HOUSE

The patterns are identical with those in the Governor Pierce ballroom (fig. 52). An interesting
handling of a stencilled border is illustrated in the detail of the stairway.

been done a generation earlier. One fact relating to the preparation of the paint was definitely handed down—that the skimmed milk which had mixed the rich colors had been "soured to an exact turn." As I entered the front door of the old house, now unoccupied, I faced a bit of wallpaper which hung loosely from the wall. Under it were two stencilled motifs, one of them the pineapple (fig. 89) for which I had been looking ever since the Moses Eaton stencils came into my possession. A green top completed the fruit in red against a background of deep warm gray. The obliging owner of the house removed the remaining section of paper which disclosed uprights in a dark mulberry-brown and a frieze of large leaves, also in Eaton's box, but found for the first time on this wall. Two stencils produced the outer edge in brown and a center in red. Oak foliage repeated the green of the pineapple leaves, and a vine of reddish-brown with cut edges was placed above the chair-rail, giving richness to the color harmony.

The two front rooms had also been stencilled, but one had received such hard wear that there was no way of recording its patterns. The other, in excellent preservation, repeated the gray of the hall and the brown in the uprights, while the leaf frieze of the hall reappeared in black and orange. The maple leaf, the orange sunflower with a brown center, the form of the baskets above the mantel, as well as the red birds with black wings and tail feathers, are details new to us, ones which we shall find again in this painter's work. Though all the motifs are in strong color, they are neutralized by the warm tone of the background.

Two sections of original plaster from a house in Alewive, in the town of West Kennebunk, have the same rich coloring, suggesting that these two houses were by the same painter. This structure was built on the West Kennebunk road in 1750 by David Thompson, a son of Richard Thompson who had acquired the land in 1714 as part of a first grant. Before the building went to pieces, two panels[27] were rescued from rooms on the second story by the late William E. Barry, architect and antiquarian, who found it necessary to chisel deep grooves in the walls before sawing them out.[28] The plaster had been made of lime ground from baked clam shells and was as hard as flint. The illustration (fig. 90) shows one piece of plaster with its hand-hewn laths at the side, just as it came out of its first setting. Though the frieze is a variant of the festoon which we have seen in Mansel Alcock's house at Hancock, New Hampshire (fig. 60), the half leaf in the scallop and the heavier tassel make it a more decorative unit, all in bright red with darker tones for the leaves. The photograph of the overmantel, taken at the time the sections were removed (fig. 90, right), shows this artisan's work better than does the

27. Now at the Tate house, Shroudwater, Portland, Maine.

28. For this detail I am indebted to Mr. Edward Brag-

don of Kennebunk, who assisted in removing the panels, and who identified the house.

panel. After seeing countless walls in shades of ochres and of pinks, with patterns super-imposed in green, red, and yellow, these new combinations of two tones of red, deep mulberry, and green on a background of warm gray have distinct character.

In the two halls of the Barry house, Kennebunk, built in 1800, stencilling was found not long ago under wallpaper when a bit of plaster was being repaired. There had been no knowledge of the decoration during the five generations the family had occupied this fine dwelling, whose doorways, mantels, and cornices follow the influence of Robert Adam and are believed by some to be the work of Samuel McIntire. Once vermilion, the wall surface (fig. 91) is today many shades of pink, brilliant and mellow, clear and warm, bearing the same treatment as that of the ballroom in the Governor Pierce house, Hillsborough, New Hampshire. The same design in black on the white ground of the border outlines the doors and the reeded wainscoting of the hall and staircase (fig. 92), for a tracing from the New Hampshire ballroom laid over it shows them to be identical in scale and design. Though faint and marred, the black festoon with the four-petaled red flower is also the same pattern as the New Hampshire frieze. The quarter-fans are defined in black on a deep ochre ground, while in the Pierce house they are against orange-red. The ornamental festoon and panels of the wall surfaces are in excellent accord with the classic forms of the woodwork. The treatment of wall spaces in panels was a form of decoration frequent in the houses of Pompeii, which was the inspiration in the French revival of Roman modes, later adopted also in America.

The chance of finding stencilled rooms or even fragments of them in Maine grows less every year, although originally they were no doubt as common as in any of the New England states. The Frost farmhouse at Eliot repeats in two rooms many of the familiar patterns. The Sadler house at Limerick, built about 1830, has a room where above the dado the walls are patterned with a border and a frieze with very small crimson quarter-fans in the corners on a buff ground. Somewhat thin in form, the festoon of the frieze lacks the good drawing of other familiar designs of this type.

From Brookfield, Vermont, on the north to Washington, Connecticut, on the south, from Kennebunk on the coast of Maine west to Ohio we have found the stencilled wall, marking out the wanderings of itinerant painters. Even in this incomplete record of their activities we can see how well these journeymen used their craft—homespun, perhaps, but intimately associated with the everyday life of its times. Whether we like their work or not, whether we smile at its crudity or envy its daring, it is nevertheless a part of our country's cultural heritage, and one amply justifying recognition in the history of the young nation's decorative arts. Moreover, a return to this type of wall treatment still offers an endless field for both traditional and new achievement. Original motifs and arrangements can be duplicated in the restoration of old houses, while the large planes of

DETAIL OF PARLOR OVERMANTEL, JOSIAH SAGE HOUSE,
SOUTH SANDISFIELD, MASSACHUSETTS

FIG. 19. STENCILLED WALL, GOODALE HOUSE, MARLBOROUGH

The patterns were stencilled in 1778 when Abner Goodale "redded up the homestead for his bride."

*Owned by Dr. and Mrs. Arthur M. Greenwood*

FIG. 32. DETAIL OF BEDROOM PATTERNS, JOSIAH SAGE HOUSE

FIG. 40. DETAIL OF PARLOR, CURTIS HICKOX HOUSE

FIG. 61. STENCILLING ON MATCHED PINE SHEATHING, ANTRIM

*Owner, Miss Louise Q. Pierce*

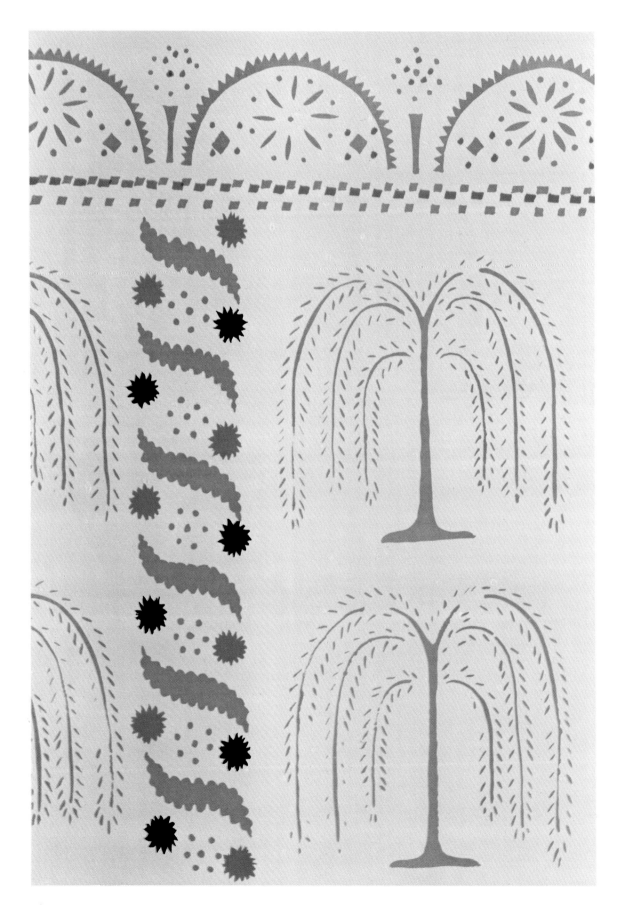

FIG. 74. WALL OF ATTIC STAIRWAY, ELISHA SMITH HOUSE

FIG. 97. HALL FLOOR BORDER DETAIL, "THE LINDENS," DANVERS, MASS. House removed to Washington, D.C., by the present owner, George M. Morris

modern architecture, with their absence of moldings and cornices, present spacious surfaces and fresh possibilities for this simple tool which has served the world through so
many ages in defining clean-cut patterns.

STENCILLED FLOORS

Walls were not the only broad surfaces for the stenciller, for floors also received
their share of his time. In fact, they may have been the first to be stencilled, since even
the least pretentious house could offer level floor boards, if not smooth plastered walls.
Be that as it may, rugs, like wallpaper, cost more in either time or money than the quickly
applied and practical stencilled pattern. The stencilled floor, which appeared after the
Revolution and continued into the forties, was apparently more widely used than is generally supposed, but the tread of countless feet brought constant need for replacement,
and few floors have been retained in their original condition.

It is surprising that an old floor could have remained covered and unknown for
several generations, but such is the history of the stencilling in the Joseph Lynde house
in Melrose, Massachusetts. Even the last descendant of the direct line, who spent ninety-
four years in this same house, had never looked beneath the rag carpets and many layers
of old newspaper under which the ornament had lain forgotten. Dating back to 1730,
the house itself was built by Joseph Lynde close to that of his brother Benjamin, and
stands today on Lynde Street, once the cow path that connected the two dwellings. It was
a large house with mammoth chimneys and many fireplaces, casement windows, and
paneling of walnut and of pine grained in imitation of curly maple. There is no exact
means of telling how soon after the building was completed the stencilling was done, but
the parlor floor was restencilled at least once with the same pattern, which had perhaps
been stored away in a closet for just such renewals. The same black design (fig. 93) first
done on a gray ground shows in places through the later coat of ochre. Evidently the last
worker took a sponge or brush and pressed it lightly at intervals to vary the set line of the
squares, which are about twelve inches in diameter.

In the "northwest chamber" of the second story is a floor (fig. 94) where the
original painting was the same as that of the parlor, but this room too had a second painting, when the worker took a new pattern and did it on ochre in yellow-green with a
few units in medium brown. On the left side of the photograph the close observer may
be able to detect one or more places where the first pattern shows. Another room has on
its raw umber boards large squares made by a black running vine centered with a wreath
of leaves. The bold designs in the house are well chosen for their purpose, and have the
quality of mosaic tiling or of parquetry in colored woods.

One example of floor stencilling has already been mentioned in connection with the work of Lydia Eldredge Williams at Ashfield. In the Red Horse Tavern in South Sudbury, Massachusetts, the floor stencilling in the Lafayette Room and in the small adjoining one (where the tulip border duplicates a wall design in the Williams house) is supposed by some to have been part of the renovation made under the supervision of Colonel Ezekiel Howe, 1746–1796, but other authorities place it early in the nineteenth century.

In another Massachusetts house, built in 1767 by Ebenezer Waters at West Sutton, a large square of original stencilling was kept when the rest of the floor was repainted, and is protected and hidden today by the valance of a large four-poster bed. It is a simple pattern (fig. 95) made of one unit, an eight-petaled flower in black, closely repeated on a deep pumpkin ground. This building has never been remodeled, and practically no changes have been made to mar either its structure or the finish. Elaborate marbleizing remains untouched on the paneling, while on the parlor wall there is a delicate stencilled pattern, unrelated to the designs which we have already recorded, composed of arabesques with a wide banding of small crosses. The paintbrush of a master hand obviously was responsible for this fine house which should be better known.

The patterning of a floor in Marblehead is unusual in its scheme of decoration. The house on Circle Street is an early one, but many alterations have modernized it until the floor has become the chief reminder of earlier days. On a ground of dark green are octagons (fig. 96) in black with gray bars, an effect achieved by first painting the floor green, then laying the octagons, probably with a stencil, and adding the gray details with another stencil. This order left both the centers of the octagons and the squares between the motifs in green, making an interesting combination in pattern and color.

An entirely different type of design is contributed by one of the best known of New England's colonial houses, which no longer stands on its original site in Danvers, Massachusetts, but has been carried, board by board, to Washington, D.C., and rebuilt there in 1936 by the new owner. Few houses of the period have richer historical associations than "The Lindens," built shortly before the Revolution by Robert Hooper, the famous "King" Hooper whom we have already mentioned as a distinguished builder. We are told he was "the wealthiest merchant of Marblehead," with ships sailing to every port in Europe and the West Indies, so it may have been one of his own vessels that brought back from England the oak "frame" which was used for the dwelling. In 1774 it served as the summer headquarters of General Gage, and after the Revolution the property was purchased by Benajah Collins. Today "The Lindens" boasts five painted or stencilled floors, some of which have been uncovered since the building was moved. The border illustrated (fig. 97) shows a vine in two shades of green with red-brown fruit which runs around the second story hall and landing.

FIG. 93. PARLOR FLOOR, JOSEPH LYNDE HOUSE, MELROSE, MASS.
The floor had been stencilled once before with the same pattern.
*Owner, Mrs. A. Lynde Walsh*

FIG. 94. BEDROOM FLOOR, JOSEPH LYNDE HOUSE
Yellow-green and brown are combined on ochre, the color scheme of many stencilled floors.

FIG. 95. BEDROOM FLOOR, EBENEZER WATERS HOUSE, WEST SUTTON, MASS.
Repetition of this single unit makes an effective floor.

*Owner, Dr. John W. Tuttle*

FIG. 96. FLOOR, MARBLEHEAD, MASS.
These more elaborate patterns suggest a floor of inlaid woods.

*Owner, Miss Hannah Atkins*

FIG. 97. HALL FLOOR BORDER DETAIL, "THE LINDENS," DANVERS, MASS.

House removed to Washington, D.C., by the present owner, George M. Morris

(Reproduced in color following page 80)

On these stencilled floors there was a great variety of design, ranging from the simple conventionalized unit to elaborate superimposed patterns, many of which have already been gathered by decorators and antiquarians. As one looks at these decorations, one marvels at the back-breaking task which was performed on hands and knees, yet they pleased the eye, were practical, and took the place of the expensive inlaid floors of wood used in some of. the early "ostentatious" dwellings.[29] Stencilled floors were also cheap substitutes for "rich Persia carpets" and the more ordinary "stout carpeting," or for the "Painted Canvass Floor-Cloths,"[30] of the kind advertised in contemporary newspapers.

## SOURCE OF PATTERNS

After these many illustrations a concluding word about the designs themselves may be worthwhile not only to show something of the influences which molded them but also to stress the individuality of their use. Although the new land was isolated by time and distance from the old, its cultural contacts and inheritance were European, and the settlers in New England brought with them the traditions of the particular section from which they came. It may be that a set of stencil patterns journeyed across the ocean in some worker's bundle, or that the memory of some stencilled wall supplied the first designs, but today few records of European walls are available.

The placement of the stencilled pattern, as we have indicated, was similar to that of the conventional wall coverings, for methodical arrangement of single units was a characteristic of the earliest wallpapers employed in the old world and the new. Both wallpaper and the other wall treatments favored by post-Revolutionary America made use of friezes, borders, and narrow pilasters to break broad surfaces into interesting spaces, and of more elaborate pattern to decorate the overmantel. In addition to following this same arrangement, stencils were also influenced in their design by these treatments. The demands of the stencil as a tool, however, conditioned to some extent the type of ornament which could be used, and, since elaborate or intricate patterns were both ineffective and difficult to execute, the units of decoration had to be simple and direct. Consequently the artisan in his variety of festoon, his vines winding about half-pilasters, or his flowers forming a frieze, simplified the patterns which came to him from wallpaper, low relief plaster, or carved woodwork. This woodwork, inspired by the Adam brothers, displayed reeding and beading on moldings and uprights, delicate wreaths encircling a miniature figure or flower, sunbursts centering broad panels, elaborate urns

29. Such as the north parlor of the Clark-Frankland house in Boston built in 1715. Besides its inlaid floor this room had elaborate oil murals.

30. *The Boston News-Letter* for November 11, 1773, lists these articles among the household furnishings of Charles Hamock to be sold at public auction.

above the fireplaces, and fluted quarter-fans in the corners. But for the stenciller, wreaths were simplified, and he centered them with a four-lobed flower or a large maple leaf. Urns were transformed into flower pots or wicker baskets, which were filled by repeating a single sprig with perhaps a bird perched stiffly on one branch or set firmly beneath. Sunbursts and quarter-fans, which were easily transferred into cut-out patterns, broke the squareness of large spaces just as they had done in the paneled and plastered treatments.

As we study the individual motifs, however, we can be sure that these usual wall treatments were not the only source of design. The heavy carved chests and other carved furniture which had come to pioneer homes may well have suggested patterns for arcaded friezes, base borders, narrow bandings, and single geometric figures. Oak leaf and acorn, pineapple or pinecone, rosette and sunburst were carved on these pieces, and, because of their bold outline, could readily be utilized for stencilled patterns. Although stripes on wallpaper sometimes simulated flower-entwined columns, Chippendale and Heppelwhite bedposts were also frequently reeded and wrapped with leaves. A number of the single wall motifs suggest the gay ornament that was painted on dower chests or fired into contemporary pottery. Conventionalized flowers (roses, tulips, cornflowers, carnations, and many-petaled daisies) occur not only in the peasant ware of Europe but in the English slipware which was imitated by the early settlers. Many familiar designs could be used alone or brightened by a spot of color. Often the individuality of stencilled walls results from the ease with which small motifs could be combined, for a flower head could be attached to almost any spray of foliage, while a heart, a rayed disc, or circle could be placed as an accent of color on a stem or in the center of a geometric pattern. In so doing, a new design was made even of a familiar motif, and each cutting of a stencil gave opportunity for some new variation. A few patterns seem to have been symbolic, used because of the personal sentiment which they represented. There can be little doubt that hearts and bells spoke of some sort of felicity and joy to many who chose them for their rooms, just as we may be sure that the small flames which Lydia Eldredge Williams placed so carefully on her walls had a particular association. The "bent bough and candle" were chosen by Governor Pierce for their holiday connotations. The eagle, whether on wall, furniture, or the prow of a ship was the emblem of liberty, and the bell may also have rung the same message; the stag was a reminder of the hunt, and the pineapple is recorded as denoting hospitality. Perhaps the willow suggested immortality, for it was often chiseled on tombstones in quiet village churchyards.

In origin many of these designs are as old as decorative art itself. The swastika has ornamented Chinese silks, vases from Melos, Croatian and Frisian woodwork, German pottery, and Indian baskets. The sunburst, the wave motif, and the heart have from the time of the Assyrians been inextricably bound up with the symbolism of creation and fertility, and the pineapple, through the pinecone used in the rituals of Ancient Greece with which it became identified, has been associated with the making of wine and later with hospitality. The festoon and wrapped column lead back through England and France to the sculptured pediment and wreathed pillar of classic Rome, which in their turn were but stone replicas of the garlands of spring or of harvest festivals hung on the temple façades in early Greece. The western world turned to the excavations of Pompeii and Herculaneum and wrought into its ornament something of what it found there. Vines and birds were frequent in late Roman and early Christian church decoration, but Chinese ornamental papers also brought into Europe delicate flowers, birds, and bending trees. Urns surmounted elaborate pillars in the villas of the Caesars, and came as well to France through Moorish Spain.

But varied as is the cultural history of the motifs, we may be sure that the knowledge of the craftsman who used any of these patterns in New England homes reached no further than their utility and adaptability to his purpose and his tools. The artistic success of his handiwork speaks well for his sense of good pattern and for the suitability of the ornament for its ends. Although distant lands left the impress of their past on his craft, we must not forget that the palm tree, the serrated leaf, the carnation, born perhaps in Persia, had their pictorial counterparts in his own yard. His tree may very naturally resemble more closely the balance of the fir, or his indented leaf that of the maple or elm which shaded his dwelling. The rose and tulip, the cornflower and pink bloomed in his own garden, and willows leaned over his brook. Whatever their decorative ancestry, these motifs were very real to him, and he carried them into a house as he would a handful of flowers. The tree that Henry Goodrich cut out of strong paper to be stencilled on some wall in Deerfield, New Hampshire, was identical with a pattern on a vase found at Knossos, Crete, from the nineteenth century B.C., a fact he overlooked. Nor did the itinerant suspect that the swastika which he tried out on the attic wall of the Sage house in South Sandisfield, Massachusetts, had been applied to a piece of pottery at Melos, and to a fragment of silk in Chinese Turkestan.

# PART TWO: STENCILLED FURNITURE

My interest in stencilled furniture began with six chairs bought in Litchfield, Connecticut. The gold fruit and leaves on the broad cross slats were badly worn, but to me it seemed an easy task to reproduce them. Gilt paint was, however, quickly discarded, for the brush utterly failed to model the rounded forms of the fruit. After many efforts I decided that the problem could be solved only by finding some old chair stenciller who still practiced the early methods. The chance discovery in Lee, Massachusetts, of a set of original stencils preserved between the leaves of an old ledger further quickened my interest. Finally, in Portland, Maine, one day I passed a window filled with stencilled chairs fresh from the hand for which I was searching, for here was the early method of gold stencilling complete in every detail. No gilt paint marred the surface, and no wash of umber darkened the sheen of the gold. George Lord, one of the last of the old chair painters, had done the work, and so began a friendship with a craftsman of eighty-seven, who from his fifteenth year had been painting chair decorations that had changed but little, for he was still using patterns which he had stencilled seventy years before.

During subsequent visits to Portland I learned the facts relating to his work from the start of his apprenticeship in 1848, when as a boy he brushed the priming coat of red on the raw wood, through the years when as foreman he was in charge of the "finishing room." While we sat in his workshop in the basement of his house, with his paints and brushes about him and his stencils carefully laid between the pages of huge portfolios, he taught me the methods of his craft, and gold stencilling was demonstrated as a simple process. On the cross bar of a chair back, for example, he spread with a large brush a thin coat of size compounded of varnish and turpentine which acted as a binder for holding the powders. In an hour or two, when the adhesive had nearly dried, he took his thin paper stencils, laid them flat on the panel, and through the openings brushed the bronzes with small velvet pads, modeling the fruits with a dexterous hand. As he worked, he relived old days and retold, literally by the hour, incident and routine pertaining to the shop. His recollections tell us that the cost of pure gold powder at sixteen dollars an ounce limited its use to only the best furniture. He applied it to pianos on rare occasions in stencilling the maker's name in "German script" and for small additional ornamentation. Worn velvet, preferably cotton, the shorter the nap the better, made the best "pounce" for spreading the metallic powders. When painted flowers were required to be centered in the stencilled scrolls on chair rails, six colors "set up" the palette and "loaded" the small square-edged brush (he called it a "swan quill") in such a manner

---

1. Pounces of velvet or chamois were of various sizes, stuffed with bits of waste or cotton. To quote Rufus Porter: "The bronze is applied by means of a little ball or roll of buff-leather termed a puff." *Scientific American*, vol. I, no. 26, 1845.

that a single stroke colored and shaded the petal of a rose. There was nothing that the old man did not want to teach me out of the store of his experience, and, as he talked, the colleagues of his early days crowded into his thoughts. There was Francis Holland, his "boss," and the three Eaton brothers of Boston, all noted for their fine work. William Eaton originated many of his own designs, and no pattern was too intricate for his knife. On one occasion young Lord, recognizing his ability, had asked for one of his stencils but had been refused with the excuse that Eaton's employers would object. Although William, "the best stenciller in New England," had gone to New Hampshire many years before, the admiration of the Portland craftsman was still alive for the skill of the older man, and he told how he had copied many of the Eaton chairs which he had seen in the shops.

A few years later, on my way to Portland, I was in Cambridge, Massachusetts, in the workshop of an artisan whose talents, acquired as a carriage painter, were now transferred to chairs and furniture. In an out-of-the-way corner of his big loft I caught sight of several volumes on a bench, between whose covers appeared the edges of some old stencils, which had long lain undisturbed, covered with dust. They had been brought to a Boston dealer by a "gatherer" of old furniture, who had "picked them up" somewhere in New Hampshire, and the chair painter had bought them solely to prevent their falling into the hands of a possible competitor, for he had no use for them himself. Three of the volumes were homemade, and the others were binders of old ledgers fitted with sheets of heavy paper. Needless to say I bought the six folios, and the next few hours revealed that I had in my possession the stencils of William Eaton, for his name or initials were cut on many of the patterns. The next day I carried them to George Lord, who had waited so long to see them. During a whole afternoon he pored over the contents of the books, which included literally hundreds of stencils, comprising flowers, leaves, veins, borders, and intricate cuttings of elaborate designs for chair backs. Some of the patterns were familiar to him, while others were not, and he made impressions of those he wanted, but whether the one which he had especially coveted was among them he forgot to say.

And so, equipped with a knowledge of the technique of the craft,[2] with this store of reminiscence from the memories of the old artisan, and with William Eaton's stencils folded away in time-worn volumes, I began gathering the material that has gone into these pages. They do not give the history of stencilled furniture with completeness, but they do illustrate some aspects of the various uses to which this method of decoration was adapted, something of the influences that formed it, and the changes which it under-

2. In defining methods of work in these pages I have given those practiced by artisans long experienced in the handling of metallic powders. Besides George Lord, I would acknowledge the experience of William Fitzemeyer, japanner, who formerly worked at India Square, Boston. He served his apprenticeship in Germany and came to this country in '46. The hand processes of applying gold leaf and bronze powder are those used by William Henry Ingalls, a chair painter of Windsor, Vermont, who succeeded his father.

went during the sweep of its long vogue. Perhaps they may serve to interpret if not to explain and justify its popularity.

To understand the development of the technique of stencilling with bronze powders as we find it in America during the opening decades of the nineteenth century, we must follow the efforts of artisans in the old world to satisfy Europe's earlier taste for the polished surfaces and gold decoration of Oriental lacquer. Although the influence of Chinese art on the countries of Western Europe reaches far back into time, it was not until after the discovery of the eastern sea routes with the subsequent establishment of a flourishing trade by the English and Dutch East India Companies that lacquer became a dominant fashion. For a while the demand was so great that special factories were set up near the trading posts for the convenience of western merchants, but it was not long before craftsmen on the Continent began to imitate this desired luxury. The archives of Amsterdam contain many seventeenth and eighteenth century references to celebrated "lack-werkers," and Chinese craftsmen, we are told, were even imported to teach the mysteries of their art. Nor was England backward in contributions, for as early as 1683 "English varnished cabinets might vie with the Oriental," and by 1697 a company of "The Patentees for Lacquering after the manner of Japan," had for sale "cabinets, secretaries, tables, stands, looking-glasses, tea-tables and chimney-pieces."[3]

Imitation lacquer was also practiced as a fashionable pastime by young and old, as the preface of the *Treatise of Japanning and Varnishing*, by Stalker and Parker, published at Oxford in 1688, attests. But more important than its warnings to these "gifted amateurs" against the "impotent fellows who pretend to teach young ladies an art in which they themselves have need to be instructed and to the disgrace of the title of Japanners, Painters and Guilders," are the formulas for making varnishes and the directions for applying metallic powders, which show the ancestry of one phase of the technique of later stencilling. Beginners may do their patterns with gold mixed with gum-water, the simplest way, but gold dust applied on a gold size is recommended as a better method.[4] I might add by way of comment that no gold paint was used by the experienced

3. Quoted by Dr. Joan Evans in *Pattern*, vol. II, p. 66.
4. Size, the binder for holding the bronze powder, was the essential element in decorating with metallic powders.

One formula an American craftsman used for his gold stencilling on wood was three or four parts of varnish to one of turpentine. To determine when the size was ready for the

japanner, for he was aware that the mixing of the powder with turpentine or other medium before it is applied robs it of its luster and gives a very different effect from that produced by spreading dry bronze directly on a sized surface.

An interesting sidelight on the popularity of japanning as a social accomplishment comes from a letter of Sir Edmund Verney written in 1689 to his daughter in school at "Great Chelsey":

> I find you have a desire to learn to Jappan, as you call it, and I approve of it; and so I shall of anything that is good and virtuous, therefore learn in God's name all Good Things, and I will willingly be at the charge so farr as I am able—though they come from Japan and from never so farr and Looke of an Indian Hue and colour, for I admire all accomplishments that will render you considerable and Lovely in the sight of God and Man.[5]

Much of the European lacquer done by amateurs and experts alike during this period was on wood, the material most common in the East, and vast quantities of elaborate furniture and small objects of all kinds were included. A variant of the same fashion was a similar surfacing of metal, which in England is first associated with the japannery of Pontypool, South Wales, where it developed following the discovery about 1660 of a heat-resisting, hard-drying varnish derived from coal. When applied under heat, this varnish produced a surface quality akin to japanned lacquer, and won for this Monmouthshire ware, generally made of thin rolled iron plate, the name of Pontypool or Usk "japan."[6] During the mid-eighteenth century, when this craft was at its height, many factories produced tea trays, cheese cradles, bread trays, urns, and innumerable small articles patterned with Chinese landscapes, figures and other designs in gold against backgrounds of "polished black," "beauteous tortoise shell," or color. From Pontypool the industry spread to Billston, from there to Wolverhampton in 1720, and later to Birmingham and London, while the works at Usk were opened in 1761 as a direct offshoot of Pontypool.

In 1772 new impetus was given to the trade when Henry Clay, a japanner of Birmingham, patented a process of pasting together sheets of thick tough paper which could be polished and either cut or molded into many shapes. On this "paper ware," later known by the French term "papier-mâché," the method of decoration was identical

---

powders or leaf required practice. Sheraton recognized the difficulty, for he wrote, "Those who are inexperienced in the art generally fall into the error of beginning to work before it is sufficiently dry." And he further suggested that the condition could be judged by "the touch of the finger which, if it slightly adhere to and bring away not the slightest degree of the size, it is in a proper condition for gilding." (*Cabinet Dictionary*, 1803, p. 224.) Another

writer, a contemporary of Lambert Hitchcock, chose the more direct term "clammy" as defining the correct state of the size. (Stokes, *Complete Cabinet Maker, and Upholsterer's Guide*, 1829.) "Tacky" is the modern word.

5. Verney: *Memoirs*, vol. II, p. 312.

6. Williams, I. J.: *Guide to the Collections of Pontypool and Usk Japan*, National Museum of Wales, Cardiff, 1926.

FIG. 98. ENGLISH JAPANNED METAL TRAY AND DETAIL

Made about 1820, the border is stencilled in gold by overlapping a single unit.

*Owned by the author*

FIG. 99. ENGLISH PAPIER-MÂCHÉ TRAY AND DETAILS
The border and band of shells are stencilled.

*Owned by the author*

with that of metal and could be done in the same works and by the same craftsmen. The handling of bronze powders on a sized surface was practiced by these japanners as a serious art, and different processes as well as ingenious gadgets were called into play throughout its development by the desire for new effects. Just when the stencil became a tool for applying metallic powder, no record tells, but this quick method of producing a design would very naturally have made an appeal to the industrialist of the later eighteenth century, when short cuts for all long processes were being sought, especially if they entailed no marked inferiority in the quality of decoration. Moreover, the stencil had in its favor the fact that it was able to produce certain types of design as no other method could.

Quite apart from their value in showing an English treatment on both tin and papier-mâché, the two tea trays (figs. 98 and 99) are excellent examples by which to illustrate two characteristic uses of the stencil. The leaf border on the rim of the first tray was stencilled by the direct and simple device of overlapping a single unit, while the broad band of flowers was done freehand as was common. On the papier-mâché tray (fig. 99) both the shells and the border are by stencil, with the exception of the highlights and small markings in metallic powders, which are spotted or lined upon the motifs before the size has dried with small "bobs"[7] or with atoms of leather drawn through the hollow of a quill to form a minute pad at the end. "Fine, hard lines and delicate shading," we are told, "could be done by a skillful workman with these odd appliances."[8] In this manner the veins of the stencilled leaves and the petals of the stencilled flowers on the border were emphasized, while the shells were mottled and lined by the same microscopic pads. This treatment accounts for the variations in detail, which to the uninitiated give the appearance of freehand brush work, pure and simple.

I have seen a similar handling of shells on a bread tray at the National Museum of Wales at Cardiff, which, together with a large tea tray, also stencilled, was attributed to the works at Usk. In a private collection at Leamington,[9] I examined a geometric design of admirable workmanship, where silver predominated in effective contrast to the dark background. In another collection a tray, probably originating at Wolverhampton, had small stencilled flower units combined with elaborate hand decoration. While the ornament of European japan was primarily applied by various freehand techniques, it is evident that some very good pieces were being done wholly or in part by the stencil. Perhaps at this point it may be helpful to interpose a distinction in definition. Although stencilling is a hand process, it introduces a mechanical method of repeating form and of giving a sharpness to outline which differs from the application of pattern through less

7. "Bob" is the workshop name of the japanner for these tools made of wool or cotton waste wrapped around a small stick handle.

8. Dickinson, G.: *English Papier-Mâché*, 1925, p. 34.
9. Owned by Mr. George Dickinson.

precise ways, and it consequently is distinguished from them in these pages. Just what could be accomplished in its own right by the stencil will, I hope, be apparent to the reader from the illustrations that are to follow.

Although the technique of stencilling with bronze powder came to America a craft perfected by the japanners of the Old World during that period when Europe had been fascinated by the metallic ornament of eastern lacquered surfaces, it was used on our shores not to vie with the wares of the Orient but to imitate the metal ormolu of the French Directory and Empire. Gold stencilling might have had little use in the cabinet making of our country had not the first quarter of the nineteenth century called for lavish gold ornament on the broad surfaces of furniture. America, short of metal workers and hard pushed to find a substitute, saw in the stencil one means of meeting this demand and in so doing developed a type of decoration essentially her own.

France and England, inspired as we have seen by the discoveries in Herculaneum and by the excavations at Pompeii in 1785, adopted not only the classical dominance of metal but also many classic motifs of design. The highly skilled workmen of France wrought out elaborate bronze bosses, clusters of fruit, bandings with many variations of the anthemion and the acanthus as mounts for mahogany and rosewood furniture. In England the metal ornament of the Regency took the form of brass inserted in veneers. To use the words of Sheraton:

> Small lines of brass are now much in use in the English furniture and looke
> very handsome in black rose and other dark wood grounds. The lines are
> made of thin brass, which is cut by gages, made by cabinet-makers for that
> purpose.[10]

Workers from across the Channel were imported to cast the more elaborate fittings, but even then they were characterized by a greater simplicity than the French.

As for America, her version was typical of a new country with comparatively limited technical resources. In the main, simplicity of structure marked the work of her cabinet makers, and, although carving was frequent, often ornate and sometimes even gilded to suggest metal, metal mounts were generally limited to what might be imported. Gold ornament in classic designs was readily supplied on the panels, columns and pedestals of her furniture by gold leaf or applied by hand with gold size overlaid with metallic powders, a process often termed "bronzing." The same designs could also be stencilled with these powders, so that we find acanthus leaves and Greek honeysuckle produced by the stencil on the capitals or bases of columns, or repeated in bandings to define or replace moldings; while fruit, flowers, and leaves were grouped in urns and baskets or massed together in conformity with the space they decorated. These three processes of gold

10. *The Cabinet Dictionary*, 1803, p. 95.

92

decoration were often combined on the same piece, giving variation of sheen and brilliancy.

FINE FURNITURE

Oddly enough stencilled decoration on mahogany and other precious woods has received little comment, while that on the "Hitchcock chair" has been the subject of frequent discussion.[11] On examples of fine American cabinet work of this period, however, stencilling appears with a finesse of workmanship and a care for detail rarely found on the furniture of ordinary woods or on the many other objects to which it was also applied, and the stencil gains a certain importance from this use.

It is difficult to localize the many chairs, tables, consoles, wardrobes, and even pianos on which the stencil was used, but the data that I have been able to gather and the pieces which I have been able to trace point to New York as the center for the best technical handling of this decoration. It was natural for this port city to have a more abundant supply of the highly-prized mahogany from Barbados and the West Indies and to attract experienced artisans. Although early New York directories list a large number of cabinet makers and gilders, whose collaboration was essential to the finished work, we look in vain for the term "stenciller" in advertisements of the time, for those who practiced the craft were known as gilders, painters, japanners, and "fancy chair" makers—all workers to whom a variety of decorative methods were taught in the course of their apprenticeship.

A piece undoubtedly from New York and showing the simplicity of line characteristic of the best "American Empire" furniture is the graceful mahogany couch (fig. 100). In its slender proportions it follows in style some of the finest examples made in England during the first decade of the century. Throughout the entire Empire period

11. An article by Mrs. Guion Thompson appeared in *Antiques*, Aug., 1923, followed by several interesting contributions in later issues by Esther Stevens Frazer (June, Sept., 1924, Jan., 1925, and Aug., 1936). These articles contain some additional bibliography. Many books on the furniture of the period at least give a brief mention of the stencilling on the Hitchcock chair as a type. References to the work on fine furniture are very few. L. V. Lockwood, for example, shows in his two volumes of *Colonial Furniture in America* (1913) a chest of drawers (c. 1820) with a mirror attached, and apart from a brief description of the piece merely comments, "About this time it became fashionable to stencil furniture" (vol. I, p. 144).

the couch or sofa was very much an item of fashion and symbol of luxury. The American of taste must have felt very like his English cousin in appreciation of it:

> In every clime riches and luxury produce habits of indolence and indulgence and these, being fostered by the excessive heat of the Eastern climate, have obtained for us that elegant and luxurious piece of furniture called a sofa which was doubtless invented by the natives of the East, on account of its allowing a reclined position, which of all others affords the most relief to the body, when overcome by lassitude or fatigue. For this reason as well as for its elegant form, the sofa has been adopted among all civilized nations, so that from the palace to the cottage *ornée*, it is now required in every room, and may therefore rank among the leading articles of our modern furniture.[12]

On this couch the stencilled and hand ornament shows classical inspiration and identifies at once the source of the design. We notice how well the stencil has molded the formal treatment of the acanthus on the rounded top of the scrolled end. The overturned tip and base of the leaf emphasize its contour and show a characteristic stencil technique. These overturned leaves usually have the under side done with an even spreading of powder that gives them a contrasting solid quality. The veins have not been made by a bob but by a curved piece of paper along which the velvet pounce has drawn the powder. The rosette on the back, but not the ornament on the seat rail and legs, has also been stencilled. It is often hard to distinguish between stencilling and precisely executed hand work, for to insure accurate rendering of symmetrical motifs to be bronzed by hand the outlines were generally transferred to the wood through a pricked pattern by a pounce filled with whiting. The design was then painted in gold size with a touch of ochre added to make the mixture "more visible," and when it was nearly dry gold powder was brushed over the pattern. In the old kits there are many of these perforated papers.

We regret there is no mark to identify the maker of this graceful piece, but its first owner, James McBride, who was born in Armagh, Ireland, became a well-known importer of Irish linens in New York, where for many years he lived in College Place. He is recorded as a "patriotic citizen" in *The Old Merchants of New York City*,[13] for, when Congress in 1813 failed in an attempt to raise a fund of sixteen million dollars, James McBride subscribed $10,000, together with a group of New York merchants who responded to the needy Government and tided over the deflated treasury after the War of 1812.

The two pianos illustrated show a much more elaborate and varied handling of the stencil. Although the first American pianoforte was made in Philadelphia in 1774,

---

12. Ackermann, Rudolph: *The Repository of Arts, Literature and Commerce*, etc., ser. 3, vol. XI, p. 367.

13. Barrett, Walter: *op. cit.*, 1864, p. 330.

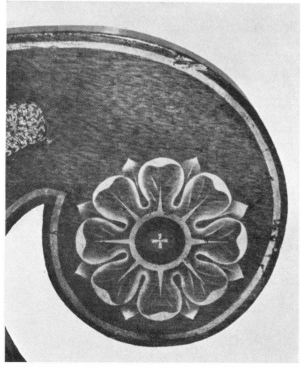

FIG. 100. MAHOGANY COUCH AND DETAILS

Dating from about 1810, the rosette on the back and the acanthus leaf on the scrolled end are stencilled.

*Owner, Mrs. John A. Vanderpoel*

FIG. 101. ROSEWOOD PIANO AND DETAIL

Made by A. & W. Geib of New York between 1822 and 1827, the gold decoration of leaves and flowers above the keyboard is stencilled. Compare the execution of the flowers with those on the rim of the tray in fig. 99.

*Valentine Museum, Richmond, Virginia*

New York became the important manufacturing center in the opening years of the next century. Trained workers from Europe saw in the new republic a growing market for their special skill. Among those who carried on the tradition of their English ancestors were the Geibs, who added their own distinction to the family reputation. John, George, Adam, and William Geib are names outstanding in the history of musical instruments in New York of the early eighteen hundreds. John Geib & Son, organ-builders, and Adam Geib, music teacher, were established by 1802, when they appear in the city directory. Later John, Jr., carried on under his own name, and in 1817 he obtained the second patent granted to a resident of New York covering "improvements in the shape and structure of the upright pianoforte." At this time Adam combined with the firm, bringing the prestige of his teaching, and undoubtedly adding to the clientèle by giving lessons at the same address. In 1819 William, a nephew, entered the concern, then located at 23 Maiden Lane, and in 1822 John evidently dropped out, for the name appears as A. & W. Geib, Piano & Musick Store. In 1827–1828 A. & W. Geib occurred for the last time, for in the following year Adam's name appeared alone; but in 1829–1830 he took a new partner, and it was Geib & Walker who carried on the business at the Maiden Lane address, and in this year one of their upright grand pianos took a gold medal at the first exhibition of The Mechanic's Institute.

This prize is testimony to the excellent craftsmanship which marks the instrument whose delicate stencilling is shown in the illustration (fig. 101). The history of the various changes in name enables us to date the work between 1822 and 1827 and also helps to decipher the faded name plate that was misread H. & W. Geib when the Valentine Museum acquired the piano in 1902 from Prestwould, the seat of the Skipwith family in Mecklenburg County, Virginia. This beautiful instrument of rosewood with its ivory and ebony keys and its sapphire velvet behind the gold-dotted lattice work must have given much pleasure to Lelia, wife of Humberston Skipwith, to whom it once belonged.

We have no special facts about the making of this particular piano, but we know that it took John Chickering more than a year to construct his first piano in 1825, for such "instruments were works of art, the completion of which was of sufficient importance to receive extended public mention."[14] Interest in music as a social accomplishment very naturally included the instruments themselves, for as an English contemporary wrote in 1826:

> The knowledge of music is now so generally diffused that musical instruments are almost an essential part of furniture, and among them we can reckon none more frequently used than the piano . . . totally unknown to our ancestors and only invented within the last half century.[15]

14. *Chickering Exhibition*, 1902, p. 1.   15. Ackermann's *Repository*, ser. 3, vol. VIII, p. 58.

The case itself confirms the dating in the type of carving and the shape of the legs, and in the bands of ornamental metal, as well as in the medallions which cover the screws fastening the legs to the body. These imitate the metal bosses marking the structural joining of the Roman bronze furniture, a feature which was carried over into the classical revival of both the French Empire and the English Regency. For us the use of gold stencilling with this metal work has special interest. In England gilding alone was used on some of the earliest piano cases, but metal was much more common. Very evidently the American craftsman did not consider the stencil an inferior decorative technique or he would not have employed the combination. The perfection of execution of the flowers and leaves shows an expertness not attained in a day and one which was not the result of casual standards.

The relation of this work to the English japanning is apparent in a comparison of the flowers with those on the English papier-mâché tray (fig. 99). The grouping has been done in much the same way, and the highlights of the petals applied in like manner. The separate touches of bronze powder are, perhaps, more obvious on the decoration above the keyboard, which is the first illustration of the bunching of flowers so typical of the stencilling of this period. Six single units made up this particular pattern, two flowers and a center for them, and three different leaves. Each flower, center, and leaf was applied separately, the ones in the foreground being stencilled before those in the background, and the veins and highlights applied as the last touches.

A very much more lavish piece of stencilling was done on the dark mahogany piano (fig. 102) from the workshop of John Tallman of Barclay Street, now in the Metropolitan Museum of New York. Giving the date as about 1825, the catalogue merely notes that the case is "profuse in gilt decoration of conventionalized designs of fruit and flowers," with no comment as to the technique. Such omissions are so frequent that they account in large measure for the lack of general knowledge of what was accomplished by able craftsmen who employed the stencil. Few associate the careful modeling, the plastic quality, the precision of veining and accented highlights, or the flexibility of arrangement with a set of cut-out patterns; nor are they prepared by the term "stencil" for the texture of fruit and leaf, or the warm transparency of thin metallic powders over the rich wood tones of the background. This quality has a peculiar beauty and did much to make stencilling so acceptable an ornament for costly furniture. As in this piano, its use with gold leaf and bronzing makes us aware that the stencil was chosen for its own contribution, and indicates that the combination of leaf gold and powder was deliberately sought by the artisan to give a contrast of tone. This contrast is brought out clearly by the urn laid on in leaf, shaded by delicate etching, and the heaped-up stencilled fruit, which takes its texture from the ground of closely-grained wood (fig. 103). The hand work or bronzing of the honeysuckle and horns of plenty above the keyboard together with

96

FIG. 102. MAHOGANY PIANO AND DETAIL

Made by John Tallman of New York in 1825, the case was elaborately stencilled. The detail from the right of the keyboard contrasts the plastic quality of the stencilled fruit and flowers with the etched gold leaf of the urn.

*Metropolitan Museum*

FIG. 103. THREE MORE DETAILS OF MAHOGANY PIANO

The lower left detail is an enlargement of the upper one and shows expert workmanship in the massed fruit and flowers from the ends of the instrument. The large flowers are made by overlapping the petal unit a variable number of times. The curved molding from the lid (lower right) is made up of a simple leaf repeated on an ebonized ground.

FIG. 104. MAHOGANY WARDROBE AND DETAILS

A New York piece of about 1825, this is a fine example of stencilling. Note especially the acanthus applied on the capital of the column.

*Museum of the City of New York*

FIG. 105. MAHOGANY CARD TABLE AND DETAIL

The stencilled bandings around the lower edges of the top and base are used as contrast to the other decoration in gold leaf on this table by George W. Miller of New York.

*Lent to the Museum of the City of New York by J. A. Lloyd Hyde*

the narrow metal bands carry out the classical spirit of the decoration. The curved molding which edges the lid of the case has a narrow stencilled border made of small pointed leaves which alternate with a bell-shaped flower, five units making the repeat. Metal was perhaps impractical on this curve, and in any case the stencil is an effective substitute. The background of the molding has been ebonized in order to give added sharpness to the design and to emphasize the finely serrated edges of the leaves.

The piano is also interesting for the ingenious placing of the stencilled pattern on the hinged drop which covers the keys when the instrument is closed, completing a balanced arrangement of massed fruit and filled urns. This placement brings together the two contemporary interpretations of the classical motifs of the abundant harvest, fruit and flowers either clustered in garlands or heaped in urns. The care with which this fine stencilling was done is shown in the details from the ends of the instrument (fig. 103). The petals of the flower were cleverly applied by overlapping a single small unit many times around a center, while the stamens were accomplished by some small pledget, probably made by wrapping a fragment of chamois about a pointed tool. Since the craftsman evidently did not want the fixed structural outline of the fruit to be too marked, he composed the pomegranates with two stencils, pouncing on his first flat pattern in thin copper with his second over it in pale gold. We must remember that various shades of gold, bronze, and copper were usually combined in the designs, just as they had been in the lacquer and japanning of the old world.

Wardrobes and clothes presses gained great popularity in the Empire period, but few of them had the well-considered proportions that distinguish the one shown in the illustration (fig. 104). Gothic influence evident in the panels is an indication of how the American cabinet maker united the different stylistic elements into something definitely his own. The piece has particular interest for us because all the ornament except the small anthemion motifs and the arrows on the pediment has been done with the stencil. The fruit and flowers retain to an unusual degree the sharpness of outline which is the province of the stencil. Every flower is clean-cut and firm; there is no overlapping of leaf edge or veining, no interference of contour, and there is excellent modulation of values in working out the perspective. The rose petals have been placed individually by fifteen applications. The outline of the apple was undoubtedly produced by a threadlike line cut as a separate stencil, a treatment so infrequent that among my original stencils only two patterns, an apple and a pear, illustrate this handling. But if this worker showed his mastery of detail in the grouping applied to both pediment and pillars, he showed even more ingenuity in fitting his stencil about the moldings of the capital of the columns. It was not easy to apply metallic powders through a thin paper pattern held close and secure on a rounded surface, and obviously the design was done in carefully planned sections. More care than usual had to be exercised in lifting only the smallest bit of the dry bronze powder on the pad so that it would not drive under the edge of the stencil or fall upon the sized surface, for to remove it meant water and fine pumice and still more patience. The band of stencilling along the base of the wardrobe is almost obliterated, but it was a single leaf unit placed at different angles.

The mahogany card table (fig. 105) shows the two border treatments most commonly found on fine furniture, and combines the two main influences on this type of design, both classic in inspiration. The narrow banding of the honeysuckle motif along the bottom of the table top has been stencilled with powder, solid and unshaded, on a blackened background in imitation of metal appliqué, and has been pointed out earlier on the molding of the piano by Tallman. The repeat on the lower base of the plinth has a single acanthus leaf alternating with another leaf of simpler structure and shows a feeling for the conventionalized form of the sculptured or carved moldings derived from Greece and Rome, with shading employed to simulate raised relief. The elaborate design on the standard is gold leaf shaded with the etching tool, which well illustrates the difference in effect between hand gilding and stencilling. The table has been marked with the name of its maker, George W. Miller of New York,[16] and I regret that I have been unable to find any record of other pieces made by this admirable craftsman who had a sure sense of line and of harmonious ornament.

It was perhaps the implications of some such dictum as that from the pen of the often quoted Ackermann that led an expert cabinet worker to make as companion pieces the secretary and console shown, for the "elegant" and the "beautiful" have been brought together both in the style of the pieces and the selection of ornament. "It is not sufficient [wrote Ackermann in 1813] that the ornaments and the colours of the furniture should correspond, but a harmony of this principle [taste] must pervade the whole; without which our endeavours to obtain the requisites of the agreeable, the elegant, or the beautiful in furniture will be defeated." The pleated sunburst of yellow silk centered with a gilt rosette, a treatment found also on some of the earliest upright pianofortes, is very "agreeable" in its rich color.

On the secretary (fig. 106) the narrow filigree border below the drawers and on the bottom molding and the upright bands edging the broad glass panel are by hand; their structure is obviously one that could not be achieved by the stencil, since there is no provision for the ties that must hold the unit together. These ties and the mitered corners clearly indicate the use of the stencil on the border outlining the doors (fig. 107). In the second detail the ties are less apparent, for the shells seem to have been done with two stencils, one slightly overlapping the other. Although this craftsman ornamented the columns with clusters of fruit and flowers, he did not find it necessary to stencil the

16. In 1822 his shop was located at 63 Division Street, and in 1828–1829 we find him at 64 Broad Street.

FIG. 106. MAHOGANY SECRETARY

The stencil provides much of the gold ornament on this handsome piece of about 1820.

*Owner, Francis H. Markoe*

FIG. 107. BORDER DETAILS OF THE SECRETARY

These two simple stencilled borders are effectively used to define the lines of the secretary.

FIG. 108. MAHOGANY CONSOLE TABLE AND DETAIL

Made as a companion piece to the secretary, this table has slight variations in its stencilled treatment.
*Owner, Francis H. Markoe*

classic acanthus on the capitals, for it was already carved there. Perhaps to give the appearance of metal, he did apply bronze powder to it, reserving the stencilled leaf for added decoration to the rounded surface of the lower drawer on which he had also massed his fruit.

Although the ornamentation of the console table (fig. 108) is close to that of the secretary, there is a definite variation in details. In the small stencilled shell or Greek honeysuckle which borders the glass panel, the same unit was placed to avoid an exact duplication, and the tip of the acanthus leaf is turned back, perhaps to adjust it better to the space. The arrangement on the console is noticeable for the elongated grapes (generally cut almost round) and for the set placing of the leaves which brings balance and formality. The very way in which any massed grouping of fruit and flowers was built tended toward variation. This stencilling, like most of that done on mahogany or rosewood, has not been marred by restoration, for such pieces have naturally been more carefully kept than those destined for everyday wear, and few would think of subjecting a piano or a highly-polished wardrobe of fine graining to a coat of black paint or to sandpaper, the fate of many a Hitchcock chair. Although the pieces in this group do not carry the name of their maker, they have been placed on the best authority as of New York origin.

These beautiful woods—for there is no finer mahogany or rosewood than that which went into the case furniture of this period—were utilized for many small articles such as clocks, knife cases, and boxes in a great diversity of shapes and sizes. They too were frequently ornamented with bronze powders. A small box of New York craftsmanship (fig. 109) combines the two decorative treatments, for the front is brush work shaded by closely etched lines, while the top and ends are stencilled with the same type of design that graced the furniture. Dark and bright tones of gold were often mixed together in an almost imperceptible shading as the powder sank into the size, but unfortunately no photograph can reproduce this subtle blending or the modeled contours lightly touched with dull copper. The background of the top has been blackened to enhance the brilliancy of its decoration, while the motif of fruit and flowers has been well adapted to the oblong space assigned to it, for a leaf could always fill a corner to give symmetry and form. Strawberries appear for the first time, and there are but few strokes of the bob or pledget, since the details are placed by the stencil. The triangular seeds of the berries resulted from a second pattern put over the outline of the fruit formed by the first stencil, and the highlights on the grapes were applied by a small separate cut-out.

Not many names of the artisans who used the stencil on fine furniture have survived until today, for this craft was so much a part of the equipment of the cabinet or
chair maker that it is difficult to identify its special workers, as we have already observed
in the brief mention of the early advertisements. We can point to an individual as a
master of this tool only when some chance has preserved a definite record, such as the old
stencils that have made known to us Thomas Jefferson Gildersleeve, "gilder," and
maker of "Furniture and Chairs of all descriptions," as the trade card of his New York
shop used to read.

Our imagination must give life and form to the few facts we have. Born in 1805,
this young lad came to New York City from Springfield, New Jersey, at about the age
of fifteen to become apprentice in the household of a friend of the family, Richard
Tweed, chair maker, in whose house on East Broadway he lived until he was twenty and
ready to open his own shop. We do not know the agreement of this apprenticeship, but
it was probably not unlike that of many another. A thorough knowledge of all aspects
of the craft was not the matter of a few months' training, but a serious business, with
mutual obligations to master and apprentice, and although there were not formal papers
of indenture, for Gildersleeve's apprenticeship was with old friends, there undoubtedly
was some definite understanding of the duties involved.

One paper of indenture, dated 1807 and preserved in the Museum of the City
of New York, not only throws light on the training of an apprentice to a gilder and maker
of "fancy chairs" but also indicates how seriously a master artisan viewed his own obligations to his craft.

> [Frederick Jereau] with the consent and approbation of two of the Alder-
> men of the City of New-York and of the Commissioners of the Alms-
> House of the said City, and of his own free will and accord, puts himself
> apprentice to Henry Dean to learn the Art, Trade and Mystery of Fancy
> chair painter & gilder for four years two months and twenty-eight days.
> [He promises during this time to serve his master faithfully,] his secrets
> keep, his lawful commands everywhere obey. He shall not waste his Mas-
> ter's goods, nor lend them unlawfully to any . . . nor contract marriage
> within the said term: at cards, dice or any other unlawful game he shall not
> play . . . he shall not absent himself day nor night from his Master's serv-
> ice, without his leave; nor haunt ale-houses, taverns nor play-houses. [The
> master agrees to] use the utmost of his endeavour to teach the said appren-
> tice in the Trade or Mystery of a fancy chair painter & Gilder and provide
> for him sufficient meat, drink, apparel, lodging, and washing, fitting for an
> apprentice, during the term . . . [and further to give the boy] one quarters
> schooling in each year and a new Bible at the expiration of the Term.

And so at the age of twenty-one Frederick Jereau would become, as did Thomas Gildersleeve, a master in his own right.

FIG. 109. MAHOGANY BOX AND DETAIL

The top is stencilled in various shades of metallic powder, while the design on the front is brush work shaded by closely-etched lines. The stencilled rosette (left), used on the two ends, is a characteristic Empire motif. The box measures five and one-quarter by ten and one-half by five inches.

*Owners, The Misses Scrugham*

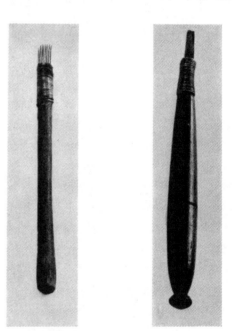

FIG. 110. BADGE AND TOOLS OF THOMAS JEFFERSON GILDERSLEEVE

The stencil knife, etching tool, box of gold powder, oval sample of flower painting on glass, and badge belonged to this New York chair maker, who worked at 237 Delancy Street.

*Museum of the City of New York*

The shop that Gildersleeve opened in 1827 was located at 237–239 Delancy Street in the upper story of his stable, back of the house. Here, in his turn with two apprentices, he worked until the house was razed to build the Delancy Street bridge, when he moved to 197 Chatham Street and opened a shop with a fellow craftsman, Madden by name. He did not retire from active business until 1861, and he died ten years later at the age of sixty-six. An incident that has come down the years shows the honesty of his business policies, which even friendship could not change. His old master's son, the notorious "Boss Tweed" who became Mayor, once suggested that the chair maker furnish certain orphan asylums and city schools with a thousand chairs, making out two bills, one to the advantage of his would-be patron, but Gildersleeve preferred to see the order placed elsewhere. And we may be sure that he carried over the same ethics to his post as receiver of taxes in the Thirteenth Ward in 1842.

One event which must have left a happier memory than his experience with the son of Richard Tweed was the parade in "Commemoration of the Triumph of Liberty in France," planned for November 25, 1830, but held, because of rain, on the 26th, in which Gildersleeve marched. His badge of white satin, yellowed but in perfect condition today was treasured as a memento of the occasion (fig. 110). In judging the importance of the event, we are apt to forget the enthusiasm with which our countrymen followed the career of the aged and popular General Lafayette, *Discipulus Washingtonis.* He was head of the armed revolutionaries, the National Guards, who for three days in July rioted in the streets of Paris, in protest against a proclamation by King Charles X, revoking the freedom of the French press, the existing franchise of the citizens at the polls, and all power vested in the delegates of the people. The eventful victory was more than a victory over the king, who was deposed in favor of the Duke of Orleans; it was one of democratic principles over autocratic government, and as such was shared by all upholders of democratic institutions.

It is probable that Gildersleeve was present at the meeting of the "Fancy and Windsor Chair Makers and Gilders of the City of New York," which was held "at the corner of Mott and Chatham streets on Wednesday evening the 17th instant," when the resolutions were adopted "That we will join our fellow-citizens in celebrating the glorious Revolution of France," and "That a committee of three be appointed to confer with the Delegates at Tammany Hall in relation to the celebration." The committee planned well, for these artisans had a conspicuous place in the procession according to a vivid contemporary description.[17] In front of the group a large banner emblematical of the trade was carried, inscribed with the mottoes, "Rest for the Weary," and "By Industry we Thrive," followed by men carrying three tri-colored chairs on which were painted

17. Myer, Moses: *New York Celebration of the Revolution in France*, 1830.

the names of Washington, Lafayette, and Jefferson. Then came a member with two small chairs and a settee, with the American and tri-colored flags and a liberty cap with the motto "We make the chair of government, the people designate the occupant." Banners with "Support the Chair" and "Liberty and Peace" added their sentiment, but the important float was an "elegant car drawn by two horses, in which two men were at work, and who during the procession manufactured a handsome curled maple cane-seat chair that was presented to Ex-President Monroe on the stage in Washington Square."

But interesting as is the account of these historic events, and significant as they were to the participants, Thomas Gildersleeve seems most real to us through the metallic powders, tools, and stencils that he used, some of which have fortunately survived. An artisan working with bronze would have in his kit several low boxes or trays generally divided into a number of compartments where he could keep his powders of different shades. These powders were pulverized metal—brass, zinc, copper, aluminum, silver, and gold, in various alloys—or metallic ores in their original color. Several packets of Gildersleeve's powders and some of the small papier-mâché boxes in which he put them have been kept. One containing a deep vermilion is very like that which can just be detected blending with the gold in the ornament of the wardrobe (fig. 104). Perhaps of even more interest than these old powders is his handmade stencil knife with its thin blade of hard tempered steel and his etching tool for the shading of gold leaf (fig. 110). The latter tool, a crude little implement but one capable of doing delicate work, was made by inserting fine needle points at one end of its small wooden handle.

Other essentials for a well-equipped kit are missing, for there are no pounces, and we do not have the square of heavy glass or sheet of tin on which the stencils themselves were cut. Tin was preferable for it prevented the blunting of the sharp blade of the knife and consequently too frequent recourse to the whetstone. The small steel punch which pierced the neat round holes centering a flower or making the beading of the rim of an urn is not among these tools. Gildersleeve employed it in many of his patterns, since small holes cut by hand left ragged edges that destroyed their decorative value. These metal punches of varying sizes were aids in giving detail to ornament, and if they were sharp, the mere pressure of the hand would neatly cut the paper laid on the hard surface.

A number of Gildersleeve's stencils, with their margins closely trimmed, were found pasted on bits of thin blue and yellow paper in a family scrapbook, where they had long been guarded (fig. 111). The usual saturation in linseed oil for toughening the cut-outs was omitted, which accounts for the strong contrast of white against black in the photograph. The rag paper was of good quality or it could never have held at the fragile ties which are here more than a mechanical means of binding the pattern together, for they are placed so as to define the structure of a flower, stem, or joint as well. The designs illustrated are only a sampling of those in the collection of forty or more patterns, which include narrow borders styled like the ones used on the cabinet furniture, rosettes and many units with which to construct fruit and floral decorations. It will be noticed that there is comparatively little variety in the basic designs placed on these important pieces of furniture: variants of the Greek honeysuckle, the acanthus, classical motifs, rosettes or bosses, fruit and flowers cover the range of ornament which was clearly conditioned by the taste of the Empire. Gildersleeve, however, was primarily a chair maker, and although on occasion he may have exercised his skill on some fine cabinet work, he did many more chairs, and his kit contains the type of pattern that was used in chair decoration from the twenties on. Fruit and flowers cut in one stencil with their leaves, pomegranates with their stems attached, a rose with its petals cut in a single unit show the direction the stencil was to travel when it became the servant of mass production. Two chairs of Gildersleeve's were preserved until recently as examples of his stencilling, but unfortunately they have been scraped and waxed and have left only a memory of "leaves and fruit."

THE  HITCHCOCK  CHAIR

Whether the stencil was first applied to the common chair so closely associated with it or to fine cabinet work, we cannot say with certainty; but from what we know of the development of the craft, we can probably assume that the fine furniture came first, while the chair, destined for everyday use, took over a fashion and a tool already established and developed it to meet the increasing demand created by a rapidly growing country. This supposition is borne out by the fact that domestic woods were stained, grained, and painted to simulate the more costly ones. A chair from Rhode Island is the earliest one for which I have found an authentic date (fig. 112). It is one of ten from the original set of twelve which were part of the dowry of Patience Harris, who married John Appleby on June 18, 1809, and which remained in the house in Stillwater to which she brought them upon her marriage. Few stencilled chairs are in better condition than these which have always been kept in the "best room." In structure they follow a contemporary type of mahogany chair, with low backs, outward curving legs, and a forward sweep of the uprights. Ackermann's *Repository* for 1809 shows under the caption of "fashionable furniture" one very similar in style, with the same convex line and the cut-out splat; in fact, it is the lines which distinguish these early chairs from those of later date when production costs were closely reckoned items in factory output, for straight legs could be turned at less expense.

Like the New York case furniture, the chair illustrated is a combination of hand work and stencilling and exhibits the same skilled craftsmanship. Pale gold leaf on the horns of plenty has been finely etched and heavier black details added by the brush. The designs on the top bar, uprights, and center of the seat rail are bronzed by hand, but those at the ends of the seat rail and on the vase turnings of the legs, together with the filling of the horns, are stencilled. Subdued shades of gold contrast with what may have originally been silver but now appears as bluish steel. Perhaps this metallic powder has undergone the same change against which the author of an English publication warned cabinet makers not many years later when he voiced the precaution that it "must be kept well stopped in a bottle and wrapped in paper" to prevent discoloration. The graining or "dyeing," as it was sometimes called, of the ground of the chair is distinctly seen in the photograph.

Although undoubtedly later, in some respects an even finer example of workmanship than the Rhode Island chair is one now in the Jeremiah Lee Mansion in Marblehead, Massachusetts, where it came from the family of Richard Pedrick (fig. 113). It is straighter in build and more closely resembles the general Hitchcock type, the frame being larger and the back proportionately longer, although this difference is less noticeable because of the additional lower crossbar. Our attention naturally focuses on the stencilling, which is done with even more care than on those owned by Patience Harris. Although the splat to be decorated is practically identical in outline, the arrangement of the fruit and leaves as well as the details on the horns differs. This second artisan apparently imposed his highlights on the fruit and grapes with small bobs, turning back and meticulously veining the tips of the long leaves and dovetailing those in the center. We are to miss this detail of execution in the majority of the "factory-made" chairs, an execution which links these two chairs with the fine furniture and suggests their source of inspiration. The two types of craftsmanship were, however, often contemporary, for even when mass production became a fact in the industry, individual artisans undoubtedly exercised their superior skill under special orders or produced work of the highest standard because they would not do otherwise. On this chair the stencilled rosette, clearly suggestive of an embossed disc, is more compact than on the Rhode Island chair, and we are less aware of the background of wood through the gold. The bronzed honeysuckle on the turned head rail is very like that on the front of the New York box (fig. 109), for the same design found many uses, and without knowing the history of ornament these early workers had an intuitive sense of what was effective.

Types of chair splats as well as of ornament frequently persisted over a period of

104

FIG. III. SOME OF GILDERSLEEVE'S STENCILS

A number of this worker's stencils were found pasted in a family scrapbook.

*Museum of the City of New York*

FIG. 112. EARLY STENCILLED CHAIR

This chair from Stillwater, Rhode Island, was part of the dowry of Patience Harris, who married John Appleby June 18, 1809.

*Owner, Miss M. C. Appleby*

FIG. 113. "HITCHCOCK TYPE" CHAIR

The stencilling on this chair is comparable to that on the finest mahogany furniture.

*Marblehead Historical Society, Marblehead, Mass.*

FIG. 114. EUNICE ALFORD HITCHCOCK

*Owner, Mrs. Mabel Roberts Moore*

time. A set of nine chairs from the Titus Whitmore house in Middle Haddam, Connecticut, dating from the eighteen twenties, carries the same horns of plenty with only slight variation and a honeysuckle motif to which the punch contributes precision of outline. A coat of dark brown grained against an undercoat of reddish brown suggests mahogany but does not give as great a contrast for the ornament as does the more typical darker finish. The staining of these chairs has been cautiously characterized by a writer in the second quarter of the century as "pretended imitation," to which we might add, "of the costly woods."

The familiar "ball and slat back," a distinct type of "fancy chair" and a modification of a late Sheraton design, should not be overlooked in its relation to stencilling. Small round balls applied between the frame and splats, a curved seat rail, and a rushed bottom distinguish this type. Armchairs and settees were made as companion pieces, their popularity lasting well through the first quarter of the nineteenth century, and they were, like the side chairs, painted in grays, greens, and yellows, with stripings of contrasting colors. A broad top carried the design which, though frequently stencilled, was more often painted by hand. It could be very elaborate as in the landscapes done in 1817 for a group of chairs to be used on the famous yacht, *Cleopatra's Barge*,[18] but the stencilled treatment was usually very simple. I have seen a yellow chair with a stencilled band of a single overlapping leaf on the back and front rail, which was identical with the smallest leaf border illustrated (fig. 138), but leaves with grapes were more common. On these light painted chairs the ground of the paneling on which the gold stencilling was laid was usually a deep olive to provide a needed contrast for the pale gold.

It is inevitable that the name of Hitchcock should already have occurred several times in these pages, for, by his ability and keen business sense in labeling the output of his factory, he identified himself with stencilled chairs so definitely that his name has become a synonym for them. Although many another preceded him, and still more were to compete with him, he does in a way stand as a symbol for the industry, since his career covers a large part of the period when this fashion was growing, flourishing, and declining, and he had an active share in forming and satisfying a popular demand by his methods of distribution. The chair which he produced met a definite need; it was strong,

18. Illustrated in *Furniture of Our Forefathers*, by Esther Singleton, on p. 557, with an account of the yacht on p. 554.

light, easy to transport by boat or over poor roads, its low cost fitted it to the small incomes of an expanding country, and above all it was decorative.

The publication during the Connecticut Tercentenary celebration of the booklet, *Hitchcock Chairs,*[19] has given us the main facts of the life and activities of the man whose name has become associated with these stencilled chairs, and whose energy and initiative are qualities so typical of those who developed the commercial life of our nation. Born in

*West view of Hitchcocksville, Barkhamsted.*

FIG. 115. CONTEMPORARY WOODCUT OF
HITCHCOCKSVILLE
Part of the chair factory may be seen at the left.

*From J. W. Barber's "Connecticut Historical
Collections etc.," 1837*

1795 at Cheshire, Connecticut, Lambert Hitchcock arrived at Barkhamsted an ambitious young man of twenty-three and modestly began by making chair parts which could be easily shipped to various sections of the country and put together at their destination. Probably by 1821 he was manufacturing completed chairs elaborately decorated, which bore the stencilled inscription "L. Hitchcock, Hitchcocksville, Connecticut, Warranted." Thus the name given the small settlement[20] (fig. 115) which grew up about the factory reached many homes. About 1826[21] a three story brick building with a cupola was erected, where almost a hundred people of the neighborhood, among them many women and children, found employment. The next two years were active ones, perhaps too active for slow methods of distribution, for in the summer of 1828 Hitchcock evidently

19. By Mabel Roberts Moore, 1933.
20. Renamed Riverton in 1866.

21. 1825 according to the *Sesqui-centenary of Barkhamsted,* p. 104.

made over his business assets to trustees for the benefit of his creditors, and a year later he was forced into bankruptcy and his personal property sold to meet the claims.

Adversity served only to test the fiber of the man and the reputation of the business that had grown so rapidly. In an advertisement from *The Connecticut Courant*, April 21, 1829, we find the auctioneers attesting that reputation of honest workmanship and integrity which went with his guarantee:

> Great Sale of chairs Wed. 22nd Apr, 1829. There will be sold in this place at auction, 500 Hitchcock chairs, cane, flag and wood seats, some entirely new patterns. Hitchcock chairs are so well known, that it is not considered necessary to give a particular description of them. Every chair is marked with his name and warranted.
>
> B. Hudson & Co., auc'rs.

Certainly no man of inferior quality could have survived the crisis, but, facing his failure squarely, Hitchcock as "agent" for the business showed the same resourcefulness that had made his first success. The factory at Hitchcocksville continued to push its products, for at least fifty-four advertisements with the identifying cut of the Hitchcock chair appeared from 1829–1832 in the papers of the near-by state capital, which supplied the news for the neighboring towns and countryside. By November 17, 1832, the claims of the creditors were satisfied, and both the *Hartford Times* and the *Courant* carried items about his resumption of the business "on his own account and responsibility," as well as the statement that "the subscriber will continue to manufacture chairs and now has on hand a large and elegant assortment of chairs made after the latest fashions and finished in the best manner."

From the phrasing of the advertisements and other available documents it seems difficult to determine just when a partnership was formed by Lambert Hitchcock and his manager, Arba Alford. In August, 1834, Alford's name appears on the announcement (fig. 116) of a new "chair store" which Hitchcock opened in Hartford, where he now lived,[22] and it was under the label of "Hitchcock, Alford & Co. Warranted" that the chairs of the later period were sold. The announcement shows that the store in Hartford was not merely the outlet for their own factory, but that it was selling the furniture of other makers as well.

On April 10, 1841, the Hitchcocksville Company, composed of Lambert Hitchcock, president, and Lambert Hitchcock, Arba Alford, and Josiah H. Sage, directors, was registered in the office of the Secretary of State as a joint stock corporation "formed for the purpose of manufacturing chairs and cabinet furniture in the towns of Barkhamsted and Colebrook in Litchfield County, Connecticut, and for the purpose of vending

---

22. In the same year Hitchcock had been elected representative from Barkhamsted to the General Assembly.

and peddling the same in this and other states." The capital stock was $15,000 which was divided into six hundred shares, each director owning two hundred. Hitchcock withdrew in the early forties to open his own factory in Unionville, Connecticut, which he operated until his death in 1852. The registration of the reorganized Alford Company,

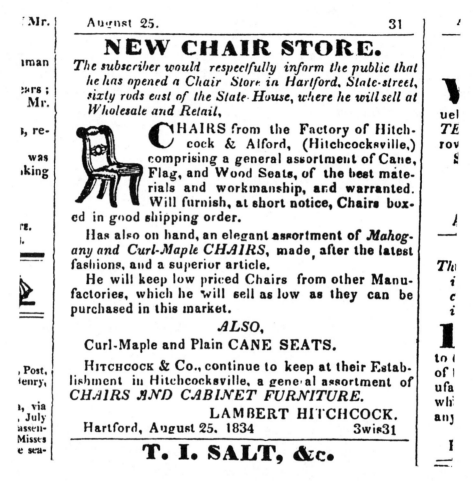

FIG. 116. HITCHCOCK & ALFORD ADVERTISEMENT
This advertisement ran in the *Connecticut Courant* and *Hartford Times* from August 25th through December, 1834.

dated April 28, 1849, indicates that Arba had taken into partnership his son Alfred and George Sanderson, but their decreased capital investment of $7,500 already suggests a declining industry. After 1853 the factory no longer made chairs but was converted into a plane manufactory by its new owners and later in 1864 into a factory for pocket rulers. When I visited it many years ago, I searched in the attic and under the eaves hoping to find some relic of the first industry, but it was clean-swept and nothing remained even to hint of the past.

But it is not from these formal records of business adventures and obstacles that we gain our most vivid impressions of this pioneer in trade. The diary[23] of his wife, Eunice Alford, whom he married in 1830 during the dark days of his failure, and his own letters make us feel the vitality and unresting energy which spurred him to find new markets and to meet keen competition. Unfortunately the love and devotion of this gentle woman was to be his for only a short time. Her sympathy and understanding did much to inspire and fortify the courage which enabled him so quickly to place his business again on a sure footing. That his ambition and his efforts were unfailing we learn from her words. Her portrait (fig. 114) painted at this period is now prized by a descendant, but the companion picture of Lambert cannot be traced.

Hitchcock may or may not have been a technical craftsman, but in these early days no detail of the business was too small for his attention, and he had reason to be confident of the merit of his own product. He evidently selected the materials carefully for his workshop, for only the best maple and birch, abundant in the surrounding hills, were chosen and then allowed to season thoroughly. He went himself to the city for many of his other necessities, and probably for new ideas as well, for his wife comments in 1833, "My husband has again started to New York accompanied by Brother Arba to buy goods for the ensuing season," suggesting that such trips were not infrequent. In fact, the previous year her diary records that they both shed tears because he expected to be gone a long time.

Some of Hitchcock's letters reveal to us the alert, progressive quality of their writer. In his search for new markets he journeyed to the frontiers, often traveling under hazards. He was an interested observer of the country through which he passed, with an eye for its business potentialities, yet his thoughts were always turning homeward to the office and factory he had left behind. Although the following letter[24] to his partner, Arba Alford, has been quoted in part by Mrs. Moore, it is worth giving in greater fullness for the character it depicts as well as for the commercial outlook it embodies. Carefully written, it is dated Chicago, October 29, 1835.

Dear Friend—
Thursday morning last I arrived in Chicago from Detroit after a journey of thirteen days, not on the most direct route to this place, but wandering through the territory from one part to another at which I wished to stop.
    My first business on my arrival was to go to the office for letters. Found one from Mr. Couch but none from you. . . . The evening mail which ar-

23. I am indebted to Mrs. Mabel Roberts Moore for    24. In the State Library, Hartford, Connecticut.
permission to quote from the diary of Eunice Hitchcock.

rives every other day from Detroit brought your letter, and I can assure you I was very glad to receive it. I am happy to hear by your letter which embraces a line from Sage that you are all well and going on prosperously. The day after I wrote you I saddled my pony, and without company took my departure from Chicago. . . . The territory of Michigan (about to become a State) so far as I have seen it is remarkably level, nothing like what we in New England should call a hill, is to be seen in crossing the whole territory, with the exception of some slight elevations in the western part, and some sand hills on the shore of Lake Michigan. . . .

Much of the soil in Michigan is very rich and productive. The oak openings are generally good, plough lands a little incline to a sandy soil, more natural to wheat than any other crop, though it provides a very good corn. . . . The road from Detroit to Chicago, called the Chicago Road, runs through the lower counties of Michigan. It is much travelled but in a bad condition. I travelled but little on this road, going at one time higher up in the territory, and at another dropping down into the upper counties of Indiana. The settlers live principally in log houses, and even the Taverns and Stage houses are of this description, except in the county towns, where generally one or more good framed public houses are found. These in some places answer the double purpose of Tavern and Court House, which, with a log jail, constitute the County Buildings.

The emigration to this territory is from all the eastern States, but more from New York and Ohio. The emigrants from the two last mentioned States stand it better than our New England people, having once had a seasoning in an atmosphere subject to fever and ague. Michigan, with the exception of Detroit and its vicinity, as you are aware, is entirely new—very few inhabitants have been here more than three years—and perhaps one half of the whole inhabitants have come in the last eighteen months—some with their buildings finished and a small piece of land under cultivation, are beginning to be comfortable. . . . The Indians for the most part have left the country. In the eastern part they are met with occasionally, but in the western part on the St. Joseph River is a tribe of 300 or 400. I passed through their settlement. They are on the Indian Reserve. They cultivate their lands and hunt. In the vicinity of this place it was common to meet an Indian with his knife. . . .

I have not room to give you many particulars of my journey from Detroit to this place. As I before stated, I followed the Main Road, but part of the way found the roads bad, and indeed some of the way I found no road at all —more like an Indian Trail. There are woods for several miles together. Occasionally fell in company with eastern men travelling through this county. Having rode my pony into the western part of Michigan, his back became so sore I was obliged to sell him. Here I fell in company with two young men, Merchants from the State of New York, who were also coming on to Chicago. Some part of the distance we came on foot, some of the way by stage, and occasionally would hire a man to bring us on a few miles. One day when travelling on foot through the woods we were overtaken by an Indian on horseback, who by signs manifested a desire to carry our valises for us, but we would not trust them on his horse. We arrived in Chicago on Tuesday last—and now from Chicago, the London of the west as some of the inhabitants call it, I write you. . . . It is a place of considerable business, and contains between four and five thousand inhabitants—has about 70 stores including groceries. There are from 20 to 25 lawyers, but these study speculation more than speeches. There are 12 physicians, 6 clergymen, and mechanics and general assistants, among which are three chair makers. I found a few acquaintances here. Perkins from Winsted is now living in Chicago. It is not that I feel indifferent in regard to our business at hand that I say so little about it in this letter. I wrote you from Detroit at considerable length in relation to it, and have not much to add at this time. I trust it will receive in all its branches your constant and strict attention. I do not now recall when our policy of insurance expires, but hope you will not let it run out. After going out to Post and Rock Rivers, I expect to return to this place, and soon after pursue my way down the Illinois River to St. Louis . . . after staying a few days at that place expect to return home by way of Cincinnati, Pittsburgh, or Philadelphia, without much delay in the route. My respect to all Friends.

The books of the factory were destroyed many years ago, and what we know of the actual details of production is fragmentary. Some of the work on undecorated chairs was done in the State prison in Wethersfield, for an inventory of the assets taken in 1828 includes a "quantity of stock for the manufacture of chairs in the hands of the Warden." In fact, it may have been the custom to "let out" much of the work, always reserving the painting and stencilling for the factory. An old man of seventy-five in a near-by town recalls that in his childhood he used to listen to the tales of an old wood worker of New Boston, who in his younger days had often gone to Hitchcocksville for loads of chair seats to cane at home, later returning the finished work.

Some of the characteristics of the "Hitchcock type" have already been suggested in the comments on the chairs shown, for there were only minor differences in this definite type, made throughout New England, New York, and along the "middle border" over a stretch of many years. We have been prepared for its strong, light construction, its squared back and its turned or broad top and cross rail suited to the ornament dictated by the Empire, and for its simple caned, rushed, or wooden seat. The uprights of the back were flattened on the front to provide a better surface for gold decoration. The large knobs on the turning of the legs were usually gilded with Dutch metal leaf, a cheap alloy but one which gave a contrast of luster to the more subdued bronze powders. The pine, maple, or hickory which went into the construction was usually painted Indian red, over-laid by a thin coat of black, grained to give a background for the bronze, while striping, usually with yellow, was part of the finish. In 1803, Sheraton had said, "black chairs look well when ornamented with yellow lines," and had given the directions for mixing the exact shade, "king's yellow and white and a trifle of orange." A protective coat of varnish was the last step. It is not difficult to identify the general type, but time, recaning, and even redecoration have usually obliterated the names of the various makers, if they troubled to mark their work at all. Hitchcock, as has been noted, was more careful, but, even so, his marked chairs are not easy to find.

The lines, as well as the inscription, indicate that the chair chosen for illustration (fig. 117) is of the early period. It is an excellent example of Hitchcock's best work, the sort that helped build the reputation of the manufacturer and expand the business. Its date is probably very close to 1826, as the slightly splayed legs, the backward curve of the uprights, and the braided edge around the caned seat suggest. A red undercoat shows through what appears to have been a deep brown, scarcely black, and the striping is a faded yellow. All of the ornament is stencilled, with the exception of that on the seat rail which, although badly defaced, bears a variant of the honeysuckle applied by hand. The luster of the stencilling is still brilliant, proving that a good alloy was used in the two shades of gold and copper. Below the rim of the vase and on the two large rosettes, spots of bronze powder were applied to vary the ground before the size had dried, a touch familiar in fine cabinet work. The whole decoration has a transparency that is lacking in later work, and the absence of leaves is noticeable in the composition of fruits, straw-berries, grapes, and flowers.

Late one dark October day this Hitchcock chair came into my possession, one of ten which I found in Tolland, Massachusetts, close to the Connecticut border line. Al-though an excellent example of the early period at its best, it had special interest for me because of one of those casual adventures common to all who are interested in things of the past. Five years earlier I had stopped at the small shop of a cabinet maker and found an old volume bound in full calf between whose pages had been slipped some fifty sten-cils, finely cut out of thin paper, still showing the rich, warm tones of the bronze. There were delicate borders, classical motifs, and round geometric designs (fig. 119) as well as one group of fifteen stencils which I had been unable to relate to any pattern. Careful examination of my new Hitchcock chair revealed that the pattern on the cross splat had been made by the identical group of single stencils over which I had so often puzzled (fig. 118). Only a few small units were missing, perhaps dropped out of the old volume. These stencils had belonged to Jarred Johnson of Brush Hill, Sheffield, Massachusetts, about whom we know little except that he was born in 1801 and became a farmer and cabinet maker. What connection he may have had with his contemporary, Lambert

112

FIG. 117. EARLY MARKED HITCHCOCK CHAIR

Dating from about 1826, this is the type of chair that earned its maker his reputation.
It is signed "L. Hitchcock, Hitchcocksville. Conn. Warranted."

*Owned by the author*

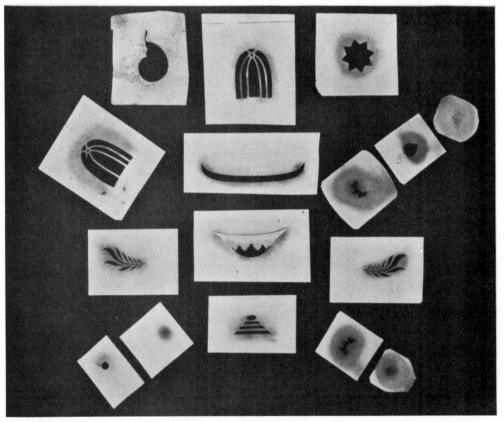

FIG. 118. DETAIL OF SAME CHAIR AND STENCILS OF JARRED JOHNSON

This group of Jarred Johnson's stencils is similar to those which constructed the design on the crossbar of the chair. Jarred Johnson (1801–1873) worked in Sheffield, Massachusetts, just over the Connecticut line.

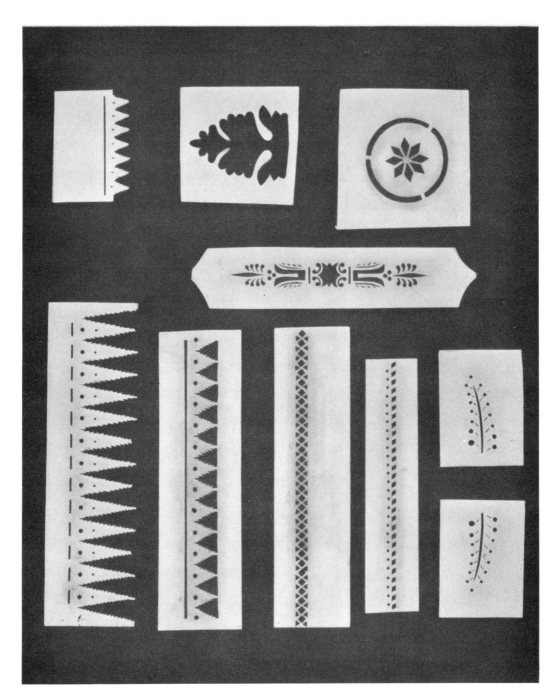

FIG. 119. BORDERS AND BANDINGS CUT BY JARRED JOHNSON

These were among the fifty stencils found between the pages of an old book.

FIG. 120. CHAIR MARKED "HITCHCOCK, ALFORD & CO. WARRANTED"
This chair illustrates the later method of veining leaves by the stencil instead of drawing powder along the edge of a curved paper.

*Owner, Homer T. Fargo*

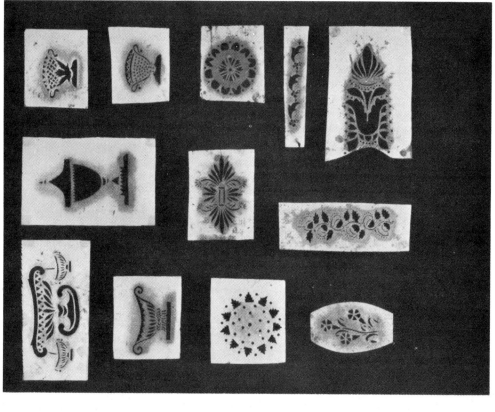

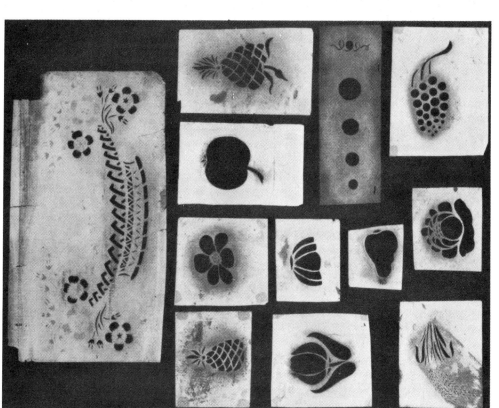

FIG. 121. STENCILS FOUND AT LEE, MASS.

Compare the bunch of grapes with that used on the crossbar in fig. 120. The influence of classic forms is seen in the small urns, rosettes, and honeysuckle.

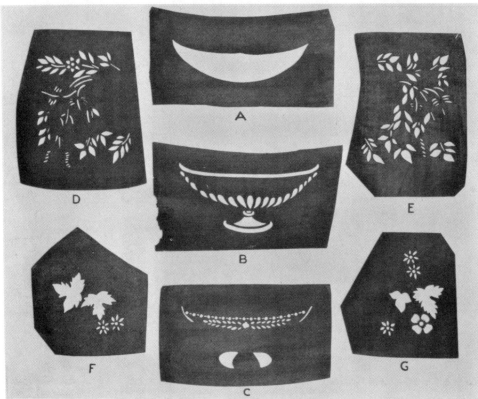

FIG. 122. CHAIR MARKED "L. HITCHCOCK" AND STENCILS
OF GEORGE LORD

This design, used by many chair painters, could be produced by the stencils of George Lord: *A* defined the bowl; *B* and *C* made the rim, the pedestal, and the decoration on the bowl; *D* and *E* provided the foliage and veins; *F* and *G* supplied the remaining leaves and flowers.

*Chair owned by Mrs. Carleton S. Roberts*

FIG. 123. STENCIL OF BOWL BY WILLIAM EATON
The same bowl and surrounding flowers and leaves are produced here
by a single cut-out.

FIG. 124. VARIANTS OF THE FILLED BOWL DESIGN
The tracings of this popular pattern were taken by a New Hampshire
chair painter from the backs of old chairs.

*The Essex Institute*

FIG. 125. ADAPTATIONS OF THE BOWL FOR FURNITURE

Other uses of the bowl are shown on the stencilled washstand (owned by Mrs. E. W. Merrifield),
a chair found in its original wrappings, and a footstool painted black and stencilled in gold.

FIG. 126. VENETIAN BLIND CORNICE WITH BOWL

Because of its flexibility, the bowl could be made to fill almost any space. It remained a favorite pattern for many years.

*Owner, William L. Warren*

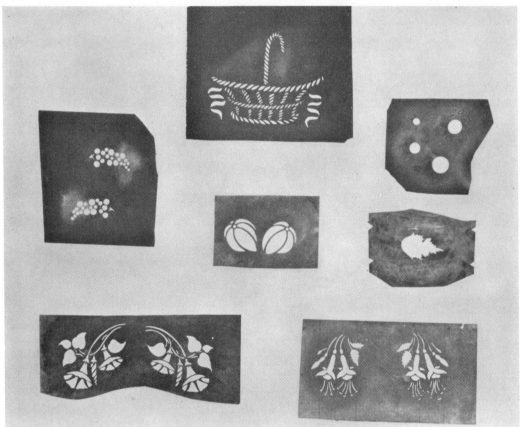

FIG. 127. FILLED BASKET AND STENCILS OF WILLIAM EATON

Like the bowl, the basket of fruit and flowers was also a common pattern. The seven stencils which produced it are also shown.

FIG. 129. STENCILS OF IVERS WHITE

These cut-outs were used by two generations, father and son, who worked at Ashburnham, Massachusetts.

FIG. 128. FLOWERS AND FRUIT BY EATON

These carefully cut stencils show Eaton's observation of detail and skilled handling of line.

FIG. 130. TWO "TURTLE BACK" CHAIRS

A comparison of the one above, found in London, England, and the one
below from Ossining, New York, suggests that the stencilled chair traveled far.

Hitchcock, record or tradition does not tell. Whether he had been attracted to the thriving factory in the comparatively near-by town of Hitchcocksville twenty-five miles away and had brought back the patterns, or whether he had merely copied the designs from some chair that had come to his own community, we can only speculate. I know of no other original stencils which have as close a connection with the Hitchcock chair, unless it is those found at Lee.

The next illustration (fig. 120) shows the work that was being done soon after 1832 by the newly reorganized partnership of Hitchcock & Alford, since it bears their trademark stencilled on the back of the seat. The set of six chairs had not far to go from their shop along the old stage route through Colebrook River to the town of New Boston, Massachusetts, where the one photographed is still owned by a descendant of the original possessor. It is in excellent condition with only the front seat rail and one upright showing the wear of a century. The horns of plenty and the urn and basket of fruit do not crowd the broad curves of the cross splats which are as smooth as satin and speak eloquently of the quality of varnish which overlaid the finished chair. To those familiar with the Hitchcock patterns, this design is well known, for it appears on both rockers and straight chairs. Evidently in these stock ornaments little was left to the initiative of the women who did much of this work. Three shades of powder were used, a pale gold, a deeper tone and copper, the pale gold defining the horns of plenty. One small item of technique helps to place the period of the stencilling since it shows a later method than those we have noted before, an outgrowth of the urge for speed. The veinings of the leaves are now being applied with a stencil in place of the slower curved paper, and this chair is the first example illustrated of the practice which was supplanting the more painstaking and less set method.

Just as the cut-outs of Jarred Johnson suggested some relationship with the early Hitchcock chair, so a single pattern in another stencil collection hints a similar connection with this Hitchcock & Alford chair. It is a bunch of grapes (fig. 121) almost identical with the one on the crossbar, and was among the seventy-odd patterns found in Lee, Massachusetts, between the pages of a paper-covered "Weekly Time Book." The name of "Reuben Goodrich, Springfield, A.D. 1842," written on the margin of the largest pattern suggests that he had once owned the group. How these stencils came into the possession of Frank Brown, a painter and repairer of furniture at East Lee, is not remembered, but it is known that he used them. They were later discovered in the barber shop of J. K. Oliver in Lee, and the last owner, from whom I bought them about twenty years ago, was a local painter. It evidently was a fairly early set, for no large single cut-outs were included except the one of the basket on which the name of Goodrich appeared. There were variations of the honeysuckle especially cut for seat rails and for the uprights of chair backs, as well as rosettes, fruits, flowers, birds, delicate borders, small urns of classic line (one urn outlined entirely by the punch), and pricked patterns for transferring the designs in hand work.

Besides the abundance of chairs which were produced, we must not forget that these same designs were decorating many other articles of domestic wood destined for distribution among the homes of the same purchasers who were eagerly buying the cane and rush seated chairs for their best rooms and the common wooden seats for their kitchens. Beds, bureaus, "wash hand-stands," tables, stools, settees, and cradle settees, to say nothing of bellows, bits of turnery such as inkstands, boxes, sleds, and even peep shows, increasingly received their share of bronze ornament. For instance, a small box bought in Hartford long ago has on its lid and ends two different urns and a border that are among those in the Lee kit. The same motifs, of course, passed from one chair maker to another, if not through the medium of a worker stencilling for several firms, as was the custom, then by the direct means of copying or adapting some popular pattern. There was no way of protecting a design by registering it as there is today. Unless we have proof positive that we are looking at an example of the very first appearance of any given pattern, we cannot with any assurance use the design alone as a basis for dating.

The name of L. Hitchcock stencilled on the back of its seat dates the chair (fig. 122) as about 1829. This particular dish of fruit and leaves and small petaled flowers on the crossbar was a favorite ornament. I illustrate it not because the chair is by Hitchcock, but because it shows a design which was used by many different craftsmen whose work extended over a period of several decades. I have seen the design among the stencils of Ivers White of Ashburnham, Massachusetts, born 1804, Willard Brooks of Hancock, New Hampshire, born 1812, William Eaton of Boston, born 1819, and George Lord of Portland, born 1833, as well as in five variants among designs rescued a generation ago by a carriage painter of Peterborough, New Hampshire, from old chair backs covered with heavy paint, which had more than likely been done by still other craftsmen. Such evidence helps to impress the fact that it is impossible to determine the exact year when a stencil either was first used or discontinued, for, as the chair painter of Portland said, "Old patterns were carried on or slightly altered with recuttings."

Nor can we always use the precise stencilled treatment as a criterion for settling the period when the work was produced, for the identical pattern might be achieved by several different handlings. A design could be composed of a number of separate stencils, or it could be cut in a single sheet. Many units produced the best result, since they allowed a variety in different tones of bronzes and more subtle shading, while a single stencil was obviously more limited, suggesting one gold for the entire design. We associate many units with the early period when more time was devoted to each piece and place the quicker method at a later date, but, although such a generalization is true in the main, like most inclusive statements, there are reservations. The seven stencils illustrated (fig.

122) are very similar to the set used to construct the urn on the Hitchcock chair, but contrary to our expectations, they are not from an early kit but from that of George Lord, who began his apprenticeship in 1848. They may have been given him by the elder Holland, who trained the boy and who provided him with his "best stencils." The single more mechanical pattern (fig. 123) was used by William Eaton, who was working earlier than Lord. All we can say, consequently, is that different treatments were being used at the same time and that the simpler and later method did not always supplant the more complex.

The order in which these seven separate units were applied is marked to show the sequence of the building of the vase, leaves, and flowers. As for the contents of this particular urn, no two treatments are identical because the fruits were not cut as a set part of this pattern. In one of the designs traced from chair slats by the New Hampshire carriage painter (fig. 124) there is a veritable harvest piled high, but on the Hitchcock chair the placing of the fruit shows its most characteristic arrangement.

## COMPOSITION AND TECHNIQUE

When we look at the variety of urns, baskets, and dishes, high and low, of all shapes and sizes, we may forget their classic ancestry and their frequent use in carving, but we immediately recognize their adaptability as motifs to conform to the spaces they must occupy, the pediment of a clock or a mirror frame, the crest of a chair, or the lid of a box. In the vase or basket which was often selected for such spaces fruit and flowers could be massed or spread out over the rim, apples and pomegranates could be cut large or small, and two or three or half a dozen, as need dictated, skillfully placed in perspective. Artisans found the grape a convenient unit to fill the odd corner of a composition, and leaves made a good background. Berries, heads of grasses, and a variety of flowers also helped to adapt the arrangement to the required proportions. This flexibility in placement and in the choice of the component parts may account for the continued recurrence of these motifs. The next four photographs (figs. 125 and 126), together with the chairs already shown, indicate the diversity both in treatment and organization of the pattern. For the washstand a tall vase was chosen, and the leaves and fruit were not only heaped into it but clustered at its base as well. On the footstool a low wide dish was used and the fruit flatly placed with an open and dispersed grouping of flowers, leaves, and grapes. For the chair a well-proportioned urn was selected and simply filled with peaches and crisp leafage arranged to fit into the panel made by the narrow striping. The perfect clarity of the ornament has been kept, however, more by chance than intent, for not many years ago this chair was discovered still in its original wrappings. The cornice for Venetian blinds combines a variety of decorative units with interest focused on the central dish whose contents conform to the ornamental outline. These admirable devices were advertised in the Colonies as early as 1769 in the *Pennsylvania Chronicle* where they were commended as "the greatest preserver of anything of the kind ever invented" since they kept out "the scorching rays of the sun."

After seeing these many finished patterns, it may be interesting to have another more detailed object lesson, showing just how the single stencils were placed to compose the decoration. When the wicker basket (fig. 127) had been stencilled, the fruits were settled in the two ends and grapes added one by one. Other units of flowers and small berries then shaped the design to the desired dimensions, and finally leaves were stencilled to soften the outline and merge the pattern with the background. The relation of foreground to middle distance was carefully kept in mind, and only the tip of the leaf and a portion of the pomegranate were used.

In all of this early stencilling the success of the work depended equally on the ability of the artisan and on the patterns, for, unless the units were well designed and sharply cut, the completed decoration was awkward. Whatever else it might contain, no stencil outfit could be complete without its full quota of urns and a variety of fruit and flowers, and in many old stencils the varied forms of the fruit showed excellent draughtsmanship. Strawberries and bilberries, cherries, apples, plums, pears, and even the lemon, were a part of the repertoire. Moreover, they were very often designed with an alert observation of the characteristics of an individual pear or cherry. In the cuttings by William Eaton (fig. 128), we notice the pains with which the cherries and their stems have been drawn, as well as the leaves and blossom end of the apple which show a feeling for the details of growth. Under a cunning knife the ties could become a distinctive element of the design, instead of merely a means of holding together the pattern.

One of my oldest collections of stencils came from an old house in Ashburnham, Massachusetts, formerly an important center of chair making, where the White family had lived for at least three generations in a large house on its Main Street. Josiah was a carpenter, Ivers a chair stenciller and coach painter, and William Fred an ornamental sign painter. Some years after the latter's death an auction which disposed of the hoardings of a century and a half took place. Apparently not an article had ever been thrown out, for old uniforms, fire buckets, furniture, tools, paints, and brushes jostled each other, overflowing from room to room. Papers, piled high in the corners, had been picked over for valuable stamps and records during the interval when the doors had remained unlocked, but the stencils had been undisturbed until they came from the auction block into my possession.[25] They had been the tools of Ivers (1804–1884), who had first placed them between the pages of old account books. I did not find in the neighborhood any of the chairs which Ivers had done, although some recently stood in the parlor of a near-by house. Six excellent examples, I was told, had been taken away by a man who had offered the son a fabulous price for some worthless trinket and a paltry amount for the fine chairs, an offer which was readily accepted. The chairs were paid for immediately and taken away, but the following day and its successors failed to bring the stranger to pay for and carry off his first purchase.

The stencils themselves numbered several hundred patterns, most of them cut on oiled paper now as dark in tone as old parchment (fig. 129). A small pineapple in two parts was done on the page of a copybook, the rounded letters of its once familiar precept, "Commendation commonly animates mankind," broken by the clean-cut incisions. Many pages of letters did similar service. Several designs were in thin brass, a material which could stand rough handling but was difficult to cut, especially in intricate patterns. There were the usual single motifs: leaves, flowers, fruit, rosettes, and horns of plenty, as well as sharp little borders, many patterns for cross slats completed by two or more cutouts, and a few negative stencils, the only ones I have found. In a negative stencil the paper around the ornament is cut away, leaving the motif free. When, for example, it is laid on the rim of a black tin tray, the pounce spreads the bronze as a background, and the design remains silhouetted in the original black, while a second stencil adds the veins.

The patterns did not long remain in the dog-eared volumes, for the son, William Fred, used them in his turn, but his work was not done with the pounce and soft bronze powders but with a brush dipped in heavy gold paint or in thick, blatant reds and greens. These frail patterns with the paint hardened into lumps upon many of them were touched with alien hands in this work of a second generation, and give indication of a craft come upon evil days, when designs might remain the same but methods had changed. More suited to this heavy hand are a group of trotting horses, stiffly executed on small squares of lead, perhaps intended for children's sleds.

In searching for more information about the family, I met Mr. Edgar Willard, eighty-nine years old and formerly a chair maker of the same town. Although he could add little to our knowledge of the three Whites, he had much to tell of the construction and export of chairs during and before the Civil War. At this period they were shipped across the water to England,[26] where trade in the product was well established by 1850. The chair parts were knocked together, but not glued, before decoration by stencil or brush; they were then taken apart, packed twelve in a box, and carried to the station in

25. Through Mr. Stephen Van Rensselaer, Peterborough, New Hampshire.

26. The only information I could secure concerning the making of stencilled chairs in England was that "they are sometimes seen," which in no way answered my question. A London authority on English woodwork said that chairs of this order may possibly have been made locally in small quantities in some village.

great loads as the first lap of their long journey. Payment was in gold, which meant doubling the American dollar, an incentive for any manufacturer.

Two "turtle-back" chairs (fig. 130) bear out Mr. Willard, for one was found in Beauchamp Place, London, and the other in Ossining, New York. The former was traced to Edinburgh, where it was bought more than twenty years ago, but nothing further could be learned of its history. To date them both about 1830 could not be far wrong. The old clipper ships carried many an object of American production to foreign ports, and chairs, that could so easily be knocked down and boxed for shipping, must have frequently been a part of the cargo, for the collector today makes his finds in Spain or China. In addition there were always those Americans who went to foreign lands and took with them their household possessions. So it is not hard to account for the appearance of a stencilled chair of "foreign" make in Edinburgh. That the Beauchamp Place chair is American-made there is little doubt, for the two are very alike in line, with due allowance for the difference in the front stretchers and for the legs of the London chair which had been cut about three inches. The likeness is most striking in the vines of the uprights, which have only the variations that so readily occur in any two hand cuttings, while the unusual cluster of three flower heads on the two panels, although not clearly seen in the photographs, is the same both in outline and treatment. The quality of the work on both is good; even battering and hard wear have not robbed the bronze on the second chair of its brilliancy, though a coat of red has obliterated the design on the top rail.

The pineapple, which had already become a common decorative motif by the end of the eighteenth century and continued in favor during the first decades of the nineteenth, was used in many of the fruit groupings. In furniture it was carved on bedposts, sofas, and even pulpits; on woodwork it was used over the pediments of doors, to center fanlights and on pilasters; on stencilled walls it appeared, as we have seen, in reds and greens on friezes and panels. Although the actual fruit was not known until after the discovery of Guadeloupe in 1493 by Columbus, this pattern goes back to the Orient, where, as the "pinecone" it occurs in highly decorative forms in textiles. In Greece the same cone was associated with the grape in the making of wine, and it may be a transfer of this classic association that made the Georgian period consider the pineapple as the emblem of hospitality and so use the motif. We know that in New England there was a

FIG. 131. CHAIR RAIL WITH PINEAPPLE MOTIF

This illustrates the process of shaping a pineapple by overlapping a single unit thirty-four times, a painstaking and unusual means of forming this fruit, done about 1830.

FIG. 132. PINEAPPLE OF SIMPLIFIED FORM

A quicker method of constructing a pineapple was used above, for a cross section (below left) has been overlapped seven times, only the width desired being used. The leaves of the fruit, however, were done by repeating a single unit (below right).

FIG. 133. CHEST STENCILLED WITH PINEAPPLES

The pineapple complete in one stencil has been used for the border of this chest of about 1820 from Cambridge, New York.

*Owner, Stephen Van Rensselaer*

FIG. 134. CHAIR WITH MASSED FLOWERS AND FRUIT
First owned by the Rev. Rufus Pomeroy of Otis, this chair rivals in its workmanship
the best cabinet furniture.

*Owner, George Norton*

FIG. 135. CHAIR BY JOHN L. HULL

Dating about 1838, this admirable example was stencilled over a dark green ground
by John Hull, a cabinet and coffin maker.

*Owner, Mrs. R. W. Beebe*

knowledge of its symbolic significance, but its obviously decorative quality is sufficient to account for its appearance on the stencilled chair.

The pineapple was a design that might be achieved in several ways by the stencil. An illustration of the patience which could be expended in the making of a single pineapple is a New England chair, where thirty-four applications of a small cut-out produced the fruit (fig. 131). This design was cunningly built by overlapping the unit, a method that also offered a choice of powders by which to round and shade the heavy motif. Incidentally, the unit treatment is here carried out to a somewhat unusual degree, for each of the small flowers was individually placed, and to the single stencil which formed eight of the leaves seven additional ones were added separately. A chair bought in New York (fig. 132) illustrates a much quicker process of constructing the same fruit. Instead of thirty-four repetitions of a small unit, seven cross sections, increasing in width from the topmost point to the base, were placed in succession. The work is flatter in quality and more conventionalized than is the more laborious method. Repetition of a single leaf, in this instance, gave the leafage at the bottom. A chest of about 1820 (fig. 133), found at Cambridge, New York, has a sampler's variety of design. Some artisan evidently emptied out the treasures of his entire kit, for it displays a great array of lyres, birds, heads of wheat, acorns, hearts clustered in a circle, and two overflowing baskets. The pineapples are conspicuous, done in the simplest way by a single pattern for both fruit and leaves, and the ties readily follow the lines of growth. The more usual cutting of this motif was in three parts, two for the leafage, and one for the body, allowing more flexibility in the adjustment of the design, so that base and top could be slightly detached from the fruit or made to overlap.

More frequent in the massing of fruit than the large pineapple were the smaller peaches, plums, pomegranates, grapes, and berries. These motifs were favorites for chairs as well as for polished cabinet pieces, though few patterns called for more skill in arrangement. If the fruit and leaves were to appear natural, the relationships of each unit must be carefully studied, and the placement and modeling done with the utmost precision, for there was no convenient basket or urn to guide the eye or to center the design. It is not often that one sees this treatment more capably handled than on the chairs which once belonged to the Reverend Rufus Pomeroy (1785–1867) of Otis, Massachusetts (fig. 134). There is nothing by which to name the maker, for neither the extraordinary sheen of the gold nor the pattern identifies it as a Hitchcock chair, but it may have been made at the Robertsville factory[27] by some especially skilled worker. Fine

27. A collection of stencils burned some twenty-odd years ago might have given a clue to the chair's origin, or thrown light on the patterns and tools which once had been used at Robertsville. A little brass-studded trunk filled with the stencils of Chloe Loomis Fleming, once a worker in the Hitchcock shop, but chiefly identified with the near-by Robertsville factory, had been kept for many years by her daughter, who had carried it about from place to place, until they were finally destroyed to save further moving.

cutting of leaf veins and tendrils, as well as the highlights on the apples and pear, should be observed. The stems, hulls, and seeds of the strawberries were cut in a single stencil, but the bob added accents at the base of the berries and on the grapes. Equal judgment was shown in the choice and blending of the bronzes, for the leaves on the outside with their veins and the forms of the berries are done in a rich copper. Bright gold was used for the fruits, seeds, stems of the strawberries, and tendrils, and pale bronze for the grapes and motifs at the ends of the seat rail. The turned top rail of the chair required hand work, for it was practically impossible to fit a paper stencil closely enough over the contours of a three dimensional curve to prevent the powder from driving under the edges and blotching the work. Brush work furnished no hazards of this kind.

Broad gold striping defines the wide crossbar, but the fine lines are in the usual king's yellow. According to an American publication of the forties, "long camel-hair pencils [brushes] are used" for striping, and "the artist guides his hand by placing some one of his fingers in such a position that it may bear on the edge of the panels, or frame, sliding along as the hand moves with the pencils."[28] All gold striping was not done by hand, however, for in three outfits I have found stencils cut to produce narrow stripes. None exceeded six inches in length, indicating that they were not intended for edging panels but for the short straight lines. The luster of the hand work on this chair is so bright that it is hard to distinguish whether it is gold leaf or bronzing, for if a good quality of metallic powder is polished with a soft brush or cloth, the burnish closely resembles that of leaf. The condition of the size was also an important factor in producing this result.

Units and arrangements of clustered fruit and flowers could be different in character as the wooden chair (fig. 135) demonstrates. It is an admirable example of gold stencilling on a dark green ground. The ornament is composed wholly of single units, and even the leaves of the roses have been applied one by one. The name written in bold letters under the seat identifies it as the work of John L. Hull, cabinet maker and coffin maker, of Killingworth, Connecticut, now known as Clinton. His old shop, used today as the selectmen's office, is still standing on Commerce Street, where he is known to have been working up to 1838.

28. *Scientific American*, vol. I, Oct. 9, 1845.

FIG. 136. LEAVES FOUND WITH JARRED JOHNSON'S STENCILS
Green leaves were often pressed between sheets of paper and transferred an
exact impression ready for cutting.

FIG. 137. LEAF STENCILS BY WILLIAM EATON

Note the delicate work of the veinings and the naturalistic outline of the individual leaves.

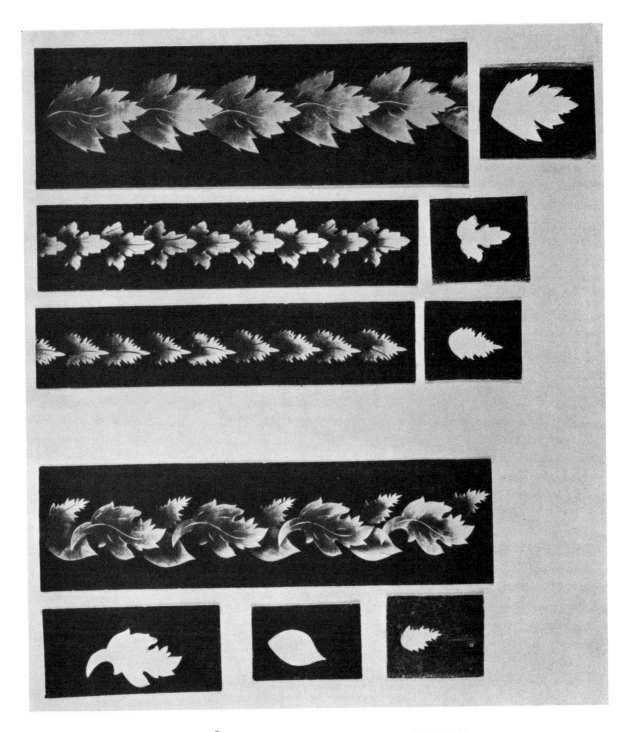

FIG. 138. LEAF BORDERS AND THEIR STENCILS

Repetition of leaves offered a great many possibilities for making effective borders. Gold, copper, and silver powders were often combined to give variation of tone.

FIG. 139. CHEST WITH LEAF BORDER AND DETAIL
This chest is supposed to have come from the Hitchcock factory.

*Owner, Mrs. Goddard Du Bois*

Perhaps no single motif was handled as often and in as many different ways as the leaf. Capable of great variation, it was adapted to many decorative treatments. Massed in backgrounds, it gave the setting for flowers and fruit; highly conventionalized as acanthus or anthemion, it was fitted to chair uprights and seat rails, to pilasters of clock and mirror frames, and to columns of wardrobes and secretaries; repeated in many arrangements in narrow bands, it bordered rims of trays and edged chests or small boxes—in fact, it was the handyman of the kit. In addition to its classic antecedents, nature furnished prototypes for this store of pattern. Often leaves were picked, pressed, and the outlines and veining duplicated. Those illustrated (fig. 136) came out of the musty volume of *Biographia Americana* in which Jarred Johnson of Brush Hill in Sheffield, Massachusetts also kept his collection of finely-cut stencils, some of which may have drawn their inspiration from these very forms. The oak or maple provided greater variety and more interesting outlines than the elm or apple. Like the fruit, most of the single leaves found in the cut-outs of these different kits are naturalistic and not stylized, so that in many instances we can recognize the tree or bush from which they came. When detached leaves for a single unit of cherries or an apple were used, we usually find the leaves botanically correct, but when chosen merely to give background they tend to be conventionalized.

The device of repeating one or more leaves in a border has had many parallels in the history of pattern, and this was perhaps one of the earliest uses to which the stencil was put with bronze powders, as in the japanned trays from England. Time brought diversity and adaptations of treatment, but the illustrations (fig. 138) show some characteristic handlings of the separate units as well as the units themselves. One can easily imagine a succession of possibilities, for the same leaf can be placed at many angles or combined with others of different shape. Once the leaf was selected, the craftsman had but to follow such instructions as those given by Francis Holland to his apprentice, George Lord: "Hold the stencil flat and firm on the sized surface; draw the pad with the powder around the edge of the leaf, avoiding an up and down motion so apt to drive the powder under the paper; then shade toward the center, leaving space for the veins."

A somewhat different border appears on a heavy chest found in Riverton, Connecticut (fig. 139), believed by its owner to have come from the Hitchcock factory or to have been made by one of its workers. On a ground of Indian red a large black diamond carries the principal patterns, a conventionalized cluster of flowers in the center and sprays in the corners, while the leaf border around the outside of the cover is varied at the corners with the same large flowers used in the diamond. The initials A. H. suggest that the chest was made for some special owner and occasion.

There are, of course, many other examples of leaf arrangements which might be cited. A room at Rock Hall, Far Rockaway, Long Island, has a set of Venetian blind cornices of about 1800 stencilled in shades of gold on a green background with a basket of fruit and horizontal bands of overlapping leaves. A late Sheraton bed, found in Boston over thirty years ago, has a section of each post encircled by leaves stencilled with metallic powders over olive-green. A companion dressing table also shows a narrow banding of leaves stencilled on a dark ground edging the top. Perhaps there is no finer example of these leaves than the banjo clock by Simon Willard (1820–1825)[29] on which the small unit is placed obliquely at intervals along the moldings and repeated in larger scale on the bottom bracket.

Most leaf patterns were completed by veining, which could be done in several ways, and, although attention has already been called to some of the methods used, it may be worthwhile to review them again (fig. 140). The earliest custom was to draw the pad along the edge of a thin curved paper, a practice possibly taken over from oriental lacquer, where it was used for indicating the lines or "waves" of hills in the middle distance of small landscapes.[30] If veins were applied by the stencil, as was common in most of the later work, they were frequently done first as a guide for placing and shading the leaf. Veinings of very decorative character could also be made with a small punch or point. When the latter was used, the roughened under surface was removed by sandpapering so that the powder could not creep under the stencil and fur the beaded line.

Often, for contrast, fine black brush strokes veined both single leaves and conventionalized foliage, as on the scrolled ends of chair rails. In the "sample" of an old chair maker from Dublin, New Hampshire, the veins are painted in black and yellow brush strokes on the bronze powder. Overlapping leaves were a usual decoration on the columns of mirror frames and clock cases and were used to surround the many small scenes painted on the glass doors of lyre and shelf clocks, or on the top sections of mirrors. On glass the stencil was applied to the underside over a thinner size than that used on wood or metal, and a coat of black was usually brushed over the bronze as a background to give the pattern brilliancy. The glass of a mirror top from New Hampshire (fig. 141) employs a variant of the usual bronzes, for silver powder and vermilion paint have stencilled the leaves and small rosettes on a deep purple-gray, making a striking frame for the basket of fruit. A clock made by Sawin & Dyer (1800–1820) of Boston (fig. 142) shows large leaves stencilled on the glass within the carved lyre front.

29. Illustrated in *Furniture Treasury* by Wallace Nutting, vol. II, fig. 3361.

30. Koizumi, C.: *Lacquer*, p. 38, the powder was "swept down the edge of the paper . . . cut away in the shape of hills." This technique was adopted by English japanners for certain architectural details in the elaborate bronze pictures which ornamented trays and hand screens in the early nineteenth century.

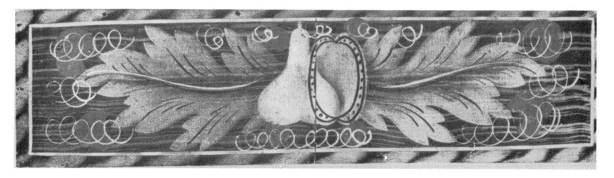

FIG. 140. FOUR METHODS OF VEINING LEAVES

In the top example, the powder was brushed along the edge of a curved paper; the veins in the second were applied through a stencil cut to fit the leaf; the third method was to use a pin-pricked stencil for the veins; at the bottom, brush strokes of black and yellow paint served the purpose.

FIG. 141. DECORATED GLASS PANEL OF A MIRROR

The outside border is stencilled in silver powder and vermilion paint.

*Owner, Mrs. Arthur E. Poole*

FIG. 142. CLOCK BY SAWIN & DYER OF BOSTON

Leaf motifs were stencilled in gold on the glass of the lyre front of this clock sometime between 1800 and 1820.

*Metropolitan Museum*

FIG. 143. SELF-PORTRAIT OF WILLIAM PAGE EATON, 1819–1904
"The best stenciller of his day."

FIG. 144. LATE CHAIR RAIL AND STENCILS

A more set method of stencilling is illustrated by this pattern and its stencils. *A* is applied to the left; the grapes of *B* are added one by one; the two fruits of *C* are done in three applications; the large leaf, *D*, is repeated at the right of the design, while the small unit of *D* provides the turnover of the central leaf.

## WILLIAM EATON

Our discussion of the types and technique of gold stencilling has already taken us from the beginning of the century well toward the half-way mark, but perhaps nothing correlates the methods of this first period and illustrates the later phases at their best as clearly as the work of William Eaton, 1819–1904 (fig. 143). Although he started work in the late thirties, he obviously had handed down to him during his apprenticeship the traditions of the craft. He learned how to build with single units, to shade and secure perspective, to apply veins both with the curved paper and with the separate stencil, and to follow the quicker process of making a complex design with as few as one or two cut-outs, for during his working years he had to compete with those who made their chair slats in a single pattern and applied their gold without shading. He achieved the technique of adding brush strokes of color on thin washes laid over the bronze powders, and he could paint flowers by hand to center chair rails, surrounding them with stencilled scrolls of bronze and silver. In fact, few extant stencil collections as completely illustrate the history of the craft as the one amassed by this Boston artisan. The day after the folios of his patterns had been discovered in the workshop of the Cambridge carriage painter, when George Lord looked through them repeating his praises of the Eaton brothers, marked the beginning of my search to find out more about their maker.

After many inquiries and a trip to New Hampshire, I finally located the farmhouse of William Eaton. It was a summer day when I made my journey down a quiet road to the two-story white house behind a low fence. It stood empty, just as it was left after the personal possessions of the family had been auctioned at the death of Harriet, the last daughter to survive, yet the tangle of lemon lilies, pink and white sweet William, and cinnamon roses among the tall grass seemed to keep the character of the artisan who had loved his garden. In the vacant rooms with their gay wallpapers there were more definite traces of Eaton's handiwork. The mantels carried touches of color, and a fire board was bright with his flowers, while on a chimney shelf stood a box of gold leaf and metallic powders, one packet still showing its original price mark of $7.00.

Other members of the family had shared his love of decoration, for a daughter had painted a bedroom floor with a pattern of strawberries and their blossoms in ivories, reds, and greens on a brown ground. In the attic I found his whetstone, its edge worn into a deep scallop by constant sharpenings of his stencil knife. In a shed I pulled out of an old barrel half filled with rubbish a sample sheet of his work on brittle paper which almost crumbled in my hands as I unrolled it. The sheet was covered with the scrolls and roses so closely associated with the memories of his skill. With it in the barrel were two of his ledgers filled with entries of his work from 1854–1869. These small, well-thumbed, copybooks with many of their pages missing are vivid records of his later days of labor, for they contain lists of chairs handled, of old patterns renewed, and of totals earned, to which we shall return.

Entries in Eaton's hand on a page of a family Bible supply additional facts about his life, for we read that William Page Eaton, son of Andrew Eaton of Marblehead and Elizabeth Page of Haverhill, was born in Salem, April 2, 1819, married Harriet Tuttle at East Boston, Massachusetts, September 3, 1840. Two years after her death in 1841, he married Harriet Gould of Weare, New Hampshire. Other entries indicate that they lived first in Chelsea, and for a short period in New Bedford, but as work was unavailable they returned to Boston. In 1845 he had a shop in Fulton Street and lived on Maverick Street, East Boston. When his family increased (he had three daughters) he bought a farm between New Boston and South Weare, New Hampshire, where his wife and children spent long summers, and where he came during the slack season or when the garden needed ploughing. When his daughter Harriet was old enough, she would relieve the pressure of work by taking his place in the shop, for she mastered the trade under his competent direction. As fashions changed and his talents were no longer wanted, he turned more and more to farming to meet the needs of his family, but he found it an occupation less congenial to his precise nature. He was recalled by one neighbor as a "city gardener," so neat were his ways about the property which pastured only three or four cows and produced little more than was needed by the small family. Every one held warm memories of Harriet, a gentle white-haired woman, who faced cheerfully "the dark days" when, after the death of her father in 1904, she was left alone on the farm, with meager resources.

The community retained more than memories of the Eaton family, for neighbors still kept some of their possessions. An old friend showed me a few stencils, part of Eaton's collection which had escaped the auction hammer. She was keeping them she said to use "on lamp shades," but the old patterns could not have survived a single minute's heat from even the smallest bulb. Another brought out a brass-studded leather box with an inscription inside the top, "Love truth more than gold," recalling George Lord's austere characterization of Eaton, but the hand work which encircled the precept revealed a love for decorative detail. All who remembered him spoke of his paintings; a carriage maker told of a sleigh ornamented with roses, which had been the talk of the countryside. His comment was, "They were *real* roses." Eaton's love of his art evidently extended beyond his working hours, for the margins of his books have casually penned designs, while bits of drawings in pencil, crayon, and water color on scraps of paper were placed between the leaves and include sketches of his house and even of himself.

In the stencils themselves we see Eaton, the artisan whom Lord considered "the

124

best worker of them all," and through the patterns we follow the later development of the craft. Eaton's cuttings of single leaves, blossoms, and fruits already shown (fig. 128) give proof of his knowledge of early treatments, but a later group of designs tell the story of the simplification of technique which placed the success of the finished ornament more upon the designer and cutter than upon individual skill of arrangement. Illustrated (fig. 144) is a more set form of producing a pattern than the filled basket already shown (fig. 127). Here the leaves are cut to fit the curve of apple and plum, but even with this much to guide him, the inexperienced worker would need a picture of the completed design before him, because it requires practice to make the proper adjustments of grapes and leaves to the space. Even this simplified application required twenty-three separate operations, to say nothing of feathering the leaf veins to bind the design to the background.

Of course, the number of cut-outs used in set patterns varied for different ornaments, but the trend was more and more toward fewer stencils. A very mechanical production but an excellent pattern drafted by Eaton (fig. 145) has a decorative quality inherent in the design itself. Little experience besides a knowledge of spreading the powder would be needed to stencil this composition, for the second cut-out is quickly fitted over the first, since each carries two sets of punched register marks. The stencils of this period, contrary to the Japanese practice, seldom had carefully placed register marks. As we look at the composite patterns in old kits, we wonder just how many of them could be accurately placed, but obviously each artisan relied on his own method. Sometimes the point of a leaf or some small detail would serve as a guide for laying the subsequent stencils.

A number of designs were cut as single stencils, especially that group intended for crossbars or "bannister backs," the shop name applied to chairs with vase-shaped backs. In Eaton's collection there are literally dozens of intricate cuttings for head rails as well as fillers for chairs of all sizes from those for children to large rockers (fig. 146). Often the crestings of the patterns indicate the shape of the fillers on which they were to be used. This kind of ornament required no shading, only the solid surface of metallic powder, and the designs themselves closely imitate elaborately chased or wrought metal fittings. There was great variety in the handling of floriated and simple scrolls and of urns or baskets. Morning glories were a favorite, perhaps because the ties could become so definite an element of the design, deftly tracing the tightly curled bud and fluting the open flower against a ground of leaves and tendrils. There were birds intent upon fly or berry, perched on branches or heads of grass. The beaded lines which often shaped the pattern to the crossbar or linked the end units together employed both small and large punches, while quick incisions added fringe and filigree. It is not surprising to find the slender ties broken when we consider the interlacing lines, and the marvel is that any of these patterns have survived, cut as they were on thin paper. These crumbling designs are

125

our only record of many patterns that would otherwise be lost, for wear and coats of paint have taken a heavy toll of the ornament placed on thousands of chairs in the period of their fashion.

In the Eaton day books chairs with vase-shaped fillers are listed as "bannister backs," a name probably derived from the heavy stone balusters whose form influenced the design of empire mahogany chair backs (fig. 159) in the early mid-nineteenth century. The ordinary chair, an imitation in soft woods, was lighter in build, but the same broad back provided not only a strong support but also a large surface for the stencil. Among the twenty-odd patterns of Eaton's which I have for these splats, fountains are numerous and of many kinds, the ornamental base giving scope for varied patterning with the punch and for the quick straight thrust of the knife (fig. 147). Jets of water could be added with a separate stencil or brushed on by hand in pale blues or grays. Delicate scrolling, vines, and narrow bandings fitted also into the contours of the splat, while patriotic emblems such as eagles, shields, and even the word "liberty" crowned by a burst of light, were sometimes woven into the patterns. This very design, less complicated in some of the details of its cutting, also appeared in a collection of stencils found some years ago at the Dyke Mill in Montague, Massachusetts, where during the fifties wooden chairs of many types were manufactured.[31] We cannot tell who did the borrowing, for there was no copyright, popularity being the one guide to the acquisition of new motifs.

By 1845, if not earlier, color was being extensively added to patterns stencilled with gold, silver, and copper powders, for a periodical of that year comments, "Silver ornaments may be tinged with various colors without losing their metallic luster," and "may be occasionally improved by outlines of opaque paints."[32] George Lord agreed that birds and shells especially should have these touches of color, and we know that Eaton followed this practice from the designs he left. One of his folios included finished "samples," showing not only the usual handlings of the bronze powders but also birds and shells done in color. The birds have particular interest, for another volume contained the stencil that fashioned them, although the wings were missing (fig. 148). We may assume that after the frame of formal leaves with bird-head terminals had been stencilled, he turned to the birds, stencilling their bodies in the customary unshaded bronze, which was allowed to dry for a full day before the transparent colors were applied. Rose, blue-green, and yellow provided a gay contrast to the wings of gold. Crests and tail feathers were then added by sweeps of the loaded brush. Finally the background of small leafing branches was ingeniously made by the stencil of a little tree (not the one illustrated)

31. The design is illustrated in *The Pennsylvania Museum Bulletin*, no. 70, Feb., 1922, p. 27, together with an account of the collection. The stencils were found by the owner, Mr. Carl P. Rollins. In the two hundred and fifty pieces there is an amusing one for stencilling the squares of a checkerboard, which suggests the black and white papers made by the *dominotiers* for the game of chess.

32. *Scientific American*, vol. I, Nov. 13, 1845.

turned this way and that, until the artisan had filled the space to his satisfaction. Tinges of copper and silver brought variety to the dulled gold of the foliage, and the small-petaled flowers carried washes of red. The number of times that the stencil was applied in making this small picture shows that the late as well as the early work was at times done with much care and patience.

Eaton's sample page of shells was also stencilled in bronze first and then overlaid with color, the deep openings being shaded in crimson lake and blue, with black, white, and red opaque lines accenting the detail. Individual and clustered shells (fig. 149), which were so cleverly cut by this artisan's knife, were patterned after those which could be gathered along the shore or brought from foreign waters to decorate New England mantels. They lend themselves successfully to the requirements of the stencil, for again the spirals and ribbings are not merely a basis for the ties but an effective part of the unit. The design on the top of a late Boston rocker (fig. 150), made about 1850 by the Union Chair Company, Winsted, Connecticut, was applied by a stencil very similar to one which Eaton cut, while stencilled seaweeds and corals done with metallic powder give to it the proper deep-sea setting.

Washes of color over metallic grounds as well as the last stages of New England's development of the stencil are illustrated by the sheet taken from the barrel at the Eaton farmhouse (fig. 151). Flowers are painted by hand in bright colors and surrounded by elaborate and often intricate framings stencilled in golds, coppers, or silver. Mottoes and sentiments, which earlier had been done in fine needlework for the walls, were now quickly accomplished with the stencil, and boxes and "keepsakes" were ornamented with doves, hearts, forget-me-nots, or other symbols heavy with romance. In this outpouring of sentiment and flood of color the stencil was lost, for painted "cottage furniture" on the one hand and black walnut on the other had brought in a new vogue.

Except for the few patterns on Eaton's sample sheets we have no finished work of this expert among craftsmen, for of the thousands of chairs which went through his hands I have not as yet been able to trace a single one. They are marked, if marked at all, by the names or initials of those for whom he worked. Although in his early days he had his own workshop for a time, we know from his day books that for many years he went from shop to shop. The records are fragmentary, since many of the pages are missing, but Martin Luther Gates, Sampson V. Keen, William G. Shattuck, John L. Rogers, Neagles, George Forsyth, Charles A. Eaton (William's brother), H. S. Mills, and Ward

B. Brown are the names which occur most often. Boston was an important center of the trade, and chairs made in outlying towns were painted there to be shipped in large quantities to southern ports and even to South America, many firms having their own representatives in the larger cities.

Apart from identifying for us a few of his employers, Eaton's books reveal a factual picture of the course of his working years. Even for an excellent artisan, this occupation was at best uncertain, and it became increasingly so as the taste for walnut supplanted that for stencilled and painted chairs. The story is consequently one of decreasing periods of employment and diminishing yearly income. At the age of thirty-six we find him working forty-one weeks in the year from September 18, 1855, to September 27, 1856. There are brief statements noting illness or unemployment and records of some 5,330 pieces of furniture having passed under his brush, yielding a total income of $562.63. His average weekly earning was $11.03, varying from the week ending February 9th, which netted ninety-six cents for twenty-four cane-seated rockers with roses at four cents each, to that of February 23rd, which totaled $25.64 for sixty-eight "Crystal Pallace Grecians" at thirty-seven cents each, in addition to twenty-four cane-seated rockers with their roses at four cents. A scroll and roses on a "Jennie Lind Chair" brought twenty cents, and a child's "Round Post Bannister" three cents. The highest price received at this period was fifty cents for a "Parker Dinner Chair" or a caned-back settee. Inadequate as this income seems to us today, it was perhaps better than the average one in the fifties. Francis Holland, who married the mother of Eaton, and under whom George Lord was trained, left Portland in 1851 for Boston, where with his entire savings of $200 he acquired a house in Chelsea, so Eaton may have seemed prosperous in the eyes of his colleagues. In 1864 during the period from August 11th to December 11th he received $499.44, while in 1868 a week's work brought in $49.76, but though prices had risen, the dates of entries were more and more infrequent. This type of furniture had had its day.

In Eaton's lists are chairs of all varieties, rockers and common, spindle, bannister and cane back, caned and wooden seats, as well as chairs for office and barroom. There is an occasional group of stools or "crickets," settees and cradle settees, and now and again a desk top or a sled. The items give very brief indications of design, including scrolls, roses, shells, stag, "fancy," "floral," and "fruit," but roses are the most frequent. There is striping in gold, bronze, and copper, and we infer that he was also renewing old chairs from the repeated mention of "old Common," "old Nurse," and "old Bannister."[33]

On one of the final pages of the first book we find a tabulation of Eaton's prices that is worth recording.

33. Mr. William Crowell, a well-known craftsman of East Brooklyn, Connecticut, told me that he has found as many as eight designs stencilled one over the other on chairs he has restored.

FIG. 145. FRUIT DISH AND EATON'S STENCILS

This characteristic design appears among his stencils in many variants and may have been originated by him. Note the highlights for the grapes in the upper cut-out and the punched register marks at upper right and center of both stencils and finished product.

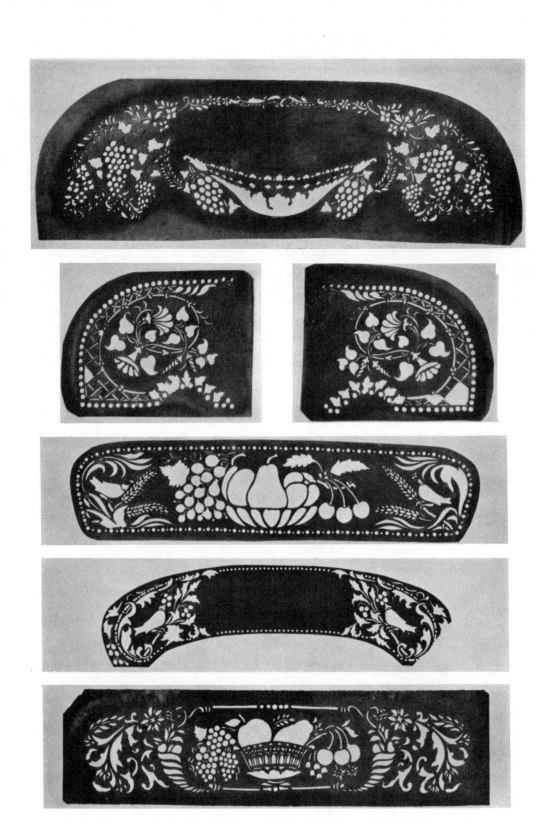

FIG. 146. EATON CUTTINGS FOR CHAIR RAILS

These patterns illustrate the skill which he brought to this later type of work.

FIG. 147. DESIGNS FOR "BANNISTER BACKS" BY EATON

Fountains were favorite decorations for the broad surfaces of these late vase-shaped chair backs. Jets of water such as the one shown completed them and were either done by the stencil or brushed in with color.

FIG. 148. EATON HEAD RAIL DESIGN AND STENCILS

This design was found in his book of finished samples with the stencil which shaped the birds. The leaf background was ingeniously made with a small tree similar to that illustrated at left.

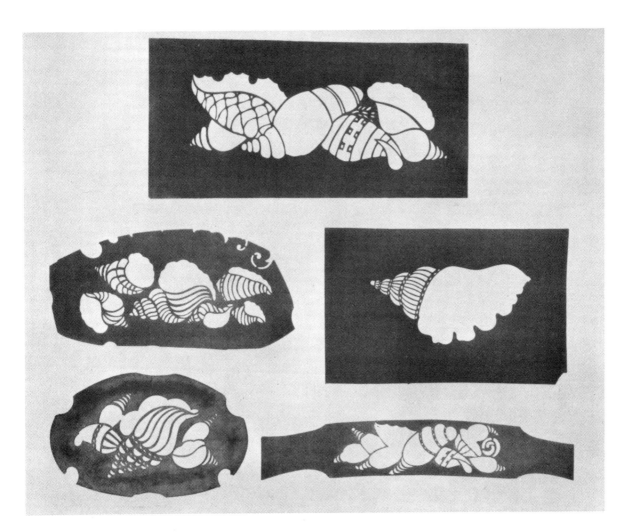

FIG. 149. SHELLS CUT BY EATON

FIG. 150. CREST OF A BOSTON ROCKER

This chair, dating about 1850 and labeled "Union Chair Co., Winsted, Connecticut," illustrates
the use of shells. In this example they were overlaid with markings in color.

FIG. 151. PAGE OF EATON'S SAMPLES

Taken from a barrel in the shed of the Eaton farmhouse, the page includes freehand flowers painted in bright colors with only their surrounding frames stencilled, and illustrates the last stage to which the art declined before extinction.

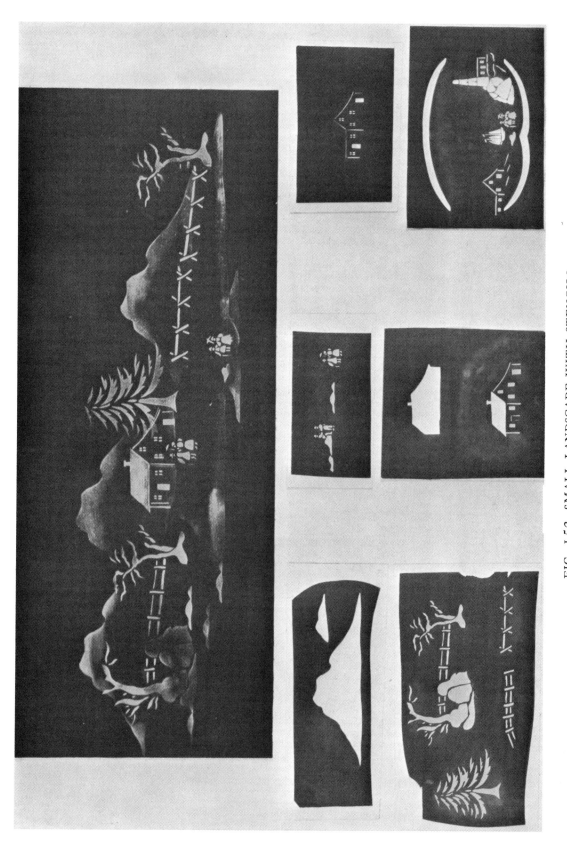

FIG. 152. SMALL LANDSCAPE WITH STENCILS

A great variety of scenes could be composed with these small cut-outs which were used on the cornices of Venetian blinds, the wide head rails of Boston rockers, and the centers of trays.

FIG. 153. THREE CORNICES FOR VENETIAN BLINDS

The scenes all appear to depict Hudson River Valley life.

*Owner, H. Armour Smith*

## Striping Cane Seats

|  | Gold | Bronze |
|---|---|---|
| Grecians | 5 | 3 |
| Round Post Bannister | 5 | 3 |
| Cane Back Rocker | 6½ | 5 |
| Half sizes | 6½ | 4 |
| Cane seat Rocker | 6 | 5 |
| Cane Back Nurse | 5½ | 4 |
| Children Grecian dinner | 6 | 4 |
| Mahogany arm dinner | 5 | 4 |
| Wood Office | 6 | 3½ |
| Cane Office | " |  |
| Cottage Grecian arm | 6½ |  |
| Ogee | 5 | 3 |
| Wood seat Rocker | 6 |  |

Scroll work according to finish

Another list from a set of chair stencils now owned by the Metropolitan Museum of Art duplicates some of this terminology, indicating that these names were more than local.[34] Written in ink on discolored brown paper, it may have been a part of an original catalogue of the patterns which were used by Cutting & Morrell, Chair Painters, 13 Church Street, Albany, New York, whose name appears in the directory of that city for 1851–1852.

| | |
|---|---|
| Wheeler's Fruit dish | 3 |
| Lilly's Plumb patern | 6 |
| Mark's Pear | 7 |
| Winsor Duck | 8 |
| Wheeler's Scroll | 9 |
| Mark's Peach | 10 |
| "      Nurse Rose | 11 |
| Office bird, etc. | 12 |
| Bailey's Com. Rock. Stripe | 13 |
| Nurse Cane      "      " | 14 |
| Child peg paterns | 15 |
| Winsor Stripes | 18 |
| Bannister Stripes | 20 |
| Seat Stripes | 22 |
| Easter Lilly for Rocker | 25 |

34. The collection, kept in the Print Department, has a wide variety of many excellent designs. In addition to small units there are numerous large cuttings for Boston rockers, including shells, flowers, and village scenes. For a child's rocker there are the letters of the alphabet cut to fit the small head-piece.

One group of these Albany patterns produced the small scenes which, from the forties on, decorated the cornices of Venetian blinds, Boston rockers, the centers of trays, and other flat surfaces. Among them are some units of a farm scene that Eaton also owned, though his are better cut. It is difficult to say with certainty just what the implications of these duplications are. At a later date, according to George Lord, one could buy stencils from certain craftsmen, and even at this time the practice may have been current. We know that the Eaton brothers guarded their stencils for the benefit of their employers, so tracings probably account for the use of an Eaton design by the Albany firm. Chairs

CUT BY WILLIAM EATON

traveled amazing distances, and the foremen of shops were alert for new designs which once secured might be improved or weakened according to the dexterity of the craftsman. When there is an opportunity of comparing a cutting of Eaton's with a similar one by another worker, he invariably profits by the comparison both in fine detail and firmness of line. Beside the stencils in daily use every old kit contained homemade transfers, sometimes as many as half a dozen of the same design being made on old bills or letters and kept for later cutting to replace broken ones.

These small pictorial designs were not thrown together in haphazard fashion but called for some creative ingenuity in their arrangement, and the single stencils for making them were of endless variety. Trees with microscopic leaves, rail and snake fences, hills, clouds, even the waves of the sea were cut as separate units. There were houses of all sizes and every type of architecture, churches with tall spires and square belfries. Funny little starched people, singly or in pairs, intently pursued their many occupations. An illustration (fig. 152) shows a group of cut-outs and a scene which it produced. The house, as was customary, required three stencils, the first blocking in the structure; the second giving the windows, door frames, and chimney top; the third defining the minor

130

details. Trees were planted at will, and fences tied together the scattered elements of the composition. Scenes of the sea were also favorites, and we find busy harbors filled with boats of all kinds, fishermen along the waterfronts, and oarsmen vigorously pulling their tiny craft. In their exact portrayals of everyday life, many of these small pictures suggest the bright lithographs of Currier and Ives.

CUT BY WILLIAM EATON

But it is in the larger cut-outs more than in these small scenes that Eaton's individual skill in handling animals and figures is apparent. The high stepping horse that pulls the sleigh and the pair that rears to the lash of the coachman's whip portray swift motion. The drawing of both is alive and rapid, and there is a distinctive character given to them by the long sweep of a knife which scissors could never achieve. These larger pictorial stencils were used in the same ways as the small scenes, but with the advantage of one quick application.

For some purposes the spirited horse, fleeing deer, or eager hunter could not take the place of more complex pictures. Three cornices for Venetian blinds (fig. 153) with views of the "majestic Hudson" are excellent examples of this type of composition, done no doubt by a New York craftsman, if we can judge by their subjects. Six of them were found in an attic of an old house in the Hudson River Valley, three still wrapped in their original papers and probably kept as a reserve supply. Others of the same series may be seen in the collection at Cooper Union Museum for the Arts of Decoration, New York City. The character of the steamboat suggests that their date would fall before 1840,[35] when these local artisans were producing under different names many late versions of Fulton's first steamboat, the *Clermont*, which made its maiden trip up this great

35. Prints of early steamboats help us to fix a more specific date, for "A fast steamboat plying on the Hudson in 1837," is very like those on the cornices. A print made in England in 1839, "Brock's Monument seen from the American side," depicts an American steamboat practically identical.

131

national waterway to Albany on August 17, 1807. At a glance one sees by the sharp, clean outlines that the boats, houses, figures, and flying birds which dot the sky are stencilled, and that the water, sky, and foliage are hand work, made by bronze powders spotted and spread on the sized surface. The cornice itself is painted green, while the end scrolls of Dutch leaf are lined in black, and a narrow gold band frames the picture.

All of the stencilled furniture which we have thus far discussed has had its designs done in bronze powders against dark grounds. Even the light colored "ball and rail" chair had a dark base as a background for its overlapping leaf or its simple panels of grapes. There was, however, another group of chairs, tables, and stands painted usually in shades of yellow, which had stencilled ornament done in bronzes by a slightly different method. To provide a dark ground necessary to make the gold visible, the design was first traced on the furniture in outline. This outline was then filled in with solid black, overlaid with size, and the separate units stencilled in the usual way. The characteristic green leaves were not stencilled, but each was put in by a single stroke of a square-end brush, while the curling tendrils were whisked on with black. The yellow wooden chair with a mottled seat (fig. 154) is a typical example of this group. The old formula for mixing the yellow was given by George Lord as white lead, medium chrome, and burnt umber, while chrome yellow (medium), Prussian blue, and raw umber mixed the favorite green.

PENNSYLVANIA FURNITURE

Gaily painted chairs and furniture of all types from chests to mirror frames are more closely associated with Pennsylvania than with New York and New England. On this furniture a good deal of stencilling was used in combination with the bright hand work so characteristic of the Pennsylvania Dutch. A bold example of their stencilling, and effective because of its brilliant color, is a pair of mirrors (fig. 155), where silver on black, copper on yellow, and gold on red give interest to an extremely simple design. There is no shading of the powder, but merely the contrast which it offers to the strong

132

FIG. 154. WOODEN CHAIR WITH
MOTTLED SEAT

The chair in yellow has on its head rail fruits stencilled in gold over a black ground.

*Owner, Miss Louise Q. Pierce*

FIG. 155. PAIR OF PENNSYLVANIA
DUTCH MIRRORS

The frames are crudely stencilled but brilliant in their coloring.

*Owner, Miss Virginia Kirkus*

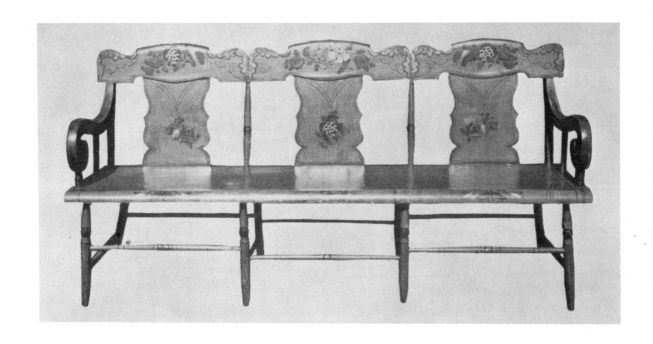

FIG. 156. PENNSYLVANIA SETTEE
AND DETAIL

On a salmon ground the green leaves
and gold ornament are by hand. Only
the grapes and the two center flowers are
stencilled.

*Owned by the author*

flat color. On chairs and settees of blue, yellow, salmon, tan, or dark tones of brown and red, the stencil was often used either to produce bronze or silver units over which color was washed, as has already been discussed in connection with shells and birds, or else to apply single motifs to a dark ground in order to emphasize the luster of the powder as in the yellow chair just described. These Pennsylvania motifs included baskets, urns, fruits, stars, flowers, and birds, all having the brilliancy of color and boldness of design which we have come to associate with peasant art. Elaborate striping was ordinarily an important part of the decoration, and metal leaf was used freely, particularly on the scrolls and turnings of the legs. A salmon pink settee (fig. 156) is a good sample of the type. All of its ornament is freehand except two stencilled motifs, the grapes and the two flowers centered on the top rail, which are stencilled in copper and silver powder on an under coating of black paint. The leaves, however, are hand painted, size being added to the color, bronze dusted over it, and black veining applied last by the brush.

The Mercer Museum at Doylestown, Pennsylvania, possesses a group of tools (fig. 157) which had belonged to an old chair painter by the name of Nees, of Manheim, Pennsylvania, who from 1820 to 1870 painted flowers and birds in natural color. Although it includes a few pricked patterns and crude stencils, his kit is chiefly composed of brushes for hand work, leather and cardboard graining tools of all sizes, and sponges and feathers for the mottling or stippling of dower chests and other furniture.

GEORGE LORD

To these pages on the use of the stencil in furniture ornament the full experience of George Lord has made many contributions, so that some additional recollections of the "last of the old chair painters" may well help to bring to the picture something of the reality with which he invested it for me, for he loved the craft and everything associated with it, though his own contacts cover mainly the period of its decay. He began his career as an ornamental chair painter in 1848 in the shop of Corey Brothers, in Portland, Maine, at the time the firm owned its own tract of timberland on Fry's Island in Lake Sebago. It was a natural vocation for the boy to choose, since his father had been a cabinet maker. Lord served his apprenticeship under Francis Holland, a good craftsman who had worked in Halifax and Boston previous to coming to Portland in 1845. The shop overlooked the Fore River at a point where the buildings of the Grand Trunk Railroad now occupy the filled-in ground. Ships were always in construction along the waterfront and vessels loading with lumber, for it was an important waterway, much used by sea-going craft. When English boats made their return trips, members of their crews often took back Boston rockers as American curiosities, carrying them on their shoulders down the bank to load them into the ship's hold. Young George must have exhibited an aptitude for the brush, for when he was eighteen he was in charge of a group of other workers. During these years he practiced all kinds of ornamental painting. In the forties it was customary to mottle the seats of wooden chairs in shades of browns, chromes, and greens by a revived eighteenth century technique. Over a coat of yellow ochre mixed with oil was brushed thin water paint of umber, Van Dyke, or burnt Sienna to which was added a drop or two of vinegar and water sweetened by molasses. Variously shaped lumps of putty then transformed the wet surface into elaborate grainings. Perhaps the original aim had been to imitate the markings of figured bird's-eye maple, burl walnut, or even the exotic amboyna, for the result took on an amazing resemblance to these woods. Illustrated (fig. 158) is an early blanket chest done by this method.

A special variation in the mottling of these chair seats had become the fashion in Boston in the fifties, and orders of the Portland firm were falling off because it was unable to produce the new effect. Lord, as foreman, was sent to Boston to learn the mysterious trick, for such the technique appeared to be, but the doors of rival chair makers were closed to him, and he returned only to report failure. A few weeks later he was at work graining a panel, and, having spread a wash of brown tempera stain over the coat of yellow oil paint, he was waiting for it partially to dry before taking the next step when there appeared in the shop a former worker, returned to Portland after a long absence, to see the "boys." He had not come empty handed, for he carried in his arms some bottles of wine with which to celebrate the reunion. To quote Lord's own words: "I quickly emptied my glass, hurried back to my panel, and, as I bent over it, drops of wine fell from my mustache upon its surface; there before my astonished eyes was the mottled effect I had been seeking so long. Thereafter we made the chairs in quantities and held our own with the Boston firms."

Lord was also an expert with the striping brush in his youth. An experienced workman could finish one hundred chairs a day if he wasted no time, and Lord was proud of having equalled this total, receiving three cents a chair or three dollars for his day's work. The "common chair" made in 1848 during his apprenticeship was sold by Corey at Portland for forty-two cents. The simple standardized design of the top bar Lord believed had been stencilled on at least twelve thousand chairs. The "Baltimore," another wooden seated chair with a design of grapes and leaves, sold for the sum of sixty-two cents. But the cane-seated contemporary "bannister back," finished to imitate rosewood, was made for the "best rooms," and brought a slightly higher price. A chair stencilled by George Lord from patterns taken out of his mildewed ledger duplicates this "bannister" exactly as it had been done during the days of his apprenticeship (fig. 159). For

134

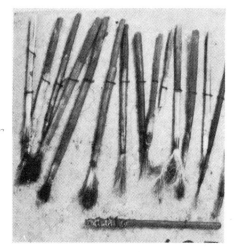

FIG. 157. KIT OF A PENNSYLVANIA CHAIR PAINTER

These brushes, stencils, feathers and leather combs for graining belonged to a chair painter of
Manheim who worked from 1820 to 1870.

*The Bucks County Historical Society, Doylestown, Pa.*

FIG. 158. MOTTLED BLANKET CHEST

Dating about 1750, the chest illustrates the same process used for graining the seats of
wooden chairs in the eighteen forties.

*Owner, Mrs. John E. Tuttle*

FIG. 159. "BANNISTER BACK" AND GEORGE LORD'S STENCILS
This chair was stencilled exactly as it had been done during Lord's apprenticeship
in 1848 from the same stencils.

FIG. 160. GEORGE F. LORD, 1833–1928

George Lord of Portland, Maine, was one of the last of the old chair painters.
He is shown still working at eighty-seven.

doing the strawberries there were very positive directions. First the seeds must be made with silver, then the forms of the berries must be shaped with red bronze and, after it had dried, a coat of transparent lake brushed over them to bring out the red, and lastly a cluster of leaves completed their grouping. Knowledge of garden fruits and their leaves and New England flowers was part of the worker's equipment, and it was a poor artisan, in the opinion of the Portland chair painter, who picked the wrong leaf for his berries or his wild rose.

So this old craftsman (fig. 160) passed on to me many of the simple but set ways of work of the ornamental painter of a century ago. Trained by the older generation whose methods were to become the yardstick for his own endeavors, he was able to bring to life the stencils piled in the crowded folios of William Eaton and to make more real to us the generation of artisans which preceded him.

### TIN   AND   VELVET

Tin and velvet should not be overlooked as surfaces for stencilling, for they are a part of the same period and fashion. With a stencil tradition in old-world japanning on metal and papier-mâché trays, we should naturally expect to find the same tool frequently giving ornament to the abundance of decorated tinware so assiduously peddled over the trade routes branching out from New England. The smithing of tin was a trade brought to the Colonies about 1740 by Edward Pattisson, who established himself in Berlin, Connecticut, and began building an industry which by 1815 in that town alone was annually converting 10,000 boxes of tin plate into finished wares. Many of the articles were decorated by hand with designs of bright colors, while others such as trays, tea caddies, and boxes of all sorts were stencilled. A candle box (fig. 161) shows a simple and hastily applied design stencilled in gold on asphaltum with roses not unlike those seen on chairs. In fact, the patterns could serve for both, since the essential treatment was the same except that the tin demanded more varnish in the size.

A tray (fig. 162) shows the later developments of stencilling, and is typical of the kind of design that was adapted to sets of varying sizes numbering anywhere from two to six. A much smaller tray with the same pattern is in the possession of the writer. Only wholesale production of these inexpensive household accessories would warrant the detail expended on the dove cote and roses. A certain amount of hand work in color enlivened

135

the bronzes, greens for trees, and blues, reds, and yellows for jacket or dress in the pictorial scenes, but even the most elaborate were quickly done when the stencil was the basis.

Every one is familiar with the type of paintings on velvet that adorned the walls of a century ago, but we do not always relate them to the stencils by which they were generally produced. "Theorem" was the term most frequently given to the stencil in connection with these pictures of baskets and bowls filled with realistic flowers and fruits which glowed with vivid color. Much of their decorative quality today is due to the texture of the white cotton velvet made yellow with age, which has brought more warmth and richness to the original tones. Whether they deserve the label of "primitives" given them by many modern collectors the reader must judge, but at any rate they had great popularity in the early years of the century. In the *New York Evening Post* of October 6, 1818, we find the following advertisement: "A few pieces of White Velvets for painting on, for sale at 150 Broadway by Philbrook & Peters." This art was fostered with other kinds of painting as part of the curriculum of those schools where young women were made proficient in "polite occupations." Yet perhaps we should not see in this craft only a feminine accomplishment, for an unnamed gentleman of parts wrote in his diary, in Georgetown, D.C., Sunday, April 22, 1832: "Verry pleasant and warm. I went down to Alexandria to take a lesson on painting on velvit and finished two pieces and it was said to be the handsomest . . . in Georgetown." Nearly a year later, after several entries showing his ardor for his new art, he wrote, "Last night I painted a piece of fruit on velvit and completed it, and think to paint a gar of flowers tonight, they are about ½ yard square." And in the following month he added, "I have been in the City to day I bought six yards white velvit for to paint on at 65 cents a yard in the evening painted a large dish with one large watermelon and a knife sticking in it which was very much admired."[36]

Although these offerings, which this gentleman planned to have framed and sent to his mother as a present, have not come down to us, a contemporary collection of origi-

36. Quoted from "Another Note on Theorem Painting," *Antiques*, vol. XXI, no. 6, June, 1932, p. 255. Further information is contained in a previous article, "Painting on Velvet," by Louise Karr (*Antiques*, September, 1931).

nal theorems used in this craft brings us near to a young hand which must have labored diligently to make the many designs contained in a portfolio preserved at the Harrison Gray Otis House in Boston.[37] When I opened the folder, I found fifty-five stencils piled in disorder, but since most of them had been carefully marked at their cutting it was easy to find which ones belonged together. This worker had delighted in the usual bunches of flowers, clusters of fruit, wicker baskets of plums, peaches, and pears. The margins of the heavy white paper in which the stencils were cut are covered to the very edge with brush marks of every color, indicating that their owner used her theorems as palettes on which to match her shades and wipe her brushes (fig. 163).

The coloring of these compositions was not a matter of chance, for the collection contains nine colored models to be copied, which were carefully sewed together as a measure of safe keeping. On the back of one is the date, June 20, 1834, and the following admonition written in a cramped hand: "This is my book. Don't you soil it." Another has her name, but it is too faint to read even with the aid of a glass. A pattern to be copied and the four stencils, bearing register marks, to compose it are illustrated (fig. 164). It was customary to plan these stencils on a "master design," indicating with numbers which parts must go into each theorem so as to give the proper colors their right positions, and one design, a pencil drawing of a basket heaped with sea shells, had only reached this stage.

Velvet painting, like most things of fashion, was introduced from across the sea, and a few rules to overcome difficulties may be gathered from *Hints to Young Practitioners in the Study of Landscape Painting, to which are added Instructions in the Art of Painting on Velvet*, an English publication of 1804 by J. W. Alston. It advises that the velvet "be well brushed with a hand-brush at the commencement of each tint that not the smallest particles of dust may be found on the surface which would prevent the tint adhering smoothly to the velvet." Gum "Astragant" or "Dragon" dissolved in water "to the consistency of oil" is suggested as a base for mixing the colors. The directions for making the "tints" are complicated and imply that prepared paints were not as easily procurable as they are today. A few years earlier, the author asserts, saffron could only be procured occasionally from French milliners, although "of late it can be purchased at different colour shops." Although this early volume does not mention the theorem as a part of the equipment, it was nevertheless used in England as a means of guiding the hand of less talented artists or of achieving results quickly. At the Victoria and Albert Museum I have seen the method applied to a pair of cream velvet fire screens on which were the figures of panthers or some similar wild animal.

The actual technique is not difficult and consists of applying paint, rather dry in consistency, to the velvet through the openings of the stencils by small stiff brushes,

37. Owned by the Society for the Preservation of New England Antiquities.

sometimes called "scrubs," while details of the units are added later with a fine brush or pen. A greater amount of freehand work seems to have been done on the landscapes in bright colors to which so many practicing this "art" aspired. Mourning pieces with their dark cypresses, tombstones, and weeping figures were also frequently done on velvet, but the less somber subjects present this phase of stencilling at its best. A still life (fig. 165) of an urn with fruits in tones of green and red on a cream ground, perhaps the masterpiece of some youthful hand, is typical of these compositions.

Thus the stencil served the tastes of our forefathers. As a tool used by a number of arts and crafts its history is long, but the ornament which it brought to the walls and furniture of the many houses of America is testimony both to its adaptability and to the enterprise and artistic integrity of the craftsmen who made it their own. The ease with which pattern could be applied commended the stencil to them; the beauty which they often achieved commends their work to us. The development of the craft, moreover, is typical of the new land, for faced with the problem of supplying inexpensively, abundantly, and practically the type of ornament Europe was favoring, individual artisans and workshops met it simply and directly by taking a well-known method and shaping it to their needs. For wall covering, bright patterns were placed on plain and tinted plastered surfaces; for ormolu and applied metal trimming, bronze powders were modeled against the background of wood or brushed on smoothly to produce flat unshaded ornament.

In meeting these problems local craftsmen contributed something unique to the art of America—an art for the many rather than the few, since countless dwellings throughout the country in this way genuinely shared the trend of "fashion" through the stencilled wall, the Hitchcock chair, and the hundred and one articles made gay with this decoration. These walls and this furniture, therefore, are bound together by more than a mere technical category, for our interest in them lies as well in the fact that there was not just an occasional room or chair but quantities of them which were present in the pattern of American life for over a half century. They are consequently our heritage to study, to know, and to appreciate.

138

FIG. 161. TIN CANDLE BOX
The design is stencilled in gold on asphaltum.
*Owner, Stephen Van Rensselaer*

FIG. 162. TIN TRAY
The stencilling is typical of the late type of pattern applied to sets of trays.
*Litchfield Historical Society, Litchfield, Conn.*

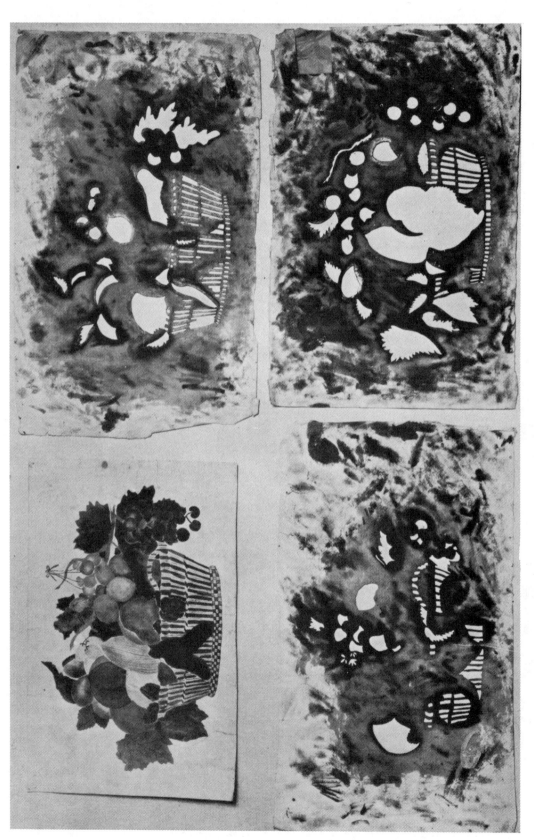

FIG. 163. PATTERN FOR VELVET PAINTING AND "THEOREMS"

The wicker basket of fruit was a favorite design. The three "theorems," as the stencils used for this work were called, are not the ones which made this particular basket, although they produced one very similar.

*Society for the Preservation of New England Antiquities*

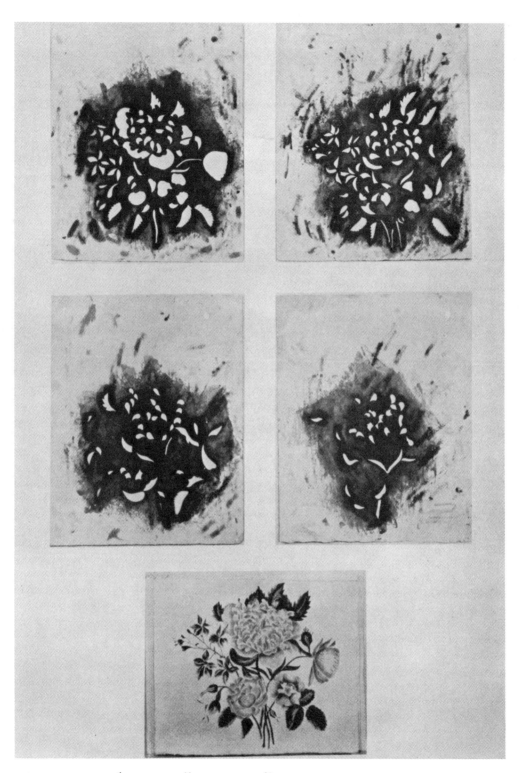

FIG. 164. FOUR "THEOREMS" AND A FINISHED PATTERN

FIG. 165. VELVET PAINTING

Elaborate pictures could easily be done by amateurs with the aid of the stencil.

*Owner, Mrs. Warren Kipp*

# THE INDEX

All houses having stencilled floors or walls are listed under Houses, the old name of the dwelling being used, as in the text, whenever possible.

"CALVARY," image print, 8
Cambridge, Mass., 88, 123
Cambridge, N. Y., 119
Canada, 48, 133
Candle box, stencilled, 135
Capers Corner, N. H., 60
Cardiff, Wales, 91
Card makers, engravings, 7 f.
Carter, Thomas Frances, *Invention of Printing in China*, 3 note 4, 7
Caves of a Thousand Buddhas, stencilling in, 3 f., 7
Chair: "ball and slat back," 105, 132; "bannister back," 125 f.; done by Lord, 134; Boston rocker by Union Chair Co., 127; from Edinburgh, 118; of Patience Harris, 103 f.; "Hitchcock," 93 and note 11, 99, 103–115; by L. Hitchcock, from Tolland, Mass., 112; by L. Hitchcock, filling of dish, 115 f.; by Hitchcock & Alford, 113; by John L. Hull, 120; illustrating filling of urn, 115 f.; in Jeremiah Lee Mansion, 104; light painted, 132; from New York, illustrating pineapple, 119; from Ossining, N. Y., 118; from Otis, Mass., illustrating massing of fruit, 119; "turtle back," 118; in Titus Whitmore house, 105
Chairs: graining of, 103, 104; by Lord, 87, 125 f.; mottling of, 134; from Pennsylvania, 132; shop names applied to, 128 f.; taken to England, 117 f., 133; of Ivers White, 117
Charlemagne, 6
Chateloy, France, wall stencilling in church at, 12
Chest: blanket, 134; stencilled, from Cambridge, N. Y., 119; stencilled, from Riverton, Conn., 121
*Chickering Exhibition*, 95 note 14
Chickering, John, 95
China, *see* Stencils, Chinese
Choir books, stencilled, 16 f.
Clark-Frankland house, inlaid floor in, 84 note 29
Clay, Henry, japanner, 90
Cleland, T. M., 1
*Cleopatra's Barge*, yacht, 105
*Clermont*, steamboat, 131
Clinton, Conn., 120
Clock, stencilled: banjo, 122; made in Boston, 122
Clouzot, Henri, 11 and note 19
Colas, René, 8
Colchester, England, stencilled wallpaper from, 15
Colebrook, Conn., 107
Colling, James K., *English Mediaeval Foliage and Coloured Decoration, etc.*, 12 and note 22
Collins, Benajah, 82

Color with gold stencilling, 87, 102, 122, 123, 126 f., 132 f., 135
Columbia Township, Ohio, 49
Composition and technique of gold or bronze stencilling, 115–122
Connecticut, 19, 24, 25, 38 f., 40, 41–48, 49 f., 55 note 19, 80, 87, 105, 106 ff., 114, 120, 121, 127, 128 note 33, 135
*Connecticut Courant, The*, advertisements in, 107 f.
*Connecticut Herald*, advertisement in, 48
Connecticut Tercentenary, 106
Console table, stencilled, 99
Coolidge, Calvin, early home of, 72 f.
Coolidge, Capt. John, 73 f.
Coolidge, Luther, 73
Copley, John Singleton, letter quoted, 21
Corey Brothers, chair makers, 133, 134
Cornices, *see* Venetian blinds
Couch, stencilled, 93 f.
Cramer, Conrad, 1
Crowell, William, ornamental painter, 128 note 33
Currier and Ives, 131
Cutting & Morrell, chair painters, 129

DANVERS, MASS., 82
Dartmouth College, fresco of, 64
de Caylus, 6
Dedham, Mass., 56
Deerfield, N. H., 66, 76, 86
Deering, N. H., 56
Deer Island, fresco of, 63
Designs: as basis for dating stencilled furniture, 114; types of, on mahogany furniture, 92 f., 103; types used on walls, 23 f., 84 ff.
Detroit, Mich., 109 f.
Dickinson, G., *English Papier-Mâché*, 91 notes 8, 9
*Domino* papers: development of, 9 ff.; use in America, 20, 22; use of borders with, 20 f.
*Dominotier*, 9 f., 21, 126 note 31
*Dominotière, La*, engraving, 10
Dossie, Robert, *The Handmaid to the Arts*, 15, 22, 74
Dover Plains, N. Y., 44 f., 49
Doylestown, Pa., 133
Dressing table, stencilled, 122
Dublin, N. H., 26, 56, 60, 122
Dufour, Joseph, 21, 54, 63
Duhamel de Monceau, *Art du Cartier*, 8 note 14
Dutch metal leaf, 111, 132
"Dyeing" of chairs to imitate costly woods, 104

EAST ANGLIA, 22; stencilling in, 13 f.